北京大学中国语言学研究中心

早期北京话珍稀文献集成 —— 西人北京话教科书汇编

主编 刘云

分卷主编 翟赟 郭利霞 陈颖

华英文义津逮

［英］禧在明 编著

北京大学出版社

图书在版编目（CIP）数据

华英文义津逮 /（英）禧在明（Walter C. Hillier）编著. —北京：北京大学出版社，2017.7
（早期北京话珍本典籍校释与研究）
ISBN 978-7-301-28489-6

Ⅰ.①华… Ⅱ.①禧… Ⅲ.①汉语—口语—研究 Ⅳ.①H193.2

中国版本图书馆CIP数据核字（2017）第153939号

书　　　名	华英文义津逮
	HUA-YING WENYI JINDAI
著作责任者	［英］禧在明（Walter C. Hillier）　编著
责任编辑	宋立文　王禾雨
标准书号	ISBN 978-7-301-28489-6
出版发行	北京大学出版社
地　　　址	北京市海淀区成府路205号　100871
网　　　址	http://www.pup.cn　新浪微博：@北京大学出版社
电子信箱	zpup@pup.cn
电　　　话	邮购部 62752015　发行部 62750672　编辑部 62753374
印　刷　者	北京京华虎彩印刷有限公司
经　销　者	新华书店
	720毫米×1020毫米　16开本　21印张　344千字
	2017年7月第1版　2018年3月第2次印刷
定　　　价	80.00元

未经许可，不得以任何方式复制或抄袭本书之部分或全部内容。
版权所有，侵权必究
举报电话：010-62752024　电子信箱：fd@pup.pku.edu.cn
图书如有印装质量问题，请与出版部联系，电话：010-62756370

19世纪来华传教士记录的官话方言及其历时演变研究
（16AYY002，2016年国家社科基金重点项目）

总　序

　　语言是文化的重要组成部分，也是文化的载体。语言中有历史。

　　多元一体的中华文化，体现在我国丰富的民族文化和地域文化及其语言和方言之中。

　　北京是辽金元明清五代国都（辽时为陪都），千余年来，逐渐成为中华民族所公认的政治中心。北方多个少数民族文化与汉文化在这里碰撞、融合，产生出以汉文化为主体的、带有民族文化风味的特色文化。

　　现今的北京话是我国汉语方言和地域文化中极具特色的一支，它与辽金元明四代的北京话是否有直接继承关系还不是十分清楚。但可以肯定的是，它与清代以来旗人语言文化与汉人语言文化的彼此交融有直接关系。再往前追溯，旗人与汉人语言文化的接触与交融在入关前已经十分深刻。本丛书收集整理的这些语料直接反映了清代以来北京话、京味儿文化的发展变化。

　　早期北京话有独特的历史传承和文化底蕴，于中华文化、历史有特别的意义。

　　一者，这一时期的北京历经满汉双语共存、双语互协而新生出的汉语方言——北京话，它最终成为我国民族共同语（普通话）的基础方言。这一过程是中华多元一体文化自然形成的诸过程之一，对于了解形成中华文化多元一体关系的具体进程有重要的价值。

　　二者，清代以来，北京曾历经数次重要的社会变动：清王朝的逐渐孱弱、八国联军的入侵、帝制覆灭和民国建立及其伴随的满汉关系变化、各路军阀的来来往往、日本侵略者的占领等等。在这些不同的社会环境下，北京人的构成有无重要变化？北京话和京味儿文化是否有变化？进一步地，地域方言和文化与自身的传承性或发展性有着什么样的关系？与社会变迁有着什么样的关系？清代以至民国时期早期北京话的语料为研究语言文化自身传承性与社会的关系提供了很好的素材。

　　了解历史才能更好地把握未来。中华人民共和国成立后，北京不仅是全国的政治中心，而且是全国的文化和科研中心，新的北京话和京味儿文化或正在形成。什么是老北京京味儿文化的精华？如何传承这些精华？为把握新的地域文化形成的规律，为传承地域文化的精华，必须对过去的地域文化的特色及其形成过程进行细致的研究和理性的分析。而近几十年来，各种新的传媒形式不断涌现，外来西方文化和国内其他地域文化的冲击越来越强烈，北京地区人口流动日趋频繁，老北京人逐渐分散，老北京话已几近消失。清代以来各个重要历史时期早期北京话语料的保护整理和研究迫在眉睫。

　　"早期北京话珍本典籍校释与研究（暨早期北京话文献数字化工程）"是北京大学中国语言学研究中心研究成果，由"早期北京话珍稀文献集成""早期北京话数据库"和"早期北京话研究书系"三部分组成。"集成"收录从清中叶到民国末年反映早期北京话面貌的珍稀文献并对内容加以整理，"数据库"为研究者分析语料提供便利，"研究书系"是在上述文献和数据库基础上对早期北京话的集中研究，反映了当前相关研究的最新进展。

　　本丛书可以为语言学、历史学、社会学、民俗学、文化学等多方面的研究提供素材。

　　愿本丛书的出版为中华优秀文化的传承做出贡献！

王洪君、郭锐、刘云
2016年10月

"早期北京话珍稀文献集成"序

清民两代是北京话走向成熟的关键阶段。从汉语史的角度看，这是一个承前启后的重要时期，而成熟后的北京话又开始为当代汉民族共同语——普通话源源不断地提供着养分。蒋绍愚先生对此有着深刻的认识："特别是清初到19世纪末这一段的汉语，虽然按分期来说是属于现代汉语而不属于近代汉语，但这一段的语言（语法，尤其是词汇）和'五四'以后的语言（通常所说的'现代汉语'就是指'五四'以后的语言）还有若干不同，研究这一段语言对于研究近代汉语是如何发展到'五四'以后的语言是很有价值的。"（《近代汉语研究概要》，北京大学出版社，2005年）然而国内的早期北京话研究并不尽如人意，在重视程度和材料发掘力度上都要落后于日本同行。自1876年至1945年间，日本汉语教学的目的语转向当时的北京话，因此留下了大批的北京话教材，这为其早期北京话研究提供了材料支撑。作为日本北京话研究的奠基者，太田辰夫先生非常重视新语料的发掘，很早就利用了《小额》《北京》等京味儿小说材料。这种治学理念得到了很好的传承，之后，日本陆续影印出版了《中国语学资料丛刊》《中国语教本类集成》《清民语料》等资料汇编，给研究带来了便利。

新材料的发掘是学术研究的源头活水。陈寅恪《〈敦煌劫余录〉序》有云："一时代之学术，必有其新材料与新问题。取用此材料，以研求问题，则为此时代学术之新潮流。"我们的研究要想取得突破，必须打破材料桎梏。在具体思路上，一方面要拓展视野，关注"异族之故书"，深度利用好朝鲜、日本、泰西诸国作者所主导编纂的早期北京话教本；另一方面，更要利用本土优势，在"吾国之旧籍"中深入挖掘，官话正音教本、满汉合璧教本、京味儿小说、曲艺剧本等新类型语料大有文章可做。在明确了思路之后，我们从2004年开始了前期的准备工作，在北京大学中国语言学研究中心的大力支持下，早期北京话的挖掘整理工作于2007年正式启动。本次推出的"早期北京话珍稀文献集成"是阶段性成果之一，总体设计上"取异族之故书与吾国之旧籍互相补正"，共分"日本北京话教科书汇编""朝鲜日据时期汉语会话书汇编""西人北京话教科书汇编""清代满汉合璧文献萃编""清代官话正音文献""十全福""清末民初京味儿小说书系""清末民初京味儿时评书系"八个系列，胪列如下：

"日本北京话教科书汇编"于日本早期北京话会话书、综合教科书、改编读物和风俗纪闻读物中精选出《燕京妇语》《四声联珠》《华语跬步》《官话指南》《改订官话指南》《亚细亚言语集》《京华事略》《北京纪闻》《北京风土编》《北京风俗问答》《北京事情》《伊苏普喻言》《搜奇新编》《今古奇观》等二十余部作品。这些教材是日本早期北京话教学活动的缩影，也是研究早期北京方言、民俗、史地问题的宝贵资料。本系列的编纂得到了日本学界的大力帮助。冰野善宽、内田庆市、太田斋、鳟泽彰夫诸先生在书影拍摄方面给予了诸多帮助。书中日语例言、日语小引的翻译得到了竹越孝先生的悉心指导，在此深表谢忱。

"朝鲜日据时期汉语会话书汇编"由韩国著名汉学家朴在渊教授和金雅瑛博士校注，收入《改正增补汉语独学》《修正独习汉语指南》《高等官话华语精选》《官话华语教范》《速修汉语自通》《速修汉语大成》《无先生速修中国语自通》《官话标准：短期速修中国语自通》《中语大全》《"内鲜满"最速成中国语自通》等十余部日据时期（1910年至1945年）朝鲜教材。这批教材既是对《老乞大》《朴通事》的传承，又深受日本早期北京话教学活动的影响。在中韩语言史、文化史研究中，日据时期是近现代过渡的重要时期，这些资料具有多方面的研究价值。

"西人北京话教科书汇编"收录了《语言自迩集》《官话类编》等十余部西人编纂教材。这些西方作者多受过语言学训练，他们用印欧语的眼光考量汉语，解释汉语语法现象，设计记音符号系统，对早期北京话语音、词汇、语法面貌的描写要比本土文献更为精准。感谢郭锐老师提供了《官话类编》《北京话语音读本》和《汉语口语初级读本》的底本，《寻津录》、《语言自迩集》（第一版、第二版）、《汉英北京官话词汇》、《华语入门》等底本由北京大学图书馆特藏部提供,谨致谢忱。《华英文义津逮》《言语声片》为笔者从海外购回,其中最为珍贵的是老舍先生在伦敦东方学院执教期间,与英国学者共同编写的教材——《言语声片》。教材共分两卷:第一卷为英文卷,用英语讲授汉语,用音标标注课文的读音;第二卷为汉字卷。《言语声片》采用先用英语导入,再学习汉字的教学方法讲授汉语口语,是世界上第一部有声汉语教材。书中汉字均由老舍先生亲笔书写,全书由老舍先生录音,共十六张唱片,京韵十足,殊为珍贵。

上述三类"异族之故书"经江蓝生、张卫东、汪维辉、张美兰、李无未、王顺洪、张西平、鲁健骥、王澧华诸先生介绍,已经进入学界视野,对北京话研究和对外汉语教学史研究产生了很大的推动作用。我们希望将更多的域外经典北京话教本引入进来,考虑到日本卷和朝鲜卷中很多抄本字迹潦草,难以辨认,而刻本、印本中也存在着大量的异体字和俗字,重排点校注释的出版形式更利于研究者利用,这也是前文"深度利用"的含义所在。

对"吾国之旧籍"挖掘整理的成果,则体现在下面五个系列中:

"清代满汉合璧文献萃编"收入《清文启蒙》《清话问答四十条》《清文指要》《续编兼汉清文指要》《庸言知旨》《满汉成语对待》《清文接字》《重刻清文虚字指南编》等十余部经典满汉合璧文献。入关以后,在汉语这一强势语言的影响下,熟习满语的满人越来越少,故雍正以降,出现了一批用当时的北京话注释翻译的满语会话书和语法书。这批教科书的目的本是教授旗人学习满语,却无意中成为了早期北京话的珍贵记录。"清代满汉合璧文献萃编"首次对这批文献进行了大规模整理,不仅对北京话溯源和满汉语言接触研究具有重要意义,也将为满语研究和满语教学创造极大便利。由于底本多为善本古籍,研究者不易见到,在北京大学图书馆古籍部和日本神户市外国语大学竹越孝教授的大力协助下,"萃编"将以重排点校加影印的形式出版。

"清代官话正音文献"收入《正音撮要》(高静亭著)和《正音咀华》(莎彝尊著)两种代表著作。雍正六年(1728),雍正谕令福建、广东两省推行官话,福建为此还专门设立了正音书馆。这一"正音"运动的直接影响就是以《正音撮要》和《正音咀华》为代表的一批官话正音教材的问世。这些书的作者或为旗人,或寓居京城多年,书中保留着大量北京话词汇和口语材料,具有极高的研究价值。沈国威先生和侯兴泉先生对底本搜集助力良多，特此致谢。

《十全福》是北京大学图书馆藏《程砚秋玉霜簃戏曲珍本》之一种，为同治元年陈金雀抄本。陈晓博士发现该传奇虽为昆腔戏，念白却多为京话，较为罕见。

以上三个系列均为古籍，且不乏善本，研究者不容易接触到，因此我们提供了影印全文。

总体来说，由于言文不一，清代的本土北京话语料数量较少。而到了清末民初，风气渐开，情况有了很大变化。彭翼仲、文实权、蔡友梅等一批北京爱国知识分子通过开办白话报来"开启民智""改良社会"。著名爱国报人彭翼仲在《京话日报》的发刊词中这样写道："本报为输进文明、改良风俗，以开通社会多数人之智识为宗旨。故通幅概用京话，以浅显之笔，达朴实之理，纪紧要之事，务令雅俗共赏，妇稚咸宜。"在当时北京白话报刊的诸多栏目中，最受市民欢迎的当属京味儿小说连载和《益世余谭》之类的评论栏目，语言极为地道。

"清末民初京味儿小说书系"首次对以蔡友梅、冷佛、徐剑胆、儒丐、勋锐为代表的晚清民国京味儿作家群及作品进行系统挖掘和整理，从千余部京味儿小说中萃取代表作家的代表作品，并加以点校注释。该作家群活跃于清末民初，以报纸为阵地，以小说为工具，开展了一场轰轰烈烈的底层启蒙运动，为新文化运动的兴起打下了一定的群众基础，他们的作品对老舍等京味儿小说大家的创作产生了积极影响。本系列的问世亦将为文学史和思想史研究提供议题。于润琦、方梅、陈清茹、雷晓彤诸先生为本系列提供了部分底本或馆藏线索，首都图书馆历史文献阅览室、天津图书馆、国家图书馆提供了极大便利，谨致谢意！

"清末民初京味儿时评书系"则收入《益世余谭》和《益世余墨》，均系著名京味儿小说家蔡友梅在民初报章上发表的专栏时评，由日本岐阜圣德学园大学刘一之教授、矢野贺子教授校注。

这一时期存世的报载北京话语料口语化程度高，且总量庞大，但发掘和整理却殊为不易，称得上"珍稀"二字。一方面，由于报载小说等栏目的流行，外地作者也加入了京味儿小说创作行列，五花八门的笔名背后还需考证作者是否为京籍，以蔡友梅为例，其真名为蔡松龄，查明的笔名还有损、损公、退化、亦我、梅蒐、老梅、今睿等。另一方面，这些作者的作品多为急就章，文字错讹很多，并且鲜有单行本存世，老报纸残损老化的情况日益严重，整理的难度可想而知。

上述八个系列在某种程度上填补了相关领域的空白。由于各个系列在内容、体例、出版年代和出版形式上都存在较大的差异，我们在整理时借鉴《朝鲜时代汉语教科书丛刊续编》《〈清文指要〉汇校与语言研究》等语言类古籍的整理体例，结合各个系列自身特点和读者需求，灵活制定体例。"清末民初京味儿小说书系"和"清末民初京味儿时评书系"年代较近，读者群体更为广泛，经过多方调研和反复讨论，我们决定在整理时使用简体横排的形式，尽可能同时满足专业研究者和普通读者的需求。"清代满汉合璧文献萃编""清代官话正音文献"等系列整理时则采用繁体。"早期北京话珍稀文献集成"总计六十余册，总字数近千万字，称得上是工程浩大，由于我们能力有限，体例和校注中难免会有疏漏，加之受客观条件所限，一些拟定的重要书目本次无法收入，还望读者多多谅解。

"早期北京话珍稀文献集成"可以说是中日韩三国学者通力合作的结晶，得到了方方面面的帮助，我们还要感谢陆俭明、马真、蒋绍愚、江蓝生、崔希亮、方梅、张美兰、陈前瑞、赵日新、陈跃红、徐大军、张世方、李明、邓如冰、王强、陈保新诸先生的大力支持，感谢北京大学图书馆的协助以及萧群书记的热心协调。"集成"的编纂队伍以青年学者为主，经验不足，两位丛书总主编倾注了大量心血。王洪君老师不仅在经费和资料上提供保障，还积极扶掖新进，"我们搭台，你们年轻人唱戏"的话语令人倍感温暖和鼓舞。郭锐老师在经费和人员上也予以了大力支持，不仅对体例制定、底本选定等具体工作进行了细致指导，还无私地将自己发现的新材料和新课题与大家分享，令人钦佩。"集成"能够顺利出版还要特别感谢国家出版基金规划管理办公室的支持以及北京大学出版社王明舟社长、张凤珠副总编的精心策划，感谢汉语编辑室杜若明、邓晓霞、张弘泓、宋立文等老师所付出的辛劳。需要感谢的师友还有很多，在此一并致以诚挚的谢意。

"上穷碧落下黄泉，动手动脚找东西"，我们不奢望引领"时代学术之新潮流",惟愿能给研究者带来一些便利,免去一些奔波之苦,这也是我们向所有关心帮助过"早期北京话珍稀文献集成"的人士致以的最诚挚的谢意。

刘　云

2015年6月23日

于对外经贸大学求索楼

2016年4月19日

改定于润泽公馆

导 读

郭利霞

一、《华英文义津逮》的作者、版本和内容

（一）禧在明其人

《华英文义津逮》的作者禧在明（Walter C. Hillier，1849—1927）生于香港，爱尔兰人，英国外交官、汉学家。父亲是英国驻曼谷领事查尔斯·奚礼尔（Charles Hillier），母亲伊莱扎（Eliza）是著名传教士麦都思（Walter Henry Medhurst）之女，弟弟爱德华·盖伊·奚礼尔（Edward Guy Hillier）是香港上海汇丰银行一位受人尊敬的银行家，曾长期担任该银行驻北京经理。禧在明1867年作为英国驻华使馆翻译见习生来华，1870年任汉文副使，1880—1881年代理汉务参赞，1883—1889年任汉务参赞。甲午战争期间，任英国驻朝鲜总领事，与袁世凯交往密切。1896年10月回到英国，1901作为中国事务参赞随英国使团出使中国。1904—1908年任伦敦大学国王学院汉文教授，教授英国外交官、军官和商人汉语。1908—1910年出任清政府财政顾问，与李鸿章交好。1927年在英国去世。

禧在明著述颇丰，《语言自迩集》第二版（*A Progressive Course Designed to Assist the Student of Colloquial Chinese as Spoken in the Capital and the Metropolitan Department*，1886）就是他协助威妥玛完成的。"从第二版序言推知，这也是最好的本子"（张卫东 2002: 47）。宋桔（2013）对《语言自迩集》诸版本作了细致考证，跟第一版相比，第二版内容上有增减、替换，

中文部分的个别修订如"小车"的量词从"个"变为"辆",整体修订如初版的"你纳"改为"您纳",还添加了南北方言的讨论。

禧在明任伦敦大学汉文教授期间根据自己的汉语学习和教学经验编写了《华英文义津逮》(又译《怎样学习中国语文》,*The Chinese Language and How to Learn It: A Manual for Beginners,* 1907)。汉字部分出了单行本《常用汉字一千个》(*One Thousand Useful Chinese Characters,* 1907)。他编写过词典《袖珍英汉词典》(*An English-Chinese Pocket Dictionary,* 1910)、《袖珍英汉北京方言词典》(*An English-Chinese Dictionary of Peking Colloquial,* 1918)。此外还写过《汉文书写字母系统备忘录:申请将该系统用于打字机、莱诺铸排机或其他铸排机并应用于布莱叶盲文系统》(*Memorandum Upon an Alphabetical System for Writing Chinese: the Application of this System to the Typewriter and to the Linotype or other Typecasting and Composing Machines and its Application to the Braille System for the Blind,* 1927)和《开平煤矿案节略》(*Memorandum on the Kai Ping Mining Case,* 1908)等。

(二)《华英文义津逮》其书[①]

1.《华英文义津逮》的版本

《华英》是针对英国外交官、军官以及商人编写的初级汉语教材,体例和内容上都受到了《语言自迩集》的深刻影响,或者说二者一脉相承,特别是语音和汉字部分。禧在明生前《华英》出版过六版:1907年第一版,出版商是伦敦的 Kegan Paul, Trench, Trübner 出版公司;1909年第二版共两卷,出版商是上海的 Kelly & Walsh(别发洋行),伦敦 Kegan Paul, Trench, Trübner 出版公司第二版出版于1910年;第三版于1913年在上海和伦敦同时发行;第四版由别发洋行出版于1914年;第五版和第六版分别由伦敦 Kegan Paul,

---

[①] 以下正文中简称为《华英》。

Trench, Trübner 出版公司出版于1916年和1921年，此后1923年第六版又出版于上海，伦敦和上海又分别重印于1923年和1927年。① 笔者手头分别是1913年和1921年伦敦出版的第三版和第六版，两个版本内容完全一样。根据周磊（2011）的描述，1923年伦敦出版的第六版内容也一样。因此，这些不同版本其实是第二版多次重印，而不是严格意义的再版，第二版和第一版最大的不同是增加了第二卷，下文将详细介绍。

笔者手头还有《常用汉字一千个》（1907），每个汉字都有注音和英文释义，封面写着 Reprinted from "The Chinese Language"，相当于第一版汉字部分的抽印本。第三版中一千个汉字的编排有所不同，虽然同样是把课文中的一千个汉字按出现的先后顺序排列，但第三版汉字左边和右上角均有数字，左边的数字是部首的序号，右上角的数字则是该汉字的序号，跟序号相对的是威式拼音，后面是英文释义。举例来说，"百"左边的数字是106，在"部首表"106可查到其部首是"白"，右上角的61是它在一千个汉字中的顺序号。

《华英》第二版是最重要的一次修订，此后又重印了十几次，虽然名曰第三、四、五、六版等，内容却保持着第二版的面貌。

2. 《华英文义津逮》的内容

本文的介绍以第三版为基础，内容包括：汪大燮②的序文、禧在明所写第二版和第一版前言，列入目录的内容共297页，共八个部分：（汉语）书面语（The Written Language）、（汉语）口语（The Spoken Language）、语音表（Table of Sounds）、进阶练习（Progressive Exercises）、汉语文本（Chinese Text of Exercises）、部首表（The Radiclas）、一千汉字表（a List

---

① 版本主要参考了周磊（2011），第6页。
② 汪大燮（1860—1929），原名尧俞，字伯唐。曾任满清驻英商务大臣，民国成立后任教育总长、代理国务总理，同孙宝琦、钱能训合称"三老"。但在本书中汪大燮的序文缺失。

of One Thousand Characters）、汉字部首索引（Index of Characters Arranged Under Their Radicals）。

"（汉语）书面语"介绍了汉字造字法、书写形式等，强调要想熟练书写，除了勤于练习，没有其他捷径。"（汉语）口语"以古代押韵而现代不再押韵的诗歌为例说明语音的演变，并讨论了汉语方言（主要是官话方言）的分布，介绍了汉语语音的特点，如送气不送气的对立、汉语的四个声调。这部分最有价值的是关于书面语和口语的论述，作者开宗明义指出：通常认为中国有两种语言，即书面语和口语（1页）。对于两者的区别，有很多具体论述，如：书面语说"帽""愿""意""篱""欢"，口语则分别说"帽子""愿意""意思""篱笆""喜欢"，还有些词语书面语和口语完全不同，如"日"和"太阳/日头"。作者说：只有在舞台上，中国人才会朗诵，历史剧人物说着书面语……完全有可能把口语记下来，但实际上除了个别小说和呈堂证据外，中国人从不记录口语，如果要记下来，他们必然会转写成书面语形式（22页）。

"语音表"是威妥玛式拼音的音节表，此不赘述。

"进阶练习"包括三部分：

（1）课文中文例句对应的英文翻译以及"逐字翻译"，如"你要什么？"除了英译"What do you want"，还有逐字对译"You want what"；

（2）英文翻译下面是课文例句中的生词，每个生词后都有威氏注音及英文注释；

（3）英文翻译和生词注释之后是语法等介绍，如44页对名词的说明；53—54页对"就、可（是）、时候"以及称谓的说明；63—71页包括汉语的主动态、被动态、比较级、介词"和、对、给、替、代"等的说明。有些分析很中肯，有些明显是套用印欧语的系统，如"态"、虚拟语气等描述。

97—99页介绍了应该遵循的一些礼貌原则。后三篇课文只有英文翻译和词语注释,没有语法注释。

"汉语文本"的顺序用罗马数字标出,前六篇文本其实是短语、单句或一些小段落。如第一课(Ⅴ)首句是"这个是你的";第二课(Ⅵ)除了主体的数词,只有四句话;第三课(Ⅶ)、第四课(Ⅷ)有对话,也有单句;第五课(Ⅸ)、第六课(Ⅹ)则是复杂的句子或小段落,后三课文本是真正的成篇语料,包括三个故事:善恶报应传、神豆传、报恩狗,前两个故事改编自欧洲童话,后一个故事选自《聊斋志异》。这部分的词语可以去"进阶练习"查找,前六课生词注释前面的数字是该字(词)所在例句的序号,后三课文本中词语旁的数字对应着"进阶练习"中生词的编号,所以前六课的注释同样的编号可能对应着多个生词,后三课生词编号和注释编号一一对应,自然是为了便于查询。有个细节需要注意,"汉语文本"按照汉语的习惯,从后往前排版,一页之内从右往左排,其他部分均按照英文习惯排版。

"部首表"其实就是《康熙字典》的214个部首,按照笔画进行归类,一画的归一类,二画的归一类,以此类推,最多的是十七画。

"汉字部首索引"是将一千个汉字按部首排列,把具有相同部首的汉字排在一起,每个汉字右边的数字是"一千汉字表"中的序号,如"工^{471}"部下的"巧^{734}"表示这是一千汉字中的第734个,"工"也正是第471个汉字。因此学生按照部首很容易在一千汉字表中检索到该字,从而了解其发音和意思。

3.《华英文义津逮》第二卷的两个版本

虽然《华英》的第二卷并未在此书中附上,但作为《华英》全书比较重要的一部分,我们在此也略作介绍。《华英》第二版和第一版的区别除了替换了170多个汉字，在汉字前后加上了便于检索的数字外，还增加了12篇改编自蒲松龄《聊斋志异》的白话小说，作为教材的第二卷，这也是两个版本最大的区别。这12篇文章分别是：《赵城虎》《瞳人语》《种梨》《劳山道士》《鸟语》《菱角》《细柳》《促织》《王成》《雏鸽》《向杲》和《骂鸭》。①

笔者手头有上海别发洋行1909年第二卷的第一版和1914年的第二版，后者内容更丰富，包括五个部分：第一部分介绍了12篇故事的作者、内容，并说明该书完成后才看到翟理斯的译本，重申2000汉字完全可以满足一般的需求，学生经过两年的学习，可以毫不费力地阅读口语小说或报纸，12个故事中的表达方式是普通北方人每天说话的方式，如果学生耐心地读完能多多少少记住一些，就会发现自己即使没有北京口音，说话方式也受到了北京话的影响；第二部分是12篇故事的英文翻译，翻译前有一个勘误表；第三部分是故事中的生词解释，包括汉字、注音、英文解释，有些还有中文例句，每篇还提示了学习重点与难点；第四部分是汉字表（List of Characters），共627个汉字；第五部分是12篇故事的汉语文本。第二卷跟第一卷相互呼应，用的是北方口语，有明显的北京话色彩。

二、《华英文义津逮》的价值

（一）作为一部汉语教材

禧在明提到威妥玛的《语言自迩集》和狄考文的《官话类编》使用最广泛（23页）。《华英》影响也不小，曾作为国王学院汉语课本，并多次再版。据朱洪（2013）考察，《华英》出版后，逐步取代《语言自迩集》成为

---

① 李海军的《作为海外汉语学习教材的〈聊斋志异〉》（《湖南社会科学》2012年第4期）对禧在明改编《聊斋》的手段和原则进行了分析。

海关洋员学汉语的主体教材。江莉（2016）推测，禧在明可能意识到威妥玛的著作对初学者来说偏难，才另著此书。《华英》还受到了《官话类编》的影响，下文将具体说明。

1.《华英》对重点和难点的把握

汉语教材最基本的功能是其教学功能，对学习者来说，则是其学习功能（赵金铭 2009）。要想切实发挥这种功能，教材对教学重点、难点的把握至关重要。《华英》第二部分提到，一个资质中等的英国年轻人在法国或德国住两年，投入全部精力学习语言，两年后会熟练地说话和写作，而汉语则至少需要五六年；但另一方面，学习汉语几个月后就可以让人听懂，去旅行不需要翻译。可以说对汉语书面语和口语难度的定位基本准确。

禧在明对口语和书面语的区别有着清晰的认识，他参与编写的《语言自迩集》就要求口语与书面语兼顾，《华英》也花了很大篇幅论述口语和书面语使用场合及用词等区别。他说：中国学者认为写下来的口语形式是没学问的，但是为了教育的目的，应当忽略这种偏见（23页）。为了让学生了解书面语的特点，禧在明举了三个例子。前两例分别选自《诗经·邶风·静女》和《论语》，禧在明认为这两个例子只要借助字典的帮助都能理解。第三个例子选自清代袁枚的书信集，虽然信本身很短，但每句都有出处不同的用典。禧在明认为，如果没有大量注释，没有一个欧洲学者能看懂这封信，能看懂的中国学者恐怕也寥寥无几。不过他也敏锐地观察到了汉语书面语风格正在经历着某种变化，这一方面是因为教育体系的改变，另一方面是受到报纸的影响，因为报纸流行简明易懂的文章。把《聊斋》故事改编成白话故事是一次成功的尝试，也是一大创举。

禧在明强调语音的重要性："如果没有好的开端，以后纠正就很困难了。"（24页）尤其重视口语中的声调：对中国人来说这是自然而然的事，对外国人却是难以逾越的困难,以"不要鸡、不要急、不要挤、不要记"为例说明了汉语中声调的重要性(20页)。口音差远没有声调不准糟糕(35页)。准确描写了三声变调:两个三声在一起第一个往往读成二声或一声(36页)。

以"人"和"仁"、"一个兵"和"一块冰"等为例说明量词对于区分词语的重要性,指出汉语有几十个量词,每个量词适用于一定数量的名词(21页)。

在第一版序言中,禧在明把汉语学习比作爬山,"熟练掌握本书的一千个汉字,理论上而言,至少已经完成了三分之一的路程"。为了让学生对汉字在总体上有一个清晰的认识,他花费了大量篇幅,从造字方法、书法、汉字的传播和影响等方面对汉字进行了全面的分析。以"福"为例说明汉字的笔顺结构等(33页)。禧在明还对握笔姿势和汉字笔顺进行了不厌其烦的说明。"部首表""部首索引"某种程度上是对汉字结构的分析。

2. 编排方式、注释及学习理念

《华英》语素和词语并举,如75页注释12既有"商、量",又有"商量";76页注释14既有"利、害",也有"利害"。这种对汉字或语素的重视并非禧在明首创,比《华英》早的《英华合璧》(*Mandarin Primer*)[①]和《官话类编》(*A Course of Mandarin Lessons: Based on Idiom*)[②]均是这样的编排方式,如《英华合璧》第八版第25课的生词表中,既有"功、劳",又有"功劳";《官话类编》1900年版53课生词表既有"云、彩",又有"云彩",且连续排列。《华英》显然是受到了《官话类编》的影响。

---

① 《英华合璧》是内地会英国籍传教士鲍康宁(Frederick William Baller, 1852—1922)编写的教材,1887年第一版,其中第八版作了重要的修订和扩充,基本奠定了以后几版的基础。

② 作者狄考文(Calvin Wilson Mateer, 1836—1908),1892年第一版,《官话类编》的编写得到过鲍康宁的帮助。

周磊（2011）剔除掉《华英》"词表"中的174个"非词成分"后，对剩下的1036个词与《（汉语水平）词汇等级大纲》进行对比，发现甲级词406个，乙级词228个，初级词汇占1000词的60%以上。周磊（2011）认为《华英》最明显的缺陷是词汇分配不合理，第一课75个词，第二课16个词，第三课99个词，第四课88个词、第五课493个词、第六课448个词。其实禧在明在序言中明言"用六个月的时间掌握这些汉字"，由于这六篇文本在内容上并没有多少关联，所以拆开学习完全没问题。

刘珣（2006:312）认为教材体现了语言教学最根本的两个方面：教什么和如何教。在如何教这一点上，禧在明对语法、语用的点拨式注释也可圈可点，如区分"不、没"的小窍门是记住"不"不跟"有"一起用，"没"不跟"是"一起用，"没"多用于过去的行为，这样就大大降低了选择的困难。又如：使用人称代词"你"时要特别注意，称呼关系较近较为亲密的人、地位比你低的人、同辈或者晚辈、或者是父母叫他们的孩子，才能用"你"，对陌生人称"你"则不礼貌。在区分"你"和"您、您纳"后，禧在明说明这种细微区别很重要，因为中国人很讲究礼貌，如果忽视了这些约定俗成的表达，会让中国人产生被蔑视的联想（54页）。可以说，《华英》的语法注释点到为止，而对影响交际的一些因素包括非语言因素则详加说明。如：遇到朋友时，如果你骑着马或坐在马车里，从礼节上讲应该下马或下车，可是为了不给朋友添同样的麻烦，最好假装没看到。……如果骑在马上或坐在车里跟朋友或陌生人说话是违背礼貌原则的，除非对方是苦力阶层（98页）。

《华英》所体现出的学习理念主要包括以下三点。

强调直接用汉语思维：如果想成功地造句，就必须努力忘掉英语所有的语法结构，努力学习用汉语的方式排列句子（34页）。

掌握汉字的方法：每个字都要仔细抄在一寸见方的纸条上，背面写读音和意思。每天都复习这些汉字，努力认识每个汉字。记住的汉字可以放一周，仍然没记住的放在一起，天天复习。不认识的汉字会越来越少，过不了多久就会成功地记住这些汉字（32页）。

学习小窍门：一个词就能表达简单的肯定或否定，不过更常见的是否定形式重复问题的后半部分否定形式，如："你出去不出去？——不出去"。肯定形式则重复前半部分，即："我出去"（44页）。

从篇幅和分量来看，《华英》主要还是以汉语文本作为语言教学内容的黏合剂，语法注释均围绕着六篇文本进行，后三篇文本只有词汇注释，第二卷的12篇文章相当于泛读材料。

（二）作为二十世纪初北京话口语语料

杜轶（2016）以《华英》第一卷的语料为基础，通过和《语言自迩集》中的汉语语料和《小额》等清末小说语料对比，讨论了清末汉语的句法特点，包括"这/那样"系词语、"这么着/那么着"等10种用法。其实禧在明在第二卷第二版的前言中明确说明所用语言是北方口语乃至北京口语，因此我们得以窥见一百多年前北方话的特点。书中有很多北京官话词语和语法格式，如：知道（197页）、使（197页）、目下（192页）、多么（185页）、起点介词"打"（207页）、VP去（如209页"买东西去了"）等，[①] 也有不少对北京话的阐述，如：很多名词带两三种词尾，其中最常见的是"子"，北京话通常替换为"儿"（44页）。

《华英》选择问句的格式有"是……，还是……"和"是……，是……"，选项间有停顿，有时前后还可加语气词，如（4）—（6）。

（1）你是一个人去，还是同他们去？（205页）

---

① 参考了（郭锐 等，2017）

（2）老爷是单喝，还是对酒喝？（199页）

（3）您要什么样的钱，是要银子，是要洋钱？（200页）

（4）要办什么喜事呢，是办生日啊，是娶媳妇呢？（182页）

（5）他是走啊，还是骑马跟着您去呢？（193页）

（6）姑娘，为什么这么哭，是走迷了道儿么，还是受什么委屈呢？（169页）

反复问句有三种格式：第一种为"VP-NEG-VP"，如："他的买卖大不大？""你知道不知道？""你穿过没穿过？"第二种为"VP-NEG-V"，如："他要了钱没要？""今天早起的新闻纸有新闻没有？""您知道有好的不知道？"第三种为"VP-NEG"，如："钱拿来了没有？""他说过这个话没有？"没有"V-NEG-VP"式，符合同期北京话的特点。

可能补语的肯定和否定形式分别是"V得C/VC了"和"V不C"，如："搁得下搁不下？——搁得下/搁下了"（204页）。同期的《汉英北京官话词汇》（1911）中也有这种格式："那有一百五十斤也背动了""六个人也坐开了"。据柯理思（1995）考察，北方官话中"VC了"的格式很常见，现代北京话中这种格式已经消失。

第二卷北京话特征更明显，除了方言词"嚼过儿、小绺、您纳"等，更突出的是大量的儿化词。我们初步统计了一下，《赵城虎》有22个儿化词，《瞳人语》有35个，《种梨》有13个，《劳山道士》有27个，《鸟语》有17个，《菱角》有38个，《细柳》有58个，《促织》有66个，《王成》有58个，《雏鸽》有17个，《向杲》有46个，《骂鸭》有19个。

三、结　语

作为二十世纪初一部影响较大的初级汉语教材，禧在明编写的《华英》

包括语音、汉字、词汇、语法、语用等内容,其中对汉语的特点、汉语学习和教学不乏真知灼见。作为北方话或北京官话口语语料,第一卷的文本和第二卷的故事提供了大量句法信息,词语注释让我们得以窥见当时的词语特点,注音则让我们得以了解当时的语音面貌。

《华英》最大的不足是套用西方语法体系来分析汉语,如现在时、过去时、将来时、"态"等描写,这也是从瓦罗的《华语官话语法》(1703)开始西人常见的一种描写方式。作为一部教材,英文部分和汉语部分不同的编排方式[①]人为地给学习者增加了不必要的负担,也是一个败笔。结构上,"进阶练习"与"汉语文本"调整顺序更合理。

杜轶(2016)分析了《华英》的五种句法偏误,其中"是"的偏误除了"这个寡妇是很穷"(167页),笔者又找到几例:"瞧着是重,其实是很轻。"(191页)"你天天是起来的早,请你把我叫起来。"(206页)"他们家里是很穷。"(《赵城虎》)可能是母语负迁移造成的偏误。

总体而言,《华英》还没有像《语言自迩集》和《官话类编》那样引起广泛关注,现有研究寥寥无几,我们期待更多的学者来关注这部著作。

[①] 一页之内前者从左到右,后者从右到左,数页之间前者从前往后,后者从后往前。不过,这是当时通用的方式。

参考文献

杜　轶（2016）禧在明《华英文义津逮》反映的清末汉语句法特征，载于王澧华、吴颖主编《近代来华外交官汉语教材研究》，广西师范大学出版社，桂林。

郭　锐、翟　赟、徐菁菁（2017）汉语普通话从哪里来？——从南北官话差异看普通话词汇、语法来源，《中国言语文化学》第6期。

江　莉（2016）19—20世纪英国驻华使馆翻译学生的汉语学习（代序），载于王澧华、吴颖主编《近代来华外交官汉语教材研究》，广西师范大学出版社，桂林。

柯理思（1995）北方官话里表示可能的动词词尾"了"，《中国语文》第4期。

刘　珣（2006）《对外汉语教育学引论》，北京语言大学出版社，北京。

宋　桔（2013）《语言自迩集》诸版本及其双语同时语料价值，《语言教学与研究》第1期。

张卫东（2002）《语言自迩集》译序，《汉字文化》第2期。

赵金铭（2009）《对外汉语教学概论》，商务印书馆，北京。

周　磊（2011）《禧在明〈华英文义津逮〉研究》，上海师范大学硕士论文。

朱　洪（2013）《晚清海关洋员汉语学习初步研究》，南京大学硕士论文。

Fulton, Thomas C.（1911）*Chinese-English Mandarin Phrase Book: Peking Dialect*. Shanghai: American Presbyterian Mission Press.

THE
CHINESE LANGUAGE
AND
HOW TO LEARN IT

A MANUAL FOR BEGINNERS

BY

SIR WALTER HILLIER, K.C.M.G., C.B.

LATE PROFESSOR OF CHINESE, KING'S COLLEGE, LONDON,
FORMERLY CHINESE SECRETARY TO H.M.'S LEGATION AT PEKING
AND SOMETIME H.M.'S CONSUL-GENERAL IN KOREA

THIRD EDITION

LONDON
KEGAN PAUL, TRENCH, TRÜBNER & CO. Ltd.
BROADWAY HOUSE, 68-74, CARTER LANE, E.C.
1913

LONDON:
PRINTED BY WILLIAM CLOWES AND SONS, LIMITED,
DUKE STREET, STAMFORD STREET, S.E., AND GREAT WINDMILL STREET, W.

PREFACE TO SECOND EDITION

THE issue of a second edition of this volume has afforded the writer an opportunity of making certain alterations which it is hoped will add to the utility of the work and secure continuity between this and the second volume of the Course which was issued in 1909.

The last 180 characters in the List under Section XII. of the first edition have been struck out and others substituted for them. These are embodied in three stories contained in Section XI. of the present volume, in which exactly one thousand characters are now made use of.

In deference to a suggestion made by various critics, the Chinese text has now been placed in one section near the end of the volume, and the index of characters under their radicals has been changed by the substitution of reference numbers for the meanings given in the first edition.

Reference has been made towards the close of the first edition to a vocabulary which it was intended to embody in Volume II. After this vocabulary had been practically completed the writer came to the conclusion that the needs of the student would be more adequately met by the compilation of a comprehensive dictionary of Northern colloquial Chinese. The vocabulary was accordingly discarded, and its place has been taken by an Anglo-Chinese Colloquial Dictionary* containing over twenty thousand separate expressions.

This will enable students to find Chinese equivalents for a number of expressions which they would otherwise have great difficulty in rendering, at any rate for many years.

WALTER C. HILLIER.

PEKING, 1910.

---

* *Anglo-Chinese Dictionary of Peking Colloquial*—Sir W. Hillier. Presbyterian Mission Press, Shanghai.

PREFACE TO FIRST EDITION

THE present work is intended to meet the wants of those who think they would like to learn Chinese but are discouraged by the sight of the formidable text-books with which the aspiring student is confronted. It is especially intended for the use of Army Officers, of Missionaries, and of young business men connected with trade interests in China who wish to commence the study of the language in England with a view to continuing it in the country itself.

The exercises contained in this volume, with a total capital of one thousand words, should be mastered in six months by any one who will devote an hour or so a day to the task, and the student who has mastered a thousand words, with some of the many combinations they can be made to form, will have a sufficient stock at his command to make his ordinary wants known. If he wishes to do more than this he must turn to the larger text-books which he will then find to be much less formidable than they appear to be at first sight.

With a stock of from fifteen hundred to two thousand of the right words, if he knows how to use them, any one can speak Chinese intelligibly, and a good knowledge of the thousand words which this book contains will take the student, theoretically at any rate, at least a third of the distance. He will find the remaining two-thirds somewhat stiff climbing, but with the start that this volume will give him he will be in a position to decide when he has gone through it whether or no it is worth his while to proceed farther.

I am indebted to His Excellency Wang, the Chinese Minister in London, for the introductory page and for the inscription which appears on the cover of the book.

My thanks are also due in no small measure to Mr. Reginald Lake, of Messrs. Gilbert & Rivington, for the courteous attention he has devoted to the production of a work that has called for an exceptional amount of care and patient revision.

WALTER C. HILLIER,
KING'S COLLEGE (UNIVERSITY OF LONDON).

April, 1907.

CONTENTS

	PAGE
THE WRITTEN LANGUAGE	1
THE SPOKEN LANGUAGE	16
TABLE OF SOUNDS	25
PROGRESSIVE EXERCISES	37
CHINESE TEXT OF EXERCISES	153–217
THE RADICALS	221
A LIST OF ONE THOUSAND CHARACTERS	234
INDEX OF CHARACTERS ARRANGED UNDER THEIR RADICALS	285

THE CHINESE LANGUAGE

I.

THE WRITTEN LANGUAGE.

It is commonly asserted that there are two languages in China—the written and the spoken. This statement requires qualification, but it is sufficiently accurate to justify the treatment of the two branches as separate and distinct when attempting a popular exposition of the subject. Of the difficulty of both there can be no doubt, but as the written language presents more difficulties than the spoken, it will be convenient to reverse the usual order of things and to deal first with the former.

The genesis of the written language of China is largely a matter of conjecture, but Chinese scholars from time immemorial have been almost unanimous in the opinion that it was pictorial in origin. The subject has been dealt with by numerous Chinese writers, and those who are interested in a more scientific treatment of the matter than the following chapter is intended to present are referred to an elaborate and learned article on the subject by the late Mr. T. Watters, a profound Chinese scholar, who, in his *Essays on the Chinese Language*, deals at length with this complicated question.*
It will be sufficient for present purposes to refer to the most widely known of the Chinese authors, a scholar called Tai T'ung, who lived six hundred years ago, and wrote a treatise which is often cited as an authority in the great Lexicon of Kang Hsi, the standard dictionary of the Chinese; it is also quoted by most foreign authors of works on the Chinese language.†

---

* *Essays on the Chinese Language*, by T. Watters, Shanghai. Presbyterian Mission Press, 1889. See also an Article entitled *Prehistoric China*, by Dr. E. Faber, published in Vol. xxiv. Part 2 of the *Journal* of the North China Branch of the Royal Asiatic Society.

† A translation of the work of this author, under the title of *The Six Scripts*, has been made by Mr. L. C. Hopkins, H.M.'s Consul-General at Tientsin.

This is what Tai T'ung says with regard to the Chinese written character:

"Spoken sounds preceded written figures, and before the invention of written symbols, dealings by means of knotted cords came into existence. These were followed by cutting notches on wooden materials, which gave way, in turn, to figures representing natural objects, and forms indicative of actions, states or relations, cut out into lines to serve as counterparts of the spoken names of the same objects, actions, states or relations. With these came graving knives, and tablets for graving upon, and this was writing, the whole object of which was to make speech visible."

In tracing the evolution of the written character, Chinese scholars divide its progress into six marked stages:

1. Pictorial.
2. Indicative.
3. Suggestive compounds.
4. Deflected characters.
5. Phonetic.
6. Adoptive, or characters which are used in place of others.

Pictorial characters are those in which the forms of objects are copied, such as

Indicative characters are those which are formed by indicating the essential features of physical action, state or relation, such as

THE CHINESE LANGUAGE

Suggestive compounds are figures pointing out some property or relative circumstance. Thus, the union of the sun and moon expresses brightness; a tree or piece of wood in a doorway, obstruction; two trees, a grove, or forest; two men on the ground, the act of sitting; the sun seen through the trees, east.

Deflected characters are represented by inverted delineations of symbols, either in whole or in part.

To each of these idiograms a certain sound was attached, and the next and greatest step, the phonetic stage, was the invention of compound characters in which symbols representing sounds by which objects were named were combined with other symbols giving an indication of the sense or meaning.*

The following example will be sufficient to illustrate this idea. Let it be taken for granted that the accompanying combination of strokes—交—is pronounced *chiao*. It means, when taken singly, to blend, unite or join, though it has some eight or ten other distinct meanings in combination. Place 虫, an insect or reptile, at the side of it, and it becomes 蛟, a species of dragon; substitute 魚, a fish,

---

* Professor Giles, *China and the Chinese*, p. 29. Columbia University Press, 1902.

and it is 鮫, a shark; 犭, a dog, and it is 狡, wily, or crafty; 女, a woman, and we have 姣, handsome; 糸, silk thread, and we get 絞, to bind around, also to strangle. Now, all these characters, and many more with the same sound symbol, are read *chiao*, but, as is shown, they each have a different meaning in accordance with the character which is added to the symbol. We thus divide Chinese characters into two parts—one, the *sound* indicator, to which the name "phonetic" is generally given; the other, the *idea* indicator, which is commonly called the "radical." Every character in the Chinese language, unless it happens to be a radical itself, is divisible into these two parts. The radicals are limited in number, there being only 214 of them altogether. Some of them, such as 口 mouth, 人 man, 子 son, 魚 fish, 山 hill, 日 sun, 月 moon, are obviously pictorial, but a large number are certainly not pictorially suggestive. The character 鼻 *pi*, for instance, is a radical, and means a nose, but neither in this, its modern, nor in its primitive form can it be said to have the slightest resemblance to that organ. Yet we know, when we see it in combination, that the compound character must have something directly or indirectly to do with the nose. Thus, 齁 *hou*, to snore, 齈 *nung*, a cold in the head, 齉 *nang*, to speak through the nose; the radical on one side giving the clue to the meaning, the phonetic on the other giving the clue to the sound. One or two more instances will suffice. Radical 魚 *yü*, a fish; 鱛 *chi*, a mullet; 鱔 *shan*, an eel. Radical 風 *feng*, wind; 飄 *p'iao*, to be blown about. It will be noticed in this last character that the radical is on the right hand side, and not on the left. It seems probable that at one time it was always in a fixed position, but that variations were adopted for the sake of symmetry. There are now many Chinese characters the radical of which is placed at the top, below, or at one or other side, and in a few instances its position is determined by the fancy of the writer.

Besides being an indicator of the meaning, the radical has a further, and most important, value. By its aid it is possible to find any character in a dictionary of the Chinese language, whether purely native, or prepared for the use of the foreign student. Let us take the character 齁 for an example, the radical of which is 鼻, a nose. Now count the number of strokes in the phonetic. If we look up the radical 鼻 in the list of radicals at the beginning or end of the dictionary, as the case may be, where it will be placed in the numerical order of the strokes of which it is composed, we shall be able to trace it to its place in the body of the volume, and there we shall find the character we are in search of placed in the list of characters of five strokes ranged under that radical. In an Anglo-Chinese dictionary the sound will naturally be given as well as the meaning, but as the Chinese have, obviously, no system of spelling such as is supplied in an alphabetical language, they have to adopt another method of indicating the pronunciation. By this method of spelling, if it can be so called, which was introduced by Buddhist monks from India,* the sound of a character is given by means of two other characters of which the first is the initial and the second the final; these two are manipulated in such a way as to yield the sound required. It might here be mentioned that each Chinese word sound belongs to one of four (in composition, five) gradations of tone which can also be indicated by the above method, but an explanation of the tone system will find a more appropriate place in the remarks which follow on the spoken language.

To illustrate the Chinese method of spelling the reader is referred once more to the character 鱔, an eel, which will be found in the list of phonetics of twelve strokes under the radical 魚, a fish. Immediately below this character in the dictionary we shall find two others: one pronounced *shang*, and the next *yen*. Place them together—shangyen; eliminate the termination of the first and the initial sound of the second—sha(ngye)n—and we get *shan*, which is the sound of the character we are looking for. In the case of characters of a complicated nature in which the radical is not easily distinguishable, the dictionaries supply a further assistance by furnishing a list of these characters arranged in order of the total number of strokes, including the radical, which is shown against the character. Where characters are formed by a combination of two or more radicals there is nothing to do but try them all until the right one is discovered.

To return for a moment to the phonetics. A Chinese gets to

---

* Probably about 510 A.D.

learn these by practice at school, and knows them intuitively, but European investigators have discovered that their number is limited, for practical purposes, to something between 1,600 and 1,700, from which, by the addition of one or other of the 214 radicals, at least seven-eighths of the characters in the Chinese language, variously estimated at forty or fifty thousand, are found. It is possible, therefore, by learning these phonetics, or primitives as they are sometimes called, to make a very close guess at the sound of any Chinese character, though it must be admitted that there are many exceptions to the rule.

Illustrations have been given above of the primitive and modern forms of certain Chinese characters. The former, it may be well to repeat, are more or less conjectural, for there is probably no genuine specimen in existence of a purely pictorial character. The so-called modern form is modern only by comparison, for it dates from at least the 2nd century B.C. It probably has remained unchanged from the time of the invention of printing in China, which, according to Mr. Watters, dates from the Sui Dynasty (A.D. 589-619), and we are safe in assuming that the written language of to-day "is to all intents and purposes the written language of twenty-five hundred years ago." * The earliest genuine specimen of connected Chinese writing is to be found on certain stone blocks or cones, commonly called the "Stone Drums," † which are now deposited in the Confucian Temple at Peking. There are isolated specimens of an undoubtedly earlier date than the stone drums which have been copied from old coins and vases, but for the purposes of this chapter they need not be taken into consideration, as the originals are now probably not in existence. The exact age of the "Stone Drums" cannot be positively determined, but Chinese writers, with a few exceptions, agree in assigning them to the period of Hsuan Wang, in the Chou Dynasty, two centuries before the time of Confucius, which would make them about 2,700 years old. The inscriptions consist of poetry, written in what is known as the old seal character, commemorating one of the hunting expeditions of

---

* Professor Giles, *China and the Chinese*.

† An exception should, perhaps, be made in favour of a bronze tripod in a temple on "Silver Island," in the river Yangtsze, which is also assigned by many Chinese experts to the same date as the Stone Drums.

Hsüan Wang, who is supposed to have reigned from B.C. 827 to 781. Only a small portion of these inscriptions is legible, but a facsimile is appended of a rubbing taken from one of the stones in the Sung Dynasty (A.D. 960-1127).*

It is not until a much later period that anything like examples of a thoroughly systematized form of writing can be found. Silk preceded paper as a material for writing upon, and it was in the first century A.D. that paper was invented. The introduction of a hair pencil or brush is ascribed to a general of the Emperor Shih Huang Ti (B.C. 221).

The various styles of writing recognized as orthodox by the Chinese may be reduced to six, if we exclude a fanciful ancient form

---

* I am indebted to Dr. S. W. Bushell, C.M.G., for permission to use this specimen. An article on the Stone Drums of Peking, by Dr. Bushell, was published in Vol. viii. of the *Journal* of the North China Branch of the Royal Asiatic Society, New Series, 1873.

known as the "tadpole-headed," in which all the characters are made to terminate in a form similar to the tail of a tadpole. Of this latter form few, if any, genuine examples exist, though tradition has it that a copy of a portion of the Chinese Classics written in the "tadpole" script was discovered about the year 150 B.C. hidden away in the walls of the house originally occupied by Confucius, where it had been placed by some of his descendants to escape the burning of all written records by the Emperor Shih Huang Ti in B.C. 213. The first of the above mentioned six styles is known as the *Chuan Shu*, commonly called the "Seal character" by Europeans. It is said to date from the reign of King Hsuan (B.C. 827) whose hunting exploits are supposed to be recorded on the Stone Drums.

宋 草 行 楷 隸 篆

The next is the *Li Shu*, or style of official attendants or clerks. It was used by writers in the public offices, and possibly dates from the time of Chi'n Shih Huang Ti (B.C. 213).

宋 草 行 楷 隸 篆

The third is the *Ch'iai Shu*, or pattern style, from which all modern forms have originated. This probably dates from the beginning of the Christian Era.

宋 草 行 楷 隸 篆

The fourth, the *Hsing Shu*, may be translated as the "running hand," the pencil being carried from stroke to stroke without being raised from the paper, but no abbreviations unauthorized by the dictionaries appear to have been introduced. Date, about A.D. 200.

宋 草 行 楷 隸 篆

The fifth style, *Ts'ao tzŭ*, or "grass characters," dating from about the same period, is a freer style of the running hand than the foregoing, and is full of abbreviations which render it very difficult even to an educated native. It is still in common use, and is largely employed in Japan and Korea

亐 学 丨 朴 隷 篆

The sixth and last class, known as the *Sung T'i*, or style of the Sung Dynasty, is the printed style introduced under the Dynasty whose name it bears. It was adopted in the early part of the tenth century, and since that period it has undergone no material alterations.

宋 草 行 楷 隷 篆

A description has been given of the method of looking up characters in a dictionary by counting the number of strokes the character contains, exclusive of the radical. Some knowledge of the mode of writing is necessary for an accurate calculation of the number of strokes. The pencil, it may be well to explain, is held in a vertical position between the thumb on one side and the forefinger and second finger on the other. The following character is said to include the elements of all the strokes required in Chinese writing :—

Horizontal strokes are drawn before perpendicular ones; central strokes before those on each side; and those on the left before those on the right. A single stroke often takes one, and sometimes two, curves, as on the left side of the above character, which is formed of six strokes, in the following order:

The above brief description will, it is hoped, enable the reader to understand something of the form and structure of this marvellous script, which has been for ages past, and still continues to be, the medium of communication between a vast proportion of the human race. In its present form it is read and understood, not only throughout the whole dominions of an Empire embracing—to take the popular estimate—three hundred and sixty millions of human beings, but it is also extensively used in adjacent kingdoms. In Korea, the Chinese Classics are studied in all the schools and exert no inconsiderable influence on the character of the nation, while Chinese is the common vehicle of official correspondence; in the Loochoo Islands many of the inhabitants read it fluently; in Tonking a knowledge of it is possessed by the educated classes; while in Japan it still constitutes the basis of the written language. Ever since the days of Confucius it has practically remained unchanged in construction, and the style of books published two thousand years ago differs little from the written language of the present day. It is hardly to be wondered at that so ancient and so widely diffused a script should be an object of veneration to the Chinese scholar, who regards it, from its universality and its adaptability to any system of speech, as vastly superior to all others. He admires it not less for its intrinsic beauty and excellence than for the vast stores of knowledge and wisdom which he considers it to embrace. To many thoughtful Chinese it is a matter of surprise that this script has not been adopted as a common medium of communication throughout the world. "Attach," they say, "what sound or pronunciation to the character you like, the meaning will still remain invariable. Why multiply scripts and invent complicated systems when you have ready to hand a language free from grammatical intricacies, a language that has stood the test of ages, and in which it has been found that no changes were necessary or desirable? It can keep pace with modern requirements, for when a new word or term has to be employed it is perfectly easy to invent a symbol to indicate it, while there is not a 'single thought, phrase or idea that is not capable of expression in Chinese." *

All this is, theoretically, true enough, but what the Chinese enthusiast loses sight of is the immense amount of study required to obtain a working knowledge of even the small proportion of the forty odd thousand characters that are required for practical purposes, while nothing but constant practice will enable any one to write these characters correctly. Chinese caligraphy is an art in which few, if any, Europeans have ever become proficient. It is possible to acquire facility in writing, but elegance of style can only be arrived at by those who have commenced to learn in childhood and have practised daily throughout the years of their educational life. There is another point overlooked by the Chinese enthusiast which is at the root of the supreme difficulty attending anything approaching to proficiency in the written language. It is not impossible to obtain a working knowledge of three, four, or five thousand symbols, which is all that a man of average education need have at his command—a knowledge of 2,000 characters would be sufficient to take one through the whole Chinese Penal Code, for instance—and if each character expressed only one word or idea, and was always limited to that one word, the difficulty would be comparatively small. But this is not the case. Almost every character, by being placed in a different position in a sentence, or used in a different combination, assumes, in some instances a different shade of meaning, and in others expresses an entirely new idea. The absence of grammar, which the language is popularly supposed to enjoy, does not present such a difficulty to the student as might be supposed. Indeed, it may be said to be somewhat of a luxury to find oneself untrammelled by the forms and accidents of grammatical rule. Number, case, mood, tense, &c., can be indicated by particles, while the value of the word which does duty impartially for noun, preposition, or verb can generally be discovered by a study of the context. The real

---

* "The works of Darwin and Mill were soon rendered into Japanese, equivalents for the many novel terms they contained being manufactured from the ideographic vocabulary, far the most elastic and capable instrument of speech that exists."—Tokio Correspondent, *The Times*, Jan. 18th, 1904.

difficulty in the comprehension and use of the written language for anything beyond the simplest purposes lies in the fact that it abounds in metaphor and allusion. The elegant writer loves to display his erudition by the employment of quotations from the books, canonical and historical, the study of which is a necessary part of his education. If he wishes to express a thought out of the common, or a complex idea, he dives into his store of recollection and quotes a word or two from the sayings of some ancient sage which are suggestive rather than perspicuous. If he wanted to speak, for instance, of the "uses of adversity" in an English composition, he would refer to a "toad's jewel," and pre-suppose the reader to be fully acquainted with the passage in Shakespeare that compares adversity to the precious jewel in the head of the toad. It is this that makes it impossible for the ordinary foreigner to do more than spell his way through a modern official document, or to understand anything but an ordinary note. In fact, it may safely be said that the average educated Chinese is incapable of expressing himself elegantly in his own language. He can understand what he reads, but he cannot write a polished letter, or turn out a finished despatch. The ancient forms of Chinese verse, or the writings of Confucius or Mencius, are child's play compared with the works of later authors, while an elegant essay, composed for an examination for example, would be almost unintelligible to an ordinary individual without the aid of a dictionary of reference or the explanations of a well-read scholar who had history at his fingers' ends, and could supply the context from which the numerous quotations are taken. In almost all Chinese composition, again, measured periods, not unlike blank verse, abound, and are esteemed by the scholar as a capital beauty of the language. Ideas, it may be said, often form the secondary object of consideration, the mode in which they are expressed claiming first attention. Thought also is stereotyped, and all the ideas which the Chinese wish to cherish or indicate are contained, as stated above, in those records which have come down to them from the sages of antiquity. Excellence in composition, therefore, consists in arranging anew orthodox phrases which are to be found in the ancient classics or in the formidable list of historical or poetical works that the scholar delights to study. Each branch, moreover, of Chinese literature possesses a peculiar style of its own. Any one who could read official Chinese, of which the *Peking Gazette* may be taken as a typical exemplar, would not necessarily be able to understand an historical work, while books on philosophy, on Buddhism or on Taoism would be almost unintelligible without a special study of their style. Modern literature can hardly be said to exist, and novels, as we understand them, are almost all placed under the ban of Imperial prohibition. They are to be found in limited numbers, it is true, but there are no modern society novels. Those which are procurable place the scene in a bygone dynasty, and few are free from objectionable episodes. The educated classes profess to despise fiction, but I suppose that there is not a single Chinese of the lettered class who has not read the few historical novels that are not in the " Index Expurgatorius," and are considered to be classics in their particular line.

I close these necessarily condensed remarks on the written language with a few examples illustrative of various styles of Chinese composition.

The first is the opening verse of an ode in which a gentleman deplores his disappointment in not meeting a lady according to engagement. It is selected, more or less at random, from the *Shih Ching*, or Book of Odes, collected by Confucius. The date is not known, but it must have been composed long before the time of Confucius, who was born B.C. 552. Against each character the meaning is placed, in order to show how it is that the Chinese language is, to a certain extent, independent of grammar or grammatical particles, and also how easy it is to arrive at the meaning of many passages of primitive Chinese. It should be noted that Chinese characters are written in columns, commencing on the right hand side of the page.

scratch	搔	love	愛	wait	俟	quiet	靜
head.	首	yet	而	I	我	girl	女
undecided	踟	not	不	at	於	her	其
halt	蹰	see	見	city wall	城	beauty	姝
				corner	隅		

Here is the rendering given in Dr. Legge's translation *:—

> How lovely is the retiring girl,
> She was to await me at a corner of the wall.
> Loving and not seeing her
> I scratch my head and am in perplexity.

* *The Chinese Classics*, Dr. Legge, Vol. i., Part 4, p. 68.

14 THE CHINESE LANGUAGE

All this is simple enough. Any one with a knowledge of the radicals and with the aid of a dictionary could make it out for himself, filling in the grammatical *lacunae* as suited his fancy. The same may be said of the following, taken from the *Lun Yu*, or collected sayings of Confucius, called by Dr. Legge the Confucian "Analects." Their antiquity is beyond question, and we may safely consider them to date from some time before the Christian Era.

yet	而	proud,	驕、	Tsze	子
happy,	樂、	how	何	Kung	貢
rich,	富	as.	如。	say	曰
yet	而	master	子	poor,	貧
like	好	say,	曰	yet	而
propriety	禮	can,	可	not	無
person	者	final particle	也、	flatter,	諂、
terminal particle	也	not as,	未若	rich, yet	富而
		poor	貧	not	無

Dr. Legge translates as follows, supplying, as before, the gaps:—

Tsze Kung said, "What do you pronounce concerning the poor man who yet does not flatter and the rich man who is not proud?" The master said, "They will do, but they are not equal to him, who, though poor, is yet cheerful, and to him who, though rich, loves the rules of propriety."

I treat my third and last example in the same manner as the foregoing, placing the more or less elementary meaning of the word against each character.

yellow	黃	drive,	驅、	at	於
cart	車	hundred	百	this	是
attendant	使者、	insects	蟲	control	司
one,		take	將	heat	烜
bright	爛	army,	軍、	inform	戒
the	其	brightness	煥	order,	令、
filled	盈	as	然	o	闍
door,	門、	burning	烈	po	伯
red	絳	few,	澤、	front	前

room.	屋	finish	畢	cloud,	雲、
		then	方	rise	起
·		fly	飛	and	而
		and	而	roll up	捲
		rise	升	mist,	霄、

The above passage is taken from a letter in the published collection of the correspondence of one Yuan Tzŭ-ts'ai, a scholar holding office at Nanking in A.D. 1716, whose style is held in high esteem. The writer condoles with a friend on the occasion of his house being burnt down. The elementary meanings of the various characters are given, as stated above, but many of these have various significations either singly or in combination, and any one with a knowledge of Chinese would be assisted in his selection by experience, as well as by examples quoted in the dictionary. Even so, there is certainly no European scholar, and probably very few Chinese, who could understand the passage without the assistance of a commentary. It consists of eight sentences, and eight elliptical quotations from various authors, none of which could be intelligibly rendered without considerable amplification of the context from which they were derived, accompanied by copious notes. It should of course be understood that the passage has been selected as an illustration of the difficulties with which the Chinese can, if they like, beset their own language. Happily it is by no means necessary for any one, even a Chinese himself, to indulge in this literary jugglery. The modern style of Chinese composition that is daily gaining ground, partly in consequence of the revised system of education, which is placing classics and poetry somewhat in the background, and also through the influence of the newspapers, which are now read by millions of people, is bringing a much simpler form of composition into vogue which can be read with comparative ease.

II.

The Spoken Language

DURING its progress through a long series of ages the Chinese spoken language, it may readily be supposed, underwent many changes. To refer to one proof alone, the specimens of ancient poetry still in existence establish this fact by the rhyming of words which have now, in many instances, no uniformity of sound. Its origin is, and must remain, a mystery in spite of the array of opinions and judgments concerning it, and as none of them can possibly be conclusive, or indeed more than purely speculative, it seems advisable to leave theory alone, and to pass on at once to modern fact. Those who are interested in the attempts to trace the origin of the language to its source, and to establish its family relationship with the great clan of human tongues, are referred once more to Mr. Watters' *Essay on the Chinese Language*, and particularly to the chapter entitled "Some Western Opinions." They will there find that it has been regarded by some as a special creation, by others as the language spoken by Noah, and Shem, the son of Noah, who moved into China in time to escape the confusion of tongues; that others, again, discover a relationship between the language of China and that of ancient Egypt, while some investigators try to prove that there is a connection between Chinese and the Hebrew tongue.

Wherever it sprang from originally, we know that the pronunciation of the language in the days of Confucius and that of the present day is so dissimilar as to make it a matter of certainty that Confucius would understand nothing of the speech that now prevails at his native place in the province of Shantung. He might, probably, according to Mr. E. H. Parker,* an eminent authority, be more at home in Korea, or Annam, or, possibly, Canton, but he certainly would be unable to understand his own remarks as recited by the modern school-boy in any part of the Empire. And it may

---

* Professor of Chinese at Owen's College, Manchester.

be as well at this stage to state that China, which, during the early part of her history was often divided into small states, is not a country in which one spoken language prevails, varied only by provincialisms, but, to quote again from Professor Giles, there are about eight well-marked dialects, all clearly of a common stock, but so distinct as to constitute eight different languages, any two of which are quite as unlike as English and Dutch. These dialects, as pointed out by Professor Giles,* fringe the coast line of China, and between Canton, on the extreme south, and Shanghai, near the mouth of the Yangtsze, we encounter no less than seven dialects, each so different from the other as to be quite unintelligible to any but a native of the particular district in which the dialect prevails. Throughout the region of the Yangtsze Valley, as it has now come to be called, and from thence northwards, we "come into the range of the great dialect, popularly known as 'Mandarin,' which sweeps round behind the narrow strip of coast occupied by the various dialects above mentioned, and dominates a hinterland constituting about four-fifths of China proper." Throughout this region, "Mandarin," or the official dialect, will be understood, and Mandarin in its purest form is now the Mandarin of Peking, or the Court dialect, which is to other forms of Mandarin somewhat as Parisian French is to the provincial dialects of France. It is to Mandarin, therefore, and especially to Pekingese Mandarin, that the following remarks will apply.

Theoretically, Chinese colloquial is not a difficult language to acquire. The street "coolie" of Peking, whose speech is practically the same as that of the highest official, has a vocabulary of a few hundred words at the outside which are amply sufficient for his wants. He can say anything he wishes to say with this stock of words, and is never at a loss for an expression. A foreign child brought up under the charge of a Chinese nurse will pick up Chinese words with much greater facility than it will imbibe English, and will be talking fluently in the vernacular long before it can do more than babble in the language of its parents, and yet a foreign adult may spend a lifetime in the country and not know ten words of Chinese. No traveller can pass two months in Japan

* *China and the Chinese,* p. 7.

C

without acquiring, without effort, a sufficient stock of words to make his wants easily known, whereas in China the stranger would leave the country after several months' sojourn with no idea of the language whatever beyond a few abusive epithets which had fastened themselves on his memory from their constant reiteration in his hearing.

"Pidgin" English, as the barbarous English spoken by the Chinese coolie or servant in Hong Kong is called, is nothing more or less than a literal translation of Chinese into English. The Englishman will pick it up in a week, and yet, if he tries to turn "pidgin" English into Chinese, he will find that at the end of twelve months he has made lamentably little progress. It may safely be said that any young Englishman of average intelligence and education who lived in France or in Germany for two years and devoted the whole of his time to the study of either language, would become a fluent speaker and writer at the end of that period. The Chinese Consular Service of Great Britain is officered by men who pass a severe competitive examination before admission, and must consequently be above the average standard of education and ability. The first two years of their career are spent in Peking, where the whole of their time is devoted to the study of the language under experienced supervision, and yet, at the end of this two years' course, there is not one of them who could personally conduct a correspondence in Chinese, translate an official document without the aid of a dictionary, or speak with sufficient fluency to act as an interpreter where important negotiations were concerned. Before they can reach this standard of proficiency they have at least five or six years of work before them.

What is the reason? There is nothing specially complicated about the language. Far from this being the case, its construction is fairly simple, much more so than that of a scientific language, German for instance, and in the matter of the expression of simple wants there is nothing difficult whatever. Yet it is not too much to say that not ten per cent. of Europeans who have devoted several years to the study of the language speak really well; that it requires from five to ten years constant practice to speak fluently, and that there is probably hardly a living instance of a European speaking Chinese so well as to be undistinguishable from a native.

On the other hand, any one who will take the trouble can acquire a sufficient vocabulary at the end of a few months to make his ordinary wants known, or to travel anywhere without the aid of an interpreter. If he wishes to get beyond this elementary stage he must make up his mind for some very up-hill work. In later chapters an attempt is made to assist the student in acquiring such a knowledge of the spoken language as will enable him to carry on an ordinary conversation. At the present stage it will suffice to indicate in general terms a few of the difficulties with which the learner has to contend, together with certain marked differences between the written and the spoken language.

The first of these difficulties is undoubtedly intonation, which, as stated above, is also an important feature in Chinese composition.

The Chinese language is restricted in the matter of sounds, of which there are, in the Peking dialect, about four hundred. It follows therefore that many words must have the same sound. In writing, this deficiency could naturally be ignored, as each ideograph speaks for itself, but, in speaking, it is evident that unless some means were devised by which words of the same sound could be distinguished, much confusion would result. But there is a system by which these sounds are sub-divided. In the first place, a considerable multiplication is effected by the expedient of duplicating many sounds having certain initial consonants by the interposition of an aspirate between the initial consonant and the vowel. By many Irishmen such a word as "chair" would be pronounced ch'air, with a strong aspirate after the ch. So, in Chinese, we have *Chi* and *Ch'i*, *tang* and *t'ang*, *pa* and *p'a*, and very many others, adding a large percentage to the number of sounds. But this number is still more appreciably increased by the pronunciation of the same sounds in different tones or inflections of the voice. Take, for instance, the sound *chi*. Under this sound are ranged no less than 135 characters, all pronounced *chi*. Although the number of conversational words pronounced *chi* is not so numerous as the written words, there is, none the less, a considerable number. We have, to quote a very few, *chi*, a chicken, *chi*, excited, *chi*, to push, *chi*, to remember. How are we to know which is which? The way they are distinguished is by intonation. The first *chi* is pronounced in an absolutely even tone, the voice neither rising nor falling, and this it is customary to indicate by chi^1. The second, which we will call chi^2, is pronounced in a rising tone something like an interrogative—chi^2?. The third, in a falling tone, chi^3, something like a tone of reproof with a rise at the end; and the fourth, chi^4, in an abrupt and somewhat dictatorial manner. To a Chinese, these tones come naturally, but to a foreign ear and tongue they present a great difficulty, to some an insurmountable difficulty, and yet, unless accurately pronounced, the word is not only as discordant as a false quantity would be in Latin, but is also extremely liable to be misunderstood.

If we wished to remark that we did not require chicken, we ought to say pu^1 yao^4 chi^1. If we said instead, pu^1 yao^3 chi^1, it would mean "do not bite the chicken," pu^1 yao^4 $chi,^2$ "do not be impatient," pu^1 yao^4 $chi,^3$ "don't shove," pu^1 yao^4 chi^4, "don't want to make a note of." It is evident, therefore, that tones are a very important element in the spoken language, indeed an all important one, and neglect or misuse of these tones will land the speaker in many and sometimes awkward, difficulties. A fluent and correct speaker will play upon these tones as the fingers of a violinist play up and down the strings of his instrument, and a false tone, apart from conveying a false meaning, is like a false note in music.

This tonic system plays a part also in Chinese composition. In poetry, and generally in prose composition, only words of a certain tone can occupy fixed places in a clause or line of a certain length, and any deviation from rule will set the line out of tune, though a regard for these rules is not necessary for purposes of clearness; rather the reverse, and they can be ignored in a document of an official or business nature.

A further aid to definiteness in conversation consists in the use of prefixes and suffixes in connection with certain nouns that stand alone in writing, and in the use of two or more words in speaking where one is used in writing. And here we come to the essential difference between the written and the spoken language. The former can be fairly called monosyllabic; the latter is undoubtedly syllabic.

To begin with the prefix. The sound $jên^2$ means man, but it also means benevolence. In speaking, we distinguish the former from the latter by the pre-position of what, for want of a better word, may be called a classifying article. The most common of these is *Ko*, best translated by the word "piece." In writing, man (or men), is indicated by one character; in speaking, it is *i ko jên*, one "piece" man, or *chi ko jen*, some "piece" man. So again, *ping*, a soldier, also ice, but in speaking, *i ko ping*, one piece soldier, *i k'uai ping*, a bit of ice. There are several dozen of these classifiers, each of which takes a certain number of nouns under its protection. Again, in the written language the character *yin*[2] is silver; in speaking, we distinguish this *yin* from many other similar sounds, and indicate that it is a substantive, by calling it *yintzŭ*; so also, in writing, *mao*, a hat, in speaking, *maotzŭ*. This rule holds good of a large number of nouns, but not of all, and there are other suffixes besides the one mentioned. As a further illustration of the syllabic nature of the spoken language a few more examples may be given. To be willing in written Chinese is *yüan*; in colloquial it is *yüani*; *i*, intention, colloquial, *issŭ*; *li*, a hedge, colloquial, *lipa*; *huan*, to rejoice, colloquial, *hsihuan*. Other expressions in the spoken language are entirely different from those in writing, as *jih*, sun, colloquial, *t'aiyang* or *jiht'ou*, but it may be said generally that there is a close analogy between the two, the essential difference lying in the fact that whereas redundancy is necessary in speaking to ensure intelligibility, the written language aims at conciseness and the elimination of all superfluity of words.

Pronunciation, apart from intonation, is a further serious impediment in the way of the speaker, such sounds as *chih*, *jih*, *tzŭ*, *ssŭ*, *tz'ŭ*, *ch'u*, etc., which are incapable of exact reproduction by any recognized system of spelling, requiring months of practice before they can be uttered correctly. And, finally, it is necessary to forget one's own idiom when trying to talk Chinese, and to remember that what in the one language seems a complicated sentence can often be rendered with great simplicity in the other. The Chinese language abounds in proverbial and idiomatic expressions. It is in the discovery of these, and the right use of them, coupled with the appropriate gestures, mannerisms and intonations, that the secret of successful speaking lies.

As a final demonstration of the distinction that is drawn between the written and the spoken languages, it may be stated that the

Chinese do not read books of a high-class character aloud to an audience. One could not imagine, for instance, a public reading of the poems of a Chinese Milton, Browning or Tennyson, or of Macaulay's Essays, for the simple reason that they would not be understood if they had not been studied beforehand by the audience, letting alone the fact that half the so-called beauties of Chinese composition gain nothing by recitation. The only instance of recitation in book language is to be found on the stage. There, historical plays are presented in which the actors talk like books, but as the audience have either read the books or know all about the incidents represented, they can follow the dialogue and understand the plot. It is quite possible to write down colloquial Chinese, but it is never so written except in a few novels or in the minutes of evidence taken in a court of Law. If a Chinese were called upon to record a conversation he would inevitably transpose it into literary form.

From what has been said above it will be realized that the popular estimate of the supreme difficulty of the Chinese language is not far wide of the mark. Fluency in speaking, as has been shown, is attainable by most people who will devote the necessary labour to its acquisition, and translation of written Chinese into a foreign language is not beyond the capacity of any diligent student, but it may safely be asserted that there is no living European who can reverse the process and turn out unaided an original Chinese composition of sufficient elegance to command the respect of a Chinese scholar. Proficiency in this direction would necessitate a life-long devotion to the study of Chinese literature to the exclusion of everything else. The late M. Stanislaus Julien might, perhaps, alone of Chinese students have laid claim to this distinction, and he, curiously enough, was unable to speak intelligibly, had never been in China in his life, and was entirely self-taught.

III.

It has been suggested in the previous section that the vocabulary of the ordinary Chinese working man does not exceed a few hundred words, and it is obvious that any one who could secure a knowledge of these words would be on the high road to an understanding of the language spoken by the Chinese coolie. A thorough working acquaintance with the vocabulary of a coolie in all its varied combinations would be sufficient for most people, as the coolie, to all intents and purposes, speaks the language which his master speaks, and if his stock of Chinese words could be handled in the way that he handles them the person who possessed this faculty would have little left to desire. The full possession of this facility is more than the few succeeding chapters profess to offer the student, but at least it is possible to supply him with a fairly representative list of words and to indicate a few of the numberless combinations which they can be made to form. If he will take the trouble to make this list his own he will find it comparatively easy to enlarge his vocabulary by the aid of text books and dictionaries. Of the former, the two most in use are the *Tzŭ Erh Chi*, by the late Sir Thomas Wade, and *Mandarin Lessons*, by the Rev. C. W. Mateer. An Anglo-Chinese glossary of words in common use will be furnished in a separate volume. The written language would require a somewhat larger stock of characters, which cannot be used in precisely the same way, but this subject will be dealt with separately. The present and succeeding chapters will deal exclusively with the colloquial form of Chinese.

It may be as well to repeat at this point that Chinese do not write as they speak, and that when we write down words as they are spoken we are, so to speak, treading on the susceptibilities of the Chinese scholar, who regards written colloquial as unscholarly, but for educational purposes the prejudice of the Chinese pedant may well be ignored. It may be asked, "Why, in this case, is it necessary for the student of colloquial Chinese to learn the character at all? Would not a transliteration of the sounds as in an alphabetical language satisfy all requirements?" The experiment has been tried, but it has never been a success, owing, amongst other causes, to the complications presented by the four intonations referred to in the previous chapter, while it is most unsatisfactory to find one's horizon limited by ignorance of the symbols used by the people themselves. There is probably no short cut to a knowledge of any language, and certainly none to Chinese. If a student will not take the small amount of trouble necessary to master eight hundred to a thousand symbols he had better leave Chinese alone.

The question of pronunciation must be faced at the outset. If the learner goes far wrong in his initial appreciation of the value of Chinese sounds he will find it difficult to correct his mistakes later on. Some Chinese sounds are incapable of production by any alphabetical combinations, and nothing but oral demonstration will make them clear, but, happily, these are few, and most of them can be spelt in such a way that any one should be able to pronounce them fairly correctly. If it were a question merely of inventing a vocabulary for the use of the English student alone the matter would be comparatively simple, but what has been aimed at by those who have tried to work out a system of spelling is to produce something of a cosmopolitan nature that shall be understood by all. The result has been that no one can understand any of the various systems elaborated without divesting himself of preconceived notions as to how certain combinations of letters should be pronounced, and beginners often go astray because they have not carefully studied the directions as to the way to read the vocabularies. Of these there are several, but the best system of transliteration is undoubtedly that elaborated by Sir Thomas Wade. It is, necessarily, not perfect, but it is probably as good as any that can be made, and in spite of much antagonism it has held its own and has outlived various systems which other scholars have endeavoured to force upon the public. All English-speaking people accept it, and though other nationalities spell many Chinese sounds in their own way, they have to fall back on the Wade system when writing for universal imformation.

The sounds as expressed in the Wade system are given below, and, in order to make them as intelligible as possible, alternative spellings in simple English form are added to each sound. If the reader will bear in mind that A is always pronounced *ar*, that I is *ee* or *i* as in French, and U *oo*, he will be saved much confusion. Other peculiarities will, to a certain extent, be indicated by the alternative spellings, and an attempt is made to show how the specially difficult sounds can be reproduced.

TABLE OF SOUNDS.

Wade system.	Approximate sound in English spelling.	Wade system.	Approximate sound in English spelling.
A	are	Ch'ien	ch'eeyen
Ai	aye, as in kite	Chih	chih. No combination of letters will exactly produce this sound. The nearest approach to it will be found in hi, of the word chivalry
An	arn, as in yarn		
Ang	arng		
Ao	ow, as in how		
Cha	char, as in charge		
Ch'a	ch'ar		
Chai	chy, as in shy		
Ch'ai	ch'y	Ch'ih	ch'ih
Chan	charn	Chin	chin, as in English
Ch'an	ch'arn	Ch'in	ch'in
Chang	charng	Ching	ching, as in sing
Ch'ang	ch'arng	Ch'ing	ch'ing
Chao	chow, as in how	Chiu	cheeoo
Ch'ao	ch'ow	Ch'iu	ch'eeoo
Chê	cher, as in church	Chiung	cheeoong
Ch'ê	ch'er	Ch'iung	ch'eeoong
Chên	chunn, as in run	Cho	chore
Ch'ên	ch'unn	Ch'o	ch'ore
Chêng	chung, as in bung	Chou	chowe, as in owe
Ch'êng	ch'ung	Ch'ou	ch'owe
Chi	chee, as in cheese	Chu	chew, as in English
Ch'i	ch'ee	Ch'u	ch'ew
Chia	cheear, as in c(hurc)h-yar(d)	Chua	chwarr; arr, as in tar
		Ch'ua	ch'warr
Ch'ia	ch'eear	Chuai	chwhy; why, as in English
Chiang	cheearng		
Ch'iang	ch'eearng	Ch'uai	ch'why
Chiao	cheeyow; ow, as in how	Chuan	chwarn; arn, as in yarn
Ch'iao	ch'eeyow	Ch'uan	ch'warn
Chieh	cheeay; ay, as in hay	Chuang	chwong
Ch'ieh	ch'eeay	Ch'uang	ch'wong
Chien	cheeyen; yen, as in hen	Chui	choey; oey, as in Joey

Wade system.	Approximate sound in English spelling.	Wade system.	Approximate sound in English spelling.
Ch'ui	ch'oey	Fei	fay, as in favour
Chun	choon; approximately, as in moon, only a little shorter	Fên	funn
		Fêng	fung, as in fungus
		Fo	for
Ch'un	ch'oon	Fou	fowe, as in owe
Chung	choong	Fu	foo, as in fool
Ch'ung	ch'oong	Ha	har
Chü	chü, the French u; the u as pronounced in Devon, as "vule," for fool. The lips must be pursed, and the tip of the tongue placed close to the front teeth	Hai	high, as in English
		Han	harn
		Hang	harng
		Hao	how, as in English
		Hei	hay
		Hên	hunn
		Hêng	hung, as in English
		Hou	hoe, as in English
Ch'ü	ch'ü	Hsi	hsee, something between she and see
Chüan	chüarn		
Ch'üan	ch'üarn	Hsia	seeare; are, as in English
Chueh	chuay; ay, as in hay		
Ch'ueh	ch'uay	Hsiang	seearng
Chun	chun; ün, as "moon," in Devon—"müne." The French u.	Hsiao	seeow; ow, as in how
		Hsieh	seeay; ay, as in hay
		Hsien	see-enn
Ch'ün	ch'ün	Hsin	hsin, something between sin and shin
Ên	unn		
Êrh	errh, the errh, like the er of her, as pronounced in Devon. The tip of the tongue should point to the roof of the mouth, which should be slightly open	Hsing	hsing
		Hsiu	seeyou; you, as in English
		Hsiung	seeyoong
		Hsü	hsü, the French u
		Hsüan	hsüarn
		Hsüeh	hsüay
		Hsün	hsün
Fa	far	Hu	who, as in English
Fan	farn	Hua	hwar; hw, as in wh'ich
Fang	farng	Huai	hwhy

Wade system.	Approximate sound in English spelling.	Wade system.	Approximate sound in English spelling.
Huan	hwarn; arn, as in tarn	K'ên	k'unn
Huang	hwong	Kêng	kung, as in hung
Hui	hway	K'êng	k'ung
Hun	hwoon	Ko	kore, as in core
Huo	hwor	K'o	k'ore
I	ee, as in see	Kou	kowe, as in owe
Jan	jan, as in the French Jeanne. The initial j is sounded as the French j, with a slight tendency towards an r	K'ou	k'owe
		Ku	koo, as in coo
		K'u	k'oo
		Kua	kwar, as in car
		K'ua	k'war
		Kuai	kwaye; aye, as in kite
Jao	jao	K'uai	k'waye
Jo	jor	Kuan	kwarn, as in tarn
Jih	jih; the ih as the i in chivalry; j as in French	K'uan	k'warn
		Kuang	kwong, as in long
		K'uang	kw'ong
Jou	jowe; owe, as in English	Kuei	kway, as in way
		K'uei	k'way
Ju	joo	Kun	kwoon, between coon and kwoon
Juan	jooarn		
Jui	jowy, as in showy	K'un	k'woon
Jun	joon	Kung	koong
Jung	joong	K'ung	k'oong
Ka	kar, as in car	Kuo	kwor
K'a	k'ar	K'uo	k'wor
Kai	kaye, as in kite	La	lar
K'ai	k'aye	Lai	laye, as in lie
Kan	karn	Lan	larn
K'an	k'arn	Lang	larng
Kang	karng	Lao	low, as in allow
K'ang	k'arng	Lei	lay, as in English
Kao	kow, as in cow	Lêng	lung
K'ao	k'ow	Li	lee
Kei	kay, as in hay	Lia	leear, as in yard
Kên	kunn	Liang	leearng

Wade system.	Approximate sound in English spelling.	Wade system.	Approximate sound in English spelling.
Liao	leeaou, as in "meeaow"	Nai	nigh, as in English
		Nan	narn
Lieh	leeay; ay, as in hay	Nang	narng
Lien	lee-enn	Nao	now, as in English
Lin	lin, as in pin	Nei	nay, as in English
Ling	ling, as in sing	Nên	nun
Liu	leeyou, as in you	Nêng	nung, as in hung
Lo	lore	Ni	nee, as in knee
Lou	low	Niang	niarng
Lu	loo	Niao	neeaow
Luan	looarn	Nieh	neeay; ay, as in hay
Lun	loon; oon a little shorter than in loon	Nien	nee-en
		Niu	neeoo
Lung	loong	No	nor
Lü	lu, the French u	Nou	no, as in English
Lüan	lüarn	Nu	noo
Lüeh	lüay; ay, as in hay	Nuan	nooarn
Ma	mar	Nung	noong
Mai	maye, as in eye	Nü	nu, the French u
Man	marn	O	or
Mang	marng	Ou	oh
Mao	mow, as in how	Pa	par
Mei	may, as in English	P'a	p'ar
Mên	munn	Pai	pie, as in English
Mêng	mung	P'ai	p'ie
Mi	mee	Pan	parn
Miao	meeaow	P'an	p'arn
Mieh	meeay; ay, as in hay	Pang	parng
Mien	me-enn	P'ang	p'arng
Min	min	Pao	pow, as in how
Ming	ming	P'ao	p'ow
Miu	meeoo	Pei	pay, as in English
Mo	more	P'ei	p'ay
Mou	mow, as in English	Pên	punn
Mu	moo	P'ên	p'unn
Na	nar, as in tar	Pêng	pung

Wade system.	Approximate sound in English spelling.	Wade system.	Approximate sound in English spelling.
P'êng	p'ung	Shou	show, as in English
Pi	pea, as in English	Shu	shoo
P'i	p'ea	Shua	shwarr, as in tar
Piao	peeaow, as in "meeaow"	Shuai	shwhy; why, as in English
P'iao	p'eeaow		
Pieh	peeay; ay, as in hay	Shuan	shwarn
P'ieh	p'eeay	Shuang	shwarng
Pien	pee-en	Shui	showy, as in English
P'ien	p'ee-en	Shun	shoon
Pin	pin	Shuo	shwor
P'in	p'in	So	sor
Ping	ping	Sou	so, as in English
P'ing	p'ing	Su	soo
Po	por	Suan	sooarn
P'o	p'or	Sui	sowey
Pou	pow, as in roe	Sun	soon
P'ou	p'ow	Sung	soong
Pu	poo	Ssŭ	szz. The nearest approach to this sound is to be found in the zz of buzz. Leave out the "bu," and put an s before zz, keeping the lips open, the teeth closed, and the tip of the tongue curled downwards and against the lower front teeth.
P'u	p'oo		
Sa	sar		
Sai	sigh		
San	sarn		
Sang	sarng		
Sao	sow, as in how		
Sê	sir		
Sên	sunn		
Sêng	sung, as in English		
Sha	shar		
Shai	shy, as in English		
Shan	sharn		
Shang	sharng	Ta	tar
Shao	shaow; ow, as in how	T'a	t'ar
Shê	sher	Tai	tie, as in English
Shên	shunn	T'ai	t'ie
Shêng	shung	Tan	tarn
Shih	shih, as in chivalry	T'an	t'arn
		Tang	tarng

Wade system.	Approximate sound in English spelling.	Wade system.	Approximate sound in English spelling.
T'ang	t'arng	Tsên	tzunn
Tao	taow, as in how	Ts'ên	ts'unn
T'ao	t'aow	Tsêng	tzung
Tê	ter	Ts'êng	ts'ung
T'ê	t'er	Tso	tzor
Tei	tay, as in pay	Ts'o	ts'or
Têng	tung, as in hung	Tsou	tzowe
T'êng	t'ung	Ts'ou	ts'owe
Ti	tea, as in English	Tsu	tzoo
T'i	t'ea	Ts'u	ts'oo
Tiao	teeaow, as in "meeaow"	Tsuan	tzooarn
T'iao	t'eeaow	Ts'uan	ts'ooarn
Tieh	teeay	Tsui	tzowey
T'ieh	t'eeay	Ts'ui	ts'owey
Tien	tee-en	Tsun	tzoon
T'ien	t'ee-en	Ts'un	ts'oon
Ting	ting	Tsung	tzoong
T'ing	t'ing	Ts'ung	ts'oong
Tiu	teeyou	Tu	too
To	tor; the o must be slightly dwelt on.	T'u	t'oo
		Tuan	tooarn
T'o	t'or	T'uan	t'ooarn
Tou	toe, as in English	Tui	towey
T'ou	t'oe	T'ui	t'owey
Tsa	tzar	Tun	toon
Ts'a	ts'ar	T'un	t'oon
Tsai	tzaye	Tung	toong
Ts'ai	ts'aye	T'ung	t'oong
Tsan	tzarn	Tzŭ	tzz; see szz. Omit bu in buzz, and substitute t before zz, keeping the teeth closed, the lips open, and tip of the tongue pointing downwards and close against the lower front teeth.
Ts'an	ts'arn		
Tsang	tzarng		
Ts'ang	ts'arng		
Tsao	tzow, as in how		
Ts'ao	ts'ow		
Tsê	tzer		
Ts'ê	ts'er		
Tsei	tzay, as in hay		

Wade system.	Approximate sound in English spelling.	Wade system.	Approximate sound in English spelling.
Tz'ŭ	t'zz	Yai	yaye, as in eye
Wa	war, as in jar	Yang	yarng
Wai	why	Yao	yaow; ow, as in how
Wan	warn, as in yarn	Yeh	yea, as in English
Wang	warng	Yen	yee-en
Wei	way, as in English	Yin	yin
Wên	one, as in English	Ying	ying
Wêng	wung	Yu	yeo, as in yeoman
Wo	wor	Yu	yu, the French u
Wu	woo	Yueh	yueh
Ya	yar	Yun	yunn

IV.

We now come to the "characters" which have been selected as likely to be of the greatest general utility. These are placed at the bottom of each page, and against each the "Wade" transliteration has been put, with the tone expressed in figures 1, 2, 3 and 4, and the meaning most commonly attached to it.

Different ways of fixing the characters on the memory will no doubt suggest themselves to individual students, but it may be of assistance to those who have no plan of campaign if a method is explained which has been pursued with fairly satisfactory results.

Each character should be carefully copied on a separate slip of paper, preferably about an inch square, and at the back of each ticket the sound, tone and meaning should be written.* These squares should be gone through daily, and an attempt should be made to identify each character. Those which are successfully identified can be placed on one side and left alone for a week; the failures should be collected separately and their inspection renewed from day to day, the identified tickets being added to the collection of successes and the failures put back to be attacked again. It will not be long before the successes predominate, and the number of failures on each subsequent revision will become encouragingly few. Proficiency in writing the characters correctly will not be easily acquired, but the writing of Chinese is a matter of secondary importance. It is always possible, in China, to obtain the services of a native clerk, and it is almost hopeless for a foreigner to attempt to write a presentable hand. This is a mere matter of practice, but, as has been previously stated, it takes many years of daily practice to arrive at good handwriting. At the same time, it is only by copying the characters that they can be successfully learnt.

In copying the characters care should be taken to form them after the recognized system. If this is not followed they will not only be hopelessly awry, but it will be difficult to count the number of strokes of which each character is composed. A correct estimate

* See Section XIII.

of these, as has been explained, is necessary when looking for a character in the dictionary. In writing characters one rule should be borne in mind. Always, when possible, commence on the left-hand side, at the top, and draw the strokes from left to right. There are exceptions to this rule, but they are not sufficiently numerous to affect the general principle. One example will suffice. 福 fu^2, prosperity, is a character with which every Chinese, literate or illiterate, is familiar; it is the best, or one of the best known characters in the language, and it is in evidence on every doorway at the new year time, not to mention other occasions, in every place where the Chinese script is known. This is how it is written, commencing with the Radical

If the same system is followed in the writing of other characters, in ninety-nine cases out of a hundred the order of the strokes will be correct.

An attempt has been made in Section II. to explain the reason why so many words in colloquial Chinese are dissyllabic, and illustrations have been given of a few words which require no amplification in writing but have to be expanded in speaking. Many of these amplifications are capable of explanation, but others are not, and the student will save himself much trouble if he will, to commence with, be satisfied to accept the fact that the double words represent the meanings given. If he wants to know why, he can work out the etymologies for himself later on.

The characters are arranged, as stated, at the foot of each page. When some fifty characters have been more or less fixed on his mind the student can begin to play with them, and to make sentences of his own, but if he wishes to play a successful game he must try to forget all the laws of English grammatical construction, and endeavour to learn how to arrange his sentences in the way that a Chinese would arrange them. If he can once get hold of this system and make it his own, half the difficulties of the language will vanish, and it is with the idea of illustrating the Chinese order of construction that, in the exercises which follow, the literal translation of the Chinese equivalent is placed opposite to each sentence. One is almost tempted to apologize for suggesting that the student should feel his way to Chinese through the channel of "pidgin" English—for that is what it practically amounts to—but, if the process is adhered to for a certain time, it will help the learner more than anything else to speak as the Chinese speak.

The acquisition of a vocabulary is, naturally, a mere question of memory, and the great difficulty to be contended with is, not the committal to memory of disjointed phrases, but the combination of these phrases in a properly constructed sentence. This is what the English paraphrase is designed to teach. It will no doubt be subjected to derision by the scientific teacher, but, none the less, the mere eccentricity of the paraphrased sentences will help to fix the order of the words, as well as individual phrases, on the mind of the beginner, and the very little grammar there is to learn will indicate itself in the process as he goes on. If he will persevere to the end of these exercises, spelling out each one for himself, writing it in the Chinese character, and not referring to the key until each sentence is complete, he will assuredly not regret the time he has spent on the labour. When he reaches the end of the examples he will have no difficulty in recognizing the characters he has made his own wherever he may meet them, and he will find, when he turns his attention to more ambitious text-books, that he will sail along with comparative ease. If the writing of the characters is considered too great a labour the English transliteration of these characters should at least be written down, but the best way to fix them on the memory is to write them constantly. When once a character has established a firm place in the memory it will remain there, with very occasional revision, for all time. It may reappear in unfamiliar combinations, the meaning of which will have to be discovered by application to the dictionary, but if any one will persevere until he has thoroughly mastered a thousand words he will find that he is in a position to have some appreciation of a novel, to read the Confucian Classics with intelligent interest, and to master the intricacies of any simple business document. He will need help at first, either that of a dictionary or of an expert, to understand any of these thoroughly, for every branch of written Chinese has its special peculiarities, but he will no longer be outside the pale, and he may count on reaching this stage after less than two years of study, though he cannot expect to speak fluently until he has polished up his knowledge in the country itself, in the midst of native surroundings.

Lastly, the tones should on no account be neglected. Some people make light of the necessity of acquiring correct intonation, but they are most assuredly wrong. It is possible that words in common use may be detected by a native even if pronounced in the wrong tone, but there are hundreds of others which will be absolutely unintelligible if the correct intonation is not given. Indeed, a bad accent is a lesser evil than inaccuracy of tone, while the absence of the latter, apart from leading to misunderstanding, is fatal to the rhythmic cadence which is a marked and pleasing feature of the spoken language. It would be almost impossible to arrive at great accuracy of pronunciation without the constant direction of a native or other competent instructor, but errors of pronunciation can, with perseverance, be corrected later on, whereas, unless the habit is formed of associating a word with its proper tone, it will be found very difficult at a later stage to make good this important omission. No written explanation can give precisely the proper note to be sounded in each tone, but an hour's oral instruction will enable any one with a quick ear to pick these up. On the other hand, some people never can learn them properly, and, consequently, often fail to make themselves understood. One golden rule should always be borne in mind in connection with the tones: *the second and third tones must almost invariably be emphasized, and the syllable never clipped.* Indeed, speaking in general terms, it may be said that if the second and third tones are looked after, the first and fourth will more or less take care of themselves. Not that they should be neglected; far from it, but they are often not sounded at all, whereas, with the exception of the character *tzŭ*, a son, when used as a substantive indicator, and a few words in the second or third tone when used as finals, it is seldom safe to neglect tones numbers two or three. The few instances in which they can be ignored will be seen in the list of new characters following each sentence. Whenever no tone mark is attached to the phonetic rendering of any of these characters it may be taken for granted that the tone is not to be sounded.

It should be noted that when two words in the third tone come together the *first almost always takes the second tone or the first.*

V.

EXAMPLES.

1. This is yours.	This piece is yours.
2. Is this yours?	This piece is yours?
3. We do not want that.	We not want that piece.
4. What do you want?	You want what.
5. Where are they?	They at where.
6. What is that?	That piece is what.
7. He is there.	He at there.
8. Where is he?	He at where.
9. What is that thing?	That piece is what thing.

1. 這 chê⁴, this.
1. 個 ko⁴, the "numerative," or "classifier" of many nouns, hereafter indicated by "piece."
1. 是 shih⁴, is.
1. 你 ni³, you.
1. 的 ti, a possessive particle, hereafter indicated by "'s," sometimes by "one," sometimes by "ing," sometimes by "ly."
1. 這 chê⁴ / 個 ko⁴ } this.
1. 你 ni³ / 的 ti } yours.
2. 麼 mo¹, the interrogative, hereafter indicated by ?. It also means "as."
3. 我 wo³, I.
3. 們 mên, the plural index of personal substantives.
3. 我 wo³ / 們 mên } we.
3. 不 pu⁴, not; used with "is," but not with "have."
3. 要 yao⁴, want.
3. 那 na⁴, that; na³, which?
3. 那 na⁴ / 個 ko⁴ } that; na³ ko⁴, which?
4. 甚 shên², used colloquially only with the following.
4. 甚 shên² / 麼 mo } what?
5. 他 t'a¹, he.
5. 那 na³ / 裏 li³ } where?
7. 在 tsai⁴, at.
7. 那 na⁴ / 裏 li³ } there.
5. 那 na⁴ / 兒 êrh } in Peking, there; na³ êrh, where?
9. 東 tung⁴, east.
9. 西 hsi¹, west.
9. 東 tung⁴ / 西 hsi¹ } thing.

10.	What are you doing?	You do what.
11.	I am not doing anything.	I not do what.
12.	Do you want it?	You want not want.
13.	Has he come?	He come ed not have.
14.	His son has come.	His son come ed.
15.	Have you brought the money?	Money bring come ed not have.
16.	Have you got any money?	You have money not have.
17.	He is inside.	He at inside.
18.	I made that.	That is I make ing.
19.	Have you seen it?	You look see ed not have.
20.	No, I have not seen it.	I not look see ed.
21.	What does that man want?	That piece man want what.
22.	I don't know what he wants.	I not know he want what.
23.	What are you doing here?	You at here do what.
24.	I am waiting for your son.	I wait your son.

---

10. 做 tso⁴, do, make.
13. 來 lai², come.
1?. 了 liao³ or lo; a sign of the past tense, hereafter indicated by "ed"; a final particle, pronounced lo; to end, finish, accomplish.
13. 沒 mei², not; used with "have," but not with "is."
13. 有 yu³, have.
14. 兒 êrh², son; in Peking used in the formation of nouns and adjectives.
14. 子 tzŭ³, son; much used in the formation of nouns.
14. 兒 êrh² / 子 tzŭ } son.
15. 錢 ch'ien², copper cash, money.
15. 拿 na², to take, seize, hold, bring.

15. 拿 na² / 來 lai² } bring.
17. 頭 t'ou², head, end, top, first, foremost.
17. 裏 li³ or / 裡 li³ } in, inside.
17. 裏 li³ / 頭 t'ou² } inside.
19. 看 k'an⁴, look; k'an¹, watch, regard.
19. 見 chien⁴, see
19. 看 k'an⁴ / 見 chien⁴ } seen.
21. 人 jên², man.
22. 知 chih¹, know.
22. 道 tao⁴, road, way.
22. 知 chih¹ / 道 tao⁴ } to know.
23. 這 chê⁴ / 裏 li³ } here.
24. 等 têng³, wait.

25.	Why are you waiting for him?	You wait him do what.
26.	He has not paid me my money.	My money he not give ed me *lo*.
27.	Sit down and wait till he comes.	Sit a sit wait he come.
28.	Is his business a large one?	His buy-sell large not large.
29.	His business is not as large as mine.	His buy-sell not have mine large.
30.	What does he sell?	He sell what
31.	I don't know what he sells.	I not know he sell what.
32.	He said your things were bought at his place.	He say your things is at he there buy ing.
33.	Did he say that?	He say ed that *lo*?
34.	Where did these men come from?	This some men is where come ing.
35.	I have not got as large a thing as that.	I not have thus large one's thing.
36.	What business does he carry on?	He do what buy-sell.
37.	He is not a tradesman.	He not is buy-sell man.
38.	I have no money to buy that.	I not have money buy that piece.
39.	When I have money I will come and buy it.	I have money, I come buy.
40.	Don't blame him; that is not his fault.	You not want speak him; that not is his fault.
41.	What did he ask you?	He ask you what.

---

26. 給 kei³, give, for, to.
27. 坐 tso⁴, sit.
28. 買 mai³, buy.
28. 賣 mai⁴, sell.
28. 買 mai³ } trade, business.
    賣 mai⁴ }
28. 大 ta⁴, great.
31. 說 shuo¹, speak, say.

34. 些 hsieh¹, some; used to form the plural of nouns.
34. 這 chê⁴ } these.
    些 hsieh¹ }
35. 那 na⁴ } thus.
    麼 mo }
40. 說 shuo¹ } to find fault with a
    人 jên² } person, to scold.
40. 不 pu⁴ } fault, wrong-do-
    是 shih⁴ } ing.
41. 問 wên⁴, ask.

42.	What things do you want?	You want what thing.
43.	I want nothing.	I not want what.
44.	Will you give me that?	You give me that not give.
45.	No, I will not.	I not give you.
46.	Have you seen my son?	My son you look see ed not have.
47.	What did he say?	He speak what talk.
48.	Don't talk.	Not want speak talk.
49.	I asked him if he wanted it and he said he didn't.	I ask him want not want; he say not want.
50.	I don't know the road.	I not know road.
51.	You ask him to wait for me.	You invite him wait me.
52.	He says he won't wait.	He say he not wait.
53.	When you asked him to sit down and wait for me, what did he say?	You invite him sit down wait, he say what.
54.	He said he wanted to buy some things and that he wouldn't wait till you came.	He say want buy things, not wait you come.
55.	He had gone before you came.	You not come ed he walk ed.
56.	What is inside that?	That inside have what.
57.	Why do you ask me?	You ask me do what.
58.	Do you think this is good?	You regard this piece good not good.
59.	In my opinion it is not very good.	At I say not is very good one.
60.	I cannot do that.	That piece I do cannot.
61.	I cannot sit there.	There I sit cannot.

---

47. 話 hua⁴, talk, language.
47. 說話 shuo¹ hua⁴ } to talk.
50. 道兒 tao⁴ 'rh } road.
51. 請 ch'ing³, please, **invite**.
53. 下 hsia⁴, below, down.

53. 坐下 tso⁴ hsia⁴ } to sit down.
55. 走 tsou³, to walk, go.
58. 好 hao³, good, well.
59. 很 hên³, very.
60. 不了 pu⁴ liao³ } cannot, cannot be done.

62.	There are none of those things left.	That piece thing not have *lo*.
63.	That is what he said before.	That is he before speak ing talk.
64.	I don't want to ask him that.	I not want ask him that.
65.	I cannot well ask him that.	I not good ask him that.
66.	If you don't come he'll scold you.	You not come he want, speak you.
67.	That doesn't matter.	That not what.
68.	When he comes I want to see him.	He come ed I want see him.
69.	Will he see me?	He see me not see me.
70.	He says he won't see any one.	He speak he what man not see.
71.	I saw you, but you didn't see me.	I look see you *lo*, you not look see ed me.
72.	If you want this I'll give it to you, but I won't give you that.	You want this piece I give you, that piece I not give you.
73.	Do you know the size of that thing?	That piece thing 's large small you know not know.
74.	No, I don't.	Not know.
75.	If I had as much money as you have I would not sell that thing.	I have you thus some piece money I not sell that piece thing.
76.	You say so, but when you have money we'll see.	You is thus say; wait you have money, look.
77.	Are you his son?	You are his son?
78.	Come up.	Up come.
79.	Come here.	Up here come.
80.	Come over here; I want to ask you something.	You pass here come; I want ask you talk.
81.	Has he been here before?	He come *kuo* not have.

---

63. 頭 t'ou² / 裏 li³ } before, in front of.
73. 小 hsiao³, little.
73. 大 ta⁴ / 小 hsiao³ } size.
75. 這 chê⁴ / 麽 mo } thus.
78. 上 shang⁴, above, up, upon, to.
80. 過 kuo⁴, to pass; a sign of the past tense.

82.	No, he has not.	He not come *kuo*.
83.	Has he made this statement before?	He speak *kuo* this piece talk, not have.
84.	It is not that there is none; he won't give me any.	Not is not have; he not give me.
85.	Did he ask for any money?	He want ed money not want.
86.	He did demand some, but I would not give him any.	He want *kuo*, I not give him.
87.	I must be off.	I want walk *lo*.
88.	Good bye!	Please.
89.	You ask him if he wants it; if he doesn't want it I'll give it to you.	You ask him want not want, he not want I give you.
90.	Have you seen this before?	This piece you look see *kuo* not [have.
91.	No, I have not seen it before.	I not look see *kuo*.
92.	Please take the upper seat.	Please above sit.
93.	He is a passer by.	He is pass come man.
94.	Has he passed by?	He pass come ed not have.
95.	I don't know whether his business is good or not.	I not know his business good not good.
96.	He can't want as many things as that.	He want cannot thus some piece things.
97.	What is inside that?	That inside have what.
98.	Ask him to come up, I have something to say.	Invite him up come; I have talk say. [good.
99.	Do you think this is good?	You regard this piece good not
100.	Yes, it's good, but not so good as that.	Good, is good, not have that piece good.
101.	This is yours, is it not?	This is yours not is.
102.	Is this yours, or is it not?	This is yours not is yours.
103.	Do you think that what he says is correct?	You regard he speak ing is, not is.
104.	Bring it here and let me see it.	Bring here come, give me look a look.

96. 些 hsieh¹ / 個 ko⁴ } some.

104. 這 chê⁴ / 裏 li³ } here.

104. 這 chê⁴ / 兒 'rh } here (Peking colloquial).

120. 外 wai⁴ / 頭 t'ou² } outside

105. Come over here and I will tell you.	You cross come, I give you speak a speak.
106. What do you want to say?	You want say what.
107. Wait till I have said it and you'll know.	Wait I speak ed you know.
108. Do you know what he said?	He say what ed, you know not [know.
109. I don't know; I've come to ask you.	I not know; I come ask you come ed.
110. Don't ask me; ask him.	Not want ask me; ask him.
111. Do as you please about waiting; if you are not here when I come I shall go.	Wait not wait, at you; I come ed, you not at here, I want walk *lo*.
112. That is not mine; I have given it to him.	That not is mine; I give ed him *lo*.
113. If you want to know whether that thing is good or not you ask him; there is nothing he doesn't know.	You want know that thing. good not good you ask him; he not have what not know ing.
114. Bring it here and let me see it.	Bring come give me look.
115. Do you know if this is the road?	This piece is road, you know not know.
116. I don't know; I have never been on this road.	I not know; I not have walk *kuo* this piece road.
117. There is a man coming; ask him.	There have man come; you ask him.
118. Can you kindly tell me where this road leads to?	Beg ask; this is to where's road.
119. That depends upon the size of the thing.	That regard thing's large small.
120. There is a huckster outside; do you want to see his things?	Outside have piece sell things one; you want see his things not want.

Any one who has taken the pains to work carefully through the foregoing sentences cannot fail to notice that the system of writing Chinese "backwards," as we might call it, applies also to a certain extent to the language. A recent writer on Japan has observed that the Japanese "speak backwards, read backwards, and write backwards." So, as far as this generalization can be accepted, do the Chinese, and it may at least be said that the order of the sentences is often inverted. The student who wishes to speak Chinese correctly must, therefore, divest himself at the outset of any idea that a Chinese sentence runs upon the same lines as an English one. It is a safe rule, in attempting to reproduce an English sentence in Chinese, to begin by cutting out all superfluities. It should, in fact, be treated as one would treat a telegraphic message and be reduced to its lowest possible dimensions; after this it may be transposed into a Chinese key, with the liberal interspersion of certain particles.

The nouns present little difficulty. One thing to bear in mind is that many of them take one of two or three endings. The most common of these is 子, which in Peking is often replaced by 兒. The termination 兒, however, is so essentially a characteristic of the Peking dialect that for general purposes it is advisable to be sparing in its use. A few indicative prefixes or "numeratives" must also be remembered, but in case of doubt it is always fairly safe to employ 個 "piece."

Another point to which attention might be called is the absence of the single affirmative or negative. "Yes" or "No" can be expressed by a single word, but they are seldom so expressed, the common form being the repetition of the latter half of a question for the negative, as in the question, "You go out not go out?" "I not go out;" the affirmative being indicated by the repetition of the first half, "I go out."

Most people at first find a difficulty in discriminating between the two negatives 不 and 沒. Only experience will enable the speaker to decide without hesitation which of the two should be employed in particular cases, but if it be borne in mind that 不 cannot be used with 有, have, nor 沒 with 是, be; further, that 沒 is generally used in connection with past action, much difficulty of selection will be removed. If we wished to say "He has not come," we must express it by 他沒有來, or, 他沒來 he *has* not come. If we said 他不來, it would mean either that he *was* not coming or that he *would* not come. So, 我不要 I *am* not wanting, *i.e.* I do not want; 我沒要 I *have* not wanted; *i.e.* I *did* not want. Attention is called to one other point; 要 not only means want, but also *will*, and is often used to mark the future tense, as 他說我沒有, 他要給我. He says that if I have not got any he *will* give me some.

VI.

The numerals present no great difficulty. The symbols from one to ten are as with us, except that the numerative 個, "piece," generally follows each figure, as 一 個, one piece, in the counting of objects. The "teens" are denoted by "ten one," "ten two," &c.; the multiples of ten by "two tens," for twenty, "three tens" thirty, and so on. The way to express hundreds, thousands, and fractional parts of round numbers, will be shown in the few examples that are given.

There are three ways of writing the numerals, which may be styled the common form, the legal form, and the abbreviated form, the last being known as the Soochow system of notation. The legal form is only used on formal documents or bills, and is equivalent to our writing numerals in words instead of in figures; the abbreviated form is employed occasionally in bills or memoranda of accounts. The three forms are given below, but it will not be necessary, for ordinary purposes, to pay attention to the legal or abbreviated forms of notation.

EXAMPLES.

一 壹 丨 i^1, one.	百 伯 pai^3, hundred.
二 貳 刂 êrh^4, two.	千 仟 ch'ien^1, thousand.
三 叁 川 san^1, three.	萬 wan^4, ten thousand, myriad.
四 肆 乂 ssŭ^4, four.	
五 伍 ߆ wu^3, five.	零 ling^2, zero, cypher.
六 陸 乚 liu^4. six.	兩 liang^3, two; used with ko, piece; a Chinese ounce or tael.
七 柒 亠 ch'i^{2,1}, seven.	
八 捌 ⸗ pa^1, eight.	
九 玖 攵 chiu^3, nine.	第 ti^4, number, the sign of the ordinal number.
十 拾 ナ shih^2, ten.	

1. Eighty-six. | Eight ten, six.
2. Four hundred and seventy-nine. | Four hundred, seven ten, nine.

3. Six hundred and five.	Six hundred, cypher, five.
4. Fifteen hundred and twenty-eight.	One thousand, five hundred, two ten, eight.
5. Three thousand and one.	Three thousand, cypher, one.
6. Fifteen thousand.	One myriad, five thousand.
7. One hundred and sixteen.	One hundred, one ten, six.
8. Two hundred and seventy-four thousand six hundred and nineteen.	Two ten seven myriad, four thousand, six hundred, ten, nine.
9. He is at the top; I am second.	He is top one piece; I am number two.
10. He has been before; I have not been before.	He is before come ing, I not come *kuo*.
11. Have you any change?	You have fractional money not have.
12. He has five sons; two of them are here, I don't where know the other three are.	He have five piece son; two piece at here, that three piece I not know at where.
13. Five times five are twenty-five.	Five five, two ten five.
14. Number fifteen.	Number ten five.
15. The fifteenth.	Number ten five piece.
16. Five taels two mace.	Five tael two mace; or, five tael two.

The student is recommended to multiply these examples for himself.

VII.

1. How much money did you give him?	You give ed him how many money.
2. I do not remember.	I not remember.
3. How many men did you see?	You look see ed how many men.
4. I saw ten or more men.	I look see ed ten several piece man.
5. All these things are yours.	These piece thing all are yours.
6. I have counted the number.	I count ed number.
7. I explained it to him.	I give him say clearly ed.
8. He does not understand what I say.	He not apprehend my talk.
9. He is not at home in the day time.	He white day not at home.
10. Did you write all these characters?	These character all is you writing?
11. There are some that I did not write.	Have, not is I write ing.

---

2. 記 chi⁴, to remember.
2. 記 chi⁴ } remember, make a
　　得 tê² }　note of
3. 多 to¹, many.
3. 少 shao³, few.
3. 多 to¹ }
　　少 shao³ } how many?
4. 幾 chi³, some, several.
4. 幾 chi³ }
　　個 ko⁴ } some, how many?
5. 都 tou¹, all.
6. 數 shu³, count.
6. 數 shu⁴ }
　　兒 êrh } number.

7. 明 ming², bright.
7. 白 pai², white, gratis, in vain.
7. 明 ming² } understand, clear-
　　白 pai² }　ly.
8. 懂 tung³, understand.
8. 懂 tung³ } understand, appre-
　　得 tê² }　hend.
9. 日 jih⁴, day.
9. 日 jih⁴ }
　　子 tzŭ } day.
9. 家 chia¹, home.
10. 字 tzŭ⁴, letters, the written [character.
10. 寫 hsieh³, write.

12. At what time did he come back?
He is what time return come ing.

13. He says he intends to come back to-morrow.
He say he to-morrow want return come.

14. When he comes back tell him I want to see him.
He return come ing time you tell him I want see him.

15. I have heard that you write very well.
I heard say you write character, write ing very good.

16. What are you talking about? I can't write.
This is what talk. I not able write character.

17. He wrote to tell me that he cannot come to-morrow.
He give me write ed one piece (fêng) letter say he to-morrow not can come.

18. I wrote to him in reply asking him to come the day after to-morrow.
I give him write ed return letter beg him day after to-morrow come.

19. He came five times and I was not at home on any occasion.
He come ed five turn, I all not at home.

---

12. 時 shih², time.
12. 候 hou⁴, wait; seldom used alone.
12. 時 shih² / 候 hou⁴ } time, when.
12. 回 hui², time, turn, return.
12. 一 i¹ / 回 hui² } one time, once.
12. 回 hui² / 來 lai² } return, afterwards.
13. 天 t'ien¹, heaven, day.
13. 明 ming² / 天 t'ien¹ } to-morrow.
14. 告 kao⁴ / 訴 su⁴ } tell.
15. 聽 t'ing¹, listen, obey.
15. 聽 t'ing¹ / 見 chien⁴ } heard.
16. 會 hui⁴, able, meet, a society.
17. 封 fêng¹, numerative of letters, to seal up a letter.
17. 信 hsin⁴, a letter, to believe, a report.
17. 一 i¹ / 封 fêng¹ / 信 hsin⁴ } a letter.
17. 信 hsin⁴ / 封 fêng¹ / 兒 êrh } an envelope.
18. 回 hui² / 信 hsin⁴ } a return letter, an answer.
18. 後 hou⁴, after, behind.
18. 後 hou⁴ / 天 t'ien¹ } the day after to-morrow.

20. If you can do it do it ; I can't.	You can do, then do; I not able.
21. I can do it, only I cannot do it well.	I can do, only is do ing not good.
22. Directly he comes back you tell him I want to see the things he has bought.	He one return come you then tell him buy ing those thing I want look.
23 What time are you going? I am going directly.	You what time go. I directly go.
24. Will this do? Yes it will do, only it is too small.	This piece suit, not suit. Suit, is suit, only is too small.
25. Who made that? He says he made it, but I don't believe him.	That is what man do ing. He say is he do ing, I but not believe.
26. I don't believe anything he says.	He say what, I all not believe.
27. If you want my things I will give them to you, but I can't give you his things.	You want my thing I then give you; I but not can give you his thing.
28. Bring that thing here and let me see it.	Take hold that piece thing bring come give me look.
29. Take as many as you want.	You want how many, then take how many.
30. That thing has no handle, how can I hold it?	That piece thing not have handle, I how hold.
31. How did you come? I walked here.	You are how come ing. I is walk ed come ing.
32. Can you come and dine with me to-morrow?	You to-morrow to me here come eat food, suit not suit.

---

20. 能 nêng², can.	30. 把兒 $\left.\begin{array}{l}\text{pa}^4\\\text{'rh}\end{array}\right\}$ handle.
20. 就 chiu⁴, then, only, at once.	
21. 就是 $\left.\begin{array}{l}\text{chiu}^4\\\text{shih}^4\end{array}\right\}$ only, but, all right.	30. 怎麼 $\left.\begin{array}{l}\text{tsên}^3\\\text{mo}\end{array}\right\}$ how.
24. 行 hsing², suit, answer, do.	32. 吃 ch'ih¹, eat.
24. 太 t'ai⁴, too, very.	32. 飯 fan⁴, food, a meal.
25. 可 k'o³, but, can.	32. 吃飯 $\left.\begin{array}{l}\text{ch'ih}^1\\\text{fan}^4\end{array}\right\}$ to dine, eat a meal.
28. 把 pa³, take hold of.	

E

33.	I am engaged to-morrow; I can't come.	I to-morrow have business, not can come.
34.	If he asks you to dinner will you go? I won't go.	He if is invite you eat food you go not go. I not go.
35.	What's to be done? I can't tell him you won't go.	This how good. I not can tell him you not go.
36.	You just tell him I am engaged.	You tell him I have business, that's it.
37.	If I tell him that he won't believe it.	I if is tell him that piece talk he not believe.
38.	I don't care whether he does or whether he doesn't.	He believe not believe I not care.
39.	Shut the door.	Take hold door shut up.
40.	The door is shut.	Door shut ed.
41.	The door is not shut to.	Door not shut up.
42.	Open the door.	Open door.
43.	Open the door.	Take hold door open open.
44.	What are you sitting there for? I am waiting till they open the door.	You sit at there do what. I wait they open door.
45.	You have made a mis-statement.	You say wrong ed.
46.	How have I made a mis-statement?	I how say wrong ed.
47.	You told me he had gone to buy things, and he had not.	You tell me he buy thing go ed. He not buy thing go.

---

33. 事 shih⁴, affair, business.
33. 情 ch'ing², feelings, disposition, affection.
33. 事 shih⁴ ⎫ business, affairs; much the same
　　情 ch'ing² ⎭ as shih⁴, above.
34. 若 jo⁴, if.
36. 就 chiu⁴ ⎫
　　是 shih⁴ ⎬ all right, that's it, that will do.
　　了 liao ⎭

38. 管 kuan³, take charge of, control, care about.
39. 關 kuan¹, shut, close, a customs station.
40. 關 kuan¹ ⎫ shut, shut to.
　　上 shang⁴ ⎭
42. 開 k'ai¹, open.
45. 錯 ts'o⁴, wrong.
47. 去 ch'ü⁴, go.

48. I didn't say so, I said he had gone out. What mistake is there about that?
49. Did you say that?
50. Yes, I did.
51. You have done that wrong.
52. I don't care whether it is wrong or not.
53. That was my fault.
54. You tell him; he won't pay any heed to what I say.
55. I went to his house to ask him about that business, but he had gone out.
56. His people said they didn't know what time he would be back, so I didn't wait.
57. Have you got it ready?
58. It will be ready to-morrow.
59. That can't be done.
60. If you don't go I must.
61. He must say which he wants; how can I know which to give him if he doesn't say?
62. Listen! Who is that talking outside?

I not say that piece talk. I say he forth go ed. This have what fault.
You say ed that piece talk?
Not wrong; is I say ing.
That piece you make wrong ed.
Wrong not wrong, I not care.

That is my fault.
You tell him; he not listen my talk.
I to his home in go ed ask him that piece affair, he forth door go ed.
He home in 's man say they not know he what time return come, I then not wait him ed.
You make complete ed not have.
To-morrow then complete.
That piece do cannot.
You not go, I must go.
He must say he want which; he not say, I how can know give him which.

You listen listen; outside is what man speak talk.

---

48. 出 ch'u¹, go forth, go out, issue.
48. 出 ch'u¹ / 去 ch'ü⁴ } go out.
48. 錯 ts'o⁴ / 兒 'rh } a mistake, fault
48. 出 ch'u¹ / 來 lai² } come out.

55. 家 chia¹, family, home.
57. 得 tê², obtain, catch a complaint.
57. 得 tê² / 了 liao } completed, that will do.
60. 得 tei³, must.
62. 外 wai⁴ / 頭 t'ou² } outside.

63. Don't on any account say that I said so.	Thousand ten thousand not want say is I say ing.
64. That is too dear; I won't buy it.	That piece too dear; I not buy.
65. This is much cheaper.	This piece cheap much *lo*.
66. Which is the front and which is the back?	Which is before, which is after.
67. I will walk in front, you walk behind.	I at front walk, you at behind walk.
68. A few days ago he said he wanted it, but afterwards he wouldn't have it.	Before several day he say he want ed; afterwards he nòt want.
69. I am telling the truth, why don't you believe me?	I say ing is true talk; you how not believe.
70. I really cannot give you that.	I truly not can give you that piece.
71. That is my affair, there is no need for you to look after it.	That is my affair; you not use look after.
72. That must not (or cannot) be done.	That do must not.
73. You know all about that; there is no occasion for me to tell you.	That piece you all know; no use I tell you.
74. That's all right; if you remember who gave it you you go and ask him when he bought it.	That all right; you if remember is what man give you ing, you then go ask him is what time buy ing.

---

63. 千 ch'ien¹ } on no account.
　　萬 wan⁴

64. 貴 kuei⁴, expensive, honour-　　[able.

65. 便 p'ien² } cheap.
　　宜 i²

65. 賤 chien⁴, cheap, common.

66. 前 ch'ien², before, front.

67. 前 ch'ien² } in front.
　　頭 t'ou²

67. 後 hou⁴ } behind.
　　頭 t'ou²

68. 後 hou⁴ } afterwards.
　　來 lai²

69. 實 shih², true, sound.

70. 實 shih² } truly, really.
　　在 tsai⁴

71. 用 yung⁴, use, employ.

72. 不 pu⁴ } cannot, must not.
　　得 tê

75.	When the weather is as hot as this what do you want to wear so many clothes for?	Weather thus hot, you wear thus many clothes do what.
76.	You call it hot? It seems to me to be cold.	You say hot? I regard cold.
77.	Is the dinner ready?	Food good ed?
78.	It will soon be ready.	Quick good ed.
79.	What's his name?	He name what.
80.	Put the chair here.	Take hold chair put at here.
81.	Did you walk or come in a carriage?	You is walk ed come ing, is sit cart come ing.
82.	He is disobedient.	He not listen talk.

75. 氣 ch'i⁴, air, vapour, breath, temper.
75. 天 t'ien¹ } weather.
　　氣 ch'i⁴
75. 熱 jo⁴, hot.
75. 穿 ch'uan¹, to wear, put on.
75. 衣 i¹ } clothes.
　　裳 shang¹
76. 冷 lêng³, cold.
78. 快 k'uai⁴, quick, sharp.
79. 姓 hsing⁴, surname, name.

80. 椅 i³ } chair.
　　子 tzŭ
80. 擱 ko¹, put, place.
81. 車 ch'ê⁴, carriage, cart.
您 nin², you sir.
您 nin² } you sir.
納 na⁴
先 hsien¹, first, before.
先 hsien¹ } before born; a
生 shêng¹   polite form of address.

There is one character in the foregoing list which deserves special attention. 就 chiu⁴, is one of the most valuable words in the spoken language, and its use is seldom out of place. Whenever a word is wanted to help out a sentence that seems to require touching up, throw in a *chiu* and you will generally be safe. It does duty, as we have seen, for "then" and for "immediately"; for "all right" and "only" when combined with 是, "is," and it often takes the place of "so." It is also used on occasion to indicate the future tense. Nothing, of course, but practice will enable the learner to be certain when it can be employed, but it should never be lost sight of, for it can be liberally introduced as an adjunct which has no special force, but gives a finish to the sentence.

The same, in a modified degree, may be said of 可, or 可是, "but," which should almost invariably be placed after the personal pronoun. The Chinese say "I but," not "but I."

Note, again, that 時候, "time," when used in the sense of "when," always takes 的 before it, as 我來的時候兒, "when I came." When used as "when," it can never take the first place in a sentence.

Caution should be exercised in the use of the personal pronoun 你, "you." This is only employed when addressing intimates or inferiors, near relations of the same or of a younger generation, or by parents to their children. To address a stranger as *ni* would not be polite. The polite form of address is 您 nin^2, or 您納, *nin-na*, and this would be used even to the commonest person who was a stranger when asking him, for instance, which was the road to a certain place. We shall come directly to other forms of address to officials of minor degree and so forth, but it might be mentioned here that persons who have no official rank or title, such as tradesmen and the like, are generally designated by the calling they follow. Thus, a man whose name was Wang and whose calling was that of a carpenter would be called Wang Mu-chiang, Carpenter Wang, the name always preceding the title; a shopkeeper would be called Wang Chang-kuei-ti, "till-keeper" Wang, or, if he was a foreman, or something of that sort, the title would be Lao-pan, "mate," or "old comrade." 先生 Hsien-shêng, "before born," or Lao-Hsien-shêng, "old before born," can be applied to most people, but it belongs properly to the lettered or teaching class who have no official status. There are many other forms of address, such as Shih-fu, "craftsman," applied to skilled mechanics, and, curiously enough, to cooks, but, to begin with, it will be found a safe rule to address all but distinctly social inferiors as *nin* or *nin-na*, "you, sir," and people to whom more consideration is due as Hsien-shêng, "before born."

The observance of these little distinctions is important, for the Chinese, as a people, are most polite in their manners towards each other, and the neglect of their conventionalities by foreigners, most of whom are not aware of them, is a fertile source of contemptuous dislike. Treat a Chinese with the conventional forms of politeness to which he is accustomed from his own people, learn to bow as he bows when accosting a stranger, and give him his proper title, and he will treat you with the respect he seldom accords to the " barbarian " who knows nothing of his language or of his customs. A knowledge of these courtesies is a valuable aid to success in conversation.

VIII.

1. I forgot to go to his house to inquire about that business, as you told me to do yesterday. | You yesterday order me to his home in go inquire that affair, I forgot ed, not go.
2. I also know he won't do. | I also know he not suit.
3. Are you still here? Why haven't you gone? | You still is here? You for what not go.
4. Because he wouldn't let me go; he heard that I hadn't had my dinner yet, and he said I must have something to eat first. I am going directly. | Because he not call me go; he heard say I yet not eat food; he say I must before eat rice. I just go.
5. Where have you come from? | You from where come.
6. I came from the country. | I from country come.
7. How far is it from here to there? | From here to there have how much road.
8. It's not far, not more than one day's journey. | Not far; not exceed one day's way.

---

1. 昨 tso², 天 t'ien¹ } yesterday.
1. 叫 chiao⁴, call, cause, order.
1. 打 ta³, beat, from, by.
1. 打 ta³, 聽 t'ing¹ } make inquiry.
1. 忘 wang⁴, forget.
2. 也 yeh³, also.
3. 還 hai², yet, still, or; huan², [repay.
3. 爲 wei⁴, for.

3. 爲 wei⁴, 甚 shên², 麼 mo } for what, why.
4. 因 yin¹, 爲 wei⁴ } because.
6. 鄉 hsiang¹, 下 hsia⁴ } the country, in the country.
7. 到 tao⁴, to, to arrive, reach.
7. 路 lu⁴, road.
8. 遠 yuan³, far.

9. Are you going there? So am I. Could you go with me?	You to there go? I also go; you with me go, suit not suit.
10. Why of course· I could. What time are you going?	How not suit. You is what time go.
11. I want a little paper to put on the top of this; you go and find me some.	I want a little paper, put at this above; you go give me seek a seek.
12. Will this do?	This piece suit not suit.
13. I am afraid it won't, it's too small.	Fear not suit; too small *lo*.
14. This will do I expect.	This piece suit *lo pa*.
15. When you have finished it tell me, and I will ask him to write to your son and tell him to come and fetch it to-morrow.	You-sir do finished ed, tell me, I then invite him give you-sir's son write one piece (*fêng*) letter call him to-morrow come take.
16. I am late.	I come late ed.
17. When will you go?	You what time go.
18. At whatever time you like.	You like what time go, then what time go.
19. Those two things are not the same size.	That two piece thing's big little not same.
20. How are they not the same? They are both alike.	How not same; all is one piece kind.

---

9. 同 t'ung², with, along with, same.
11. 點 tien³, a dot, speck, point, comma, to dot, point.
11. 一 i¹ } a little.
    點 tien³
11. 紙 chih³, paper.
11. 上 shang⁴ } above, on top of.
    頭 t'ou
11. 找 chao³, look for.
13. 怕 p'a⁴, fear, expect.
14. 罷 pa⁴, a final particle, expressing doubt, a command, an invitation.
15. 完 wan², finish, end.
16. 晚 wan³, late.
18. 愛 ai⁴, to like, be fond of.
20. 樣 yang⁴, kind, fashion.
20. 樣 yang⁴ } pattern, example.
    子 tzŭ
20. 一 i¹
    個 ko⁴ } alike, the same.
    樣 yang⁴

21. Just go and tell him that I am busy now, and ask him where he lives; if I am not busy to-morrow I will go and see him.	You just go tell him I now have affair, ask him at where live; I if is to-morrow not have affair I then go see him.
22. Where does he live? I don't know where he lives now.	He at where live. I not know he now at where live.
23. I mean to get up early to-morrow. You get up early every day; please call me.	I to-morrow want early get up. You day day is get up ing early, please you take me call get up.
24. If you don't want it, suppose you give it to me.	You not want, give me *pa*.
25. Come here; I have something to say to you.	Come *pa*; I have talk with you say.
26. What do you want to say?	You want say what.
27. Never you mind; you just come here.	That you not use care; you come, all right.
28. He arrived yesterday evening; I have not seen him yet.	He yesterday late mid-day come ed; I yet not see him.
29. He was not here last year; he won't come here this year either; I expect he will come the year after next if he doesn't come next year.	Last year he not at here; this year he also not come; he next year not come, expect he year after next want come.

---

21. 現 hsien⁴, now, ready.
21. 現 hsien⁴ / 在 tsai⁴ } now.
21. 住 chu⁴, dwell, live, tight, fast.
23. 早 tsao³, early.
23. 起 ch'i³, rise, get up.
23. 起 ch'i³ / 來 lai² } get up, commence.
23. 早 tsao³ / 起 ch'i³ } early.
25. 和 ho², with, harmonious.
28. 晚 wan³ / 晌 shang³ } evening, late afternoon.

28. 晚 wan³ / 上 shang⁴ } evening, late afternoon.
29. 年 nien², year.
29. 去 ch'u⁴ / 年 nien² } last year.
29. 今 chin¹, now.
29. 今 chin¹ / 年 nien² } this year.
29. 明 ming² / 年 nien² } next year.
29. 後 hou⁴ / 年 nien² } the year after next.

30. I expect it will rain to-day.	To-day expect want down rain.
31. That's too long; bring the short one here.	That too long; take hold short one bring come.
32. He has grown a big lad in the last few years.	This several year he grow big ed
33. Do you know the length of that board?	That board's long short you know not know.
34. He can't be short of money.	He short cannot money.
35. I am a few cash short; you might lend them to me.	I short some piece cash; you lend give me *pa*.
36. How much money does he owe you?	He owe you how much money.
37. I'll go and borrow a few cash from him.	I go from him borrow some piece cash.
38. This ought to be done by you.	This is you ought do ing affair.
39. He is ill and can't come.	He ill ed, not can come.
40. What is the matter with him.	He have what ill.
41. I don't know; all I know is that when I went to see him yesterday morning he wasn't up, and his people said that he was ill.	I not know; I only know I yesterday early go see him 's time he yet not get up; he home in 's man say he ill ed.
42. What is his name?	He name what.
43. He is an official.	He is do officer ing.
44. What post does he hold?	Do what officer.
45. He looks after government horses.	He care official horse.

30. 今天 chin¹ t'ien¹ } to-day.
30. 下 hsia⁴, below, down.
30. 雨 yü³, rain.
31. 長 ch'ang², long; chang³, to grow.
31. 短 tuan³, short.
33. 板子 pan³ tzŭ } a board.
35. 借 chieh⁴, borrow.
35. 借給 chieh⁴ kei³ } lend.
36. 該 kai¹, owe, ought.
37. 跟 kên¹, with, from, to follow.
39. 病 ping⁴, ill, illness.
43. 官 kuan¹, official, officer.
45. 馬 ma³, horse.

46. How much do you think he gave me for doing that business for him?	I give he manage that piece affair you think he give me how much money *lai cho*.
47. I know that man; he doesn't like spending money; I expect he didn't give you much.	I know that piece man; he not like spend money; he giving not much *pa*.
48. If I had known he was that sort of man I wouldn't have done it for him.	I if is know he is that fashion one man, I then not give him do.
49. He will certainly come sooner or later.	He early late certainly want come.
50. He never can make up his mind.	He ever not have decision.
51. You suggest something.	You give me forth piece opinion.
52. Walk a little quicker; if you walk as slowly as this I expect we shan't get home to-night.	Quick a little walk *pa;* you thus slow walk, fear to-day evening arrive cannot (*pu liao*) home.
53. I know what his idea was in writing this letter.	He write this piece (*fêng*) letter I know his motive.
54. If you want it you must ask him; I can't give you authority.	You want, must ask him; I not can do master.

---

46. 想 hsiang³, think.
46. 着 cho, the present participle; lai cho, sign of past tense.
49. 準 chun³, certainly, accurate, permit, sanction.
49. 定 ting⁴ (see 68).
50. 老 lao³, old, ever, always.
50. 老沒 lao³ mei²} never, for a long time.
50. 老不 lao³ pu⁴} never.

50. 主 chu³, master.
50. 意 i⁴, intention, idea.
50. 主意 chu³ i⁴} purpose, plan of action.
51. 出主意 ch'u¹ chu³ i⁴} make a suggestion, give an idea, decide on a plan.
52. 慢 man⁴, slow.
53. 意思 i⁴ ssŭ} intention, idea, meaning, motive.
54. 做主 tso⁴ chu³} give a decision, assume authority.

THE CHINESE LANGUAGE

55. You needn't ask him what the meaning of those characters is. He can't even read; how can he tell you their meaning?	You not use ask him that character have what meaning; even character still not recognize, he how can tell you character's meaning.
56. Are you going alone, or are you going with them?	You is one piece man go, or is with them go?
57. Were they asked too?	Also invit ed them *lo*?
58. Invited? Of course they were.	Why yes invit ed?
59. Put the thing down.	Take hold thing, place down.
60. Is there room to put it there?	Place succeed down, place not down.
61. There is room for it.	Place succeed down.
62. There is room for it.	Place down ed.
63. Just reflect; how can he bring all those things back with him? Tell him to bring back half, that will do.	You think one think; he how can take hold thus some piece thing all carry return come. You order him hold one half, that's it.
64. Although you say so I still don't believe it.	You although is thus say, I yet is not believe.
65. Why don't you believe?	You why not believe.
66. Because you never speak the truth.	Because you continuously (*lao*) not say true talk.
67. Why did his father beat him?	He father why beat him.

---

55. 連 lien², even, also, together with, join.

55. 認 jên⁴, to acknowledge, confess.

55. 認 jên⁴ } recognize, be ac-
    得 tê² } quainted with.

58. 可 k'o³ ⎫ yes, isn't it? yes,
    不 pu⁴ ⎬ that's so, why yes. A common
    是 shih⁴ ⎭ affirmative.

63. 帶 tai⁴ to bring or carry with one.

63. 半 pan⁴, half.

64. 雖 sui¹ }
    然 jan² } although.

67. 父 fu⁴, a father.

67. 父 fu⁴ }
    親 chi'n¹ } father.

67. 親 ch'in¹, a relative, self.

68. Because he is never at home. The last time he was out when his father called him he said he would certainly beat him the next time.

Because he continuously not at home. Upper turn he father call him 's time he not at home; he father say, lower turn he certainly will beat him.

69. What office does Mr. Hua hold?

Hua lao yeh do what officer.

70. He has no office now.

Now he not do officer.

71. Go and inquire if he is up, and if he is ask him to come over here.

You go inquire he get up ed not have. He if is get up ed, you then request him cross come.

72. He told me yesterday what his name was, but I have forgotten.

He yesterday tell me he name what, I but forgot ed.

73. Ah! I recollect, he said his name was Ch'ang.

Ah! I recollect ed; he say he name Ch'ang.

74. Have you begun that thing yet?

That thing you make begin not have.

75. Not yet, when do you want it?

Yet not make; you what time want.

76. I want it now.

I now want.

77. Will it do to-morrow?

To-morrow, suit not suit.

78. It would be better if you could do it after your dinner.

You eat ed food then do, good.

79. When I have had my dinner I'll come and do it. Will that be all right?

I eat ed food then come do, good not good.

80. That will do.

Good.

---

68. 一 i¹ 定 ting⁴, } certain, certainly.
69. 爺 yeh², father; lao³ yeh², mister.
73. 阿 a¹, an exclamation, a final particle.
73. 想 hsiang³ 起 ch'i³ 來 lai³ } remember, recall to mind.
74. 做 tso⁴ 起 chi³ 來 lai² } commence to do, put in hand.

It will by this time have been discovered that there are certain stock particles, or grammatical indicators, that govern the construction of a Chinese sentence. The mode of their use would be simple enough to learn if it were invariable, but unfortunately it is not, and there are so many ways of saying the same thing in Chinese that it is difficult to lay down hard and fast rules. It is not advisable for the student, at any rate in the earlier stages of his career, to go deeply into the question of Chinese grammar; he will pick up the rules, such as they are, as he goes along, if he will keep his eye on the English paraphrase that is placed opposite each sentence. A Chinese grammar elaborated on foreign lines would confuse him considerably at the outset, as the manner in which a sentence is constructed varies with the context. At the same time the number of characters on which the changes are rung is comparatively few, and if they are borne in mind their value as grammatical indicators will soon be appreciated. In the case of verbs, the following are the most important:—

了	過	來着	已經		
liao³	kuo⁴	lai²-cho	i³-ching¹	. .	the past tense.
			already		

要	就	將來			
yao⁴	chiu⁴	chiang¹-lai²	. .		the future.
will	then	hereafter			

或	或者	許	也許		
huo⁴	huo⁴-cho³	hsü³	yeh³-hsu³	. .	the subjunctive.
perhaps	perhaps	may or might	also might		

叫	挨	被	受		
chiao⁴	ai²	pei⁴	shou⁴	. .	indicators of passive verbs
cause	suffer	suffer	receive, endure		

THE CHINESE LANGUAGE

The mode of their use will be seen in the following illustrations:—

ACTIVE VOICE.

打 ta³, to beat.   狗 kou³, a dog.

Indicative.   Subjunctive.

PRESENT.

I beat the dog.

我　打　狗
I　beat　dog.

I may beat the dog.

我　許　打　狗
I　may　beat　dog

我　或者　要　打　狗
I　perhaps　will　beat　dog.

我　許　要　打　狗
I　may　want　beat　dog.

狗　我　許　打
dog　I　may　beat.

狗　許　打
dog　may　beat.

IMPERFECT.

I beat the dog.

我　打　了　狗　了
I　beat　ed　dog　lo.

我　把　狗　打　了
I　take　dog　beat　ed.

我　打　狗　來　着
I　beat　dog　lai　cho.
(or, I was beating the dog).

I might beat the dog.

我　許　打　狗
I　might　beat　dog.

我　許　把　狗　打　了
I　might　take　dog　beat　ed.

我　或者　要　打　狗
I　perhaps　would　beat　dog.

狗　我　許　打
dog　I　might　beat.

Indicative.

Subjunctive.

PERFECT.

I have beaten the dog.

我	打	過	狗	
I	beat	en	dog.	

狗	我	打	了	
dog	I	beat	ed.	

我	打	過	狗	了
I	beat	en	dog	lo.

狗	我	打	過	了
dog	I	beat	en	ed.

I may have beaten the dog.

狗	我	也	許	打	過
dog	I	also	might	beat	en.

狗	我	或者	也	打	了
dog	I	perhaps	also	beat	ed.

狗	我	也	許	打	來	着
dog	I	also	might	beat	lai	cho.

我	也	許	打	狗	來	着
I	also	might	beat	dog	lai	cho.

PLUPERFECT.

I had beaten the dog.

狗	我	打	來	着
dog	I	beat	lai	cho.

我	打	了	狗	了
I	beat	ed	dog	lo.

我	已經	打	了	狗	了
I	already	beat	ed	dog	lo.

I might have beaten the dog.

我	許	打	狗	來	着
I	might	beat	dog	lai	cho.

我	也	許	打	狗	來	着
I	also	might	beat	dog	lai	cho.

我	或者	也	打	狗	來	着
I	perhaps	also	beat	dog	lai	cho.

FUTURE.

I shall beat the dog.

我	要	打	狗	
I	will	beat	dog.	

我	就	要	打	狗
I	then	will	beat	dog.

我	就	打	狗	
I	then	beat	dog.	

我	就	要	把	狗	打	了
I	then	will	take	dog	beat	lo.

我	將來	要	打	狗
I	hereafter	will	beat	dog.

I shall have beaten the dog.

狗	我	已經	打	了
dog	I	already	beat	ed.

狗	我	這	就	打	了
dog	I	this	then	beat	ed.

我	已經	就	把	狗	打	了
I	already	then	take	dog	beat	ed.

我	已經	把	狗	打	了
I	already	take	dog	beat	ed.

Conditional.

I should beat the dog.

我　就　打　狗
I　then　beat　dog.

我　就　要　打　狗
I　then　will　beat　dog.

我　就　要　把　狗　打　了
I　then will take dog beat ed.

I should have beaten the dog.

我　就　打　狗
I　then　beat　dog.

我　已經　就　把　狗　打　了
I already then take dog beat ed.

狗　我　已經　打　了
dog　I　already　beat　ed.

我　就　把　狗　已經　打　了
I then take dog already beat ed.

Imperative.

Beat the dog.

打　狗
beat　dog.

打　狗　罷
beat　dog　pa.

把　狗　打　了
take　dog　beat　lo.

Let us beat the dog.

我們　把　狗　打　罷
we　take　dog　beat　pa.

我們　打　狗　罷
we　beat　dog　pa.

Infinitive.

Present.—To beat. 打

Perfect.—To have beaten the dog.

打　了　狗
beat　ed　dog.

把　狗　打　了
take　dog　beat　ed.

把　狗　打　過　了
take　dog　beat　en　lo.

Future.—To be about to beat the dog.

要 打 狗
want beat dog.

要 把 狗 打 了
want take dog beat ed.

PARTICIPLE.

Beating the dog.

打 狗
beat dog.

打 着 狗
beat ing dog.*

PASSIVE VOICE.

Indicative.   **Subjunctive.**

PRESENT.

The dog is beaten. | *The dog may be beaten.*

狗 打 了
dog beat ed.

狗 挨 打 了
dog suffer beat ed.

狗 叫 人 打 了
dog cause man beat ed.

狗 被 打 了
dog suffer beat ed.

狗 受 打 了
dog receive† beat ed.

狗 許 被 打
dog may suffer beat.

狗 或者 要 打
dog perhaps will beat.

狗 許 叫 人 打
dog may cause man beat.

狗 許 叫 人家 打
dog may cause person beat.

狗 許 挨 打
dog may suffer beat.

人家 也 許 打 狗
person also may beat dog.

* Rarely used in this connection, but in such a sentence as 坐着看, sitting down to read, or, sitting down to look, it would be quite correct.
† Rarely used with the verb to beat.

Indicative.   Subjunctive.

IMPERFECT.

The dog was beaten.   *The dog might be beaten.*

狗 挨 打 了
dog suffer beat ed.

狗 許 挨 打
dog may suffer beat.

狗 被 人 打 了
dog suffer man beat ed.

狗 或者 要 叫 人 打
dog perhaps will cause man beat.

狗 叫 人 打 了
dog cause man beat ed.

狗 也 許 叫 人 打 了
dog also may cause man beat ed.

狗 挨 了 打 了
dog suffer ed beat ed.

人家 也 許 把 狗 打 了
person also may take dog beat ed.

狗 也 許 挨 打
dog also may suffer beat.

狗 或者 是 要 打 的
dog perhaps is want beat ing.

PERFECT.

The dog has been beaten.   *The dog may have been beaten.*

狗 挨 打 了
dog suffer beat ed.

人家 許 把 狗 打 了
person may take dog beat ed

狗 挨 了 打 了
dog suffer ed beat lo.

狗 也 許 是 叫 人 打 了
dog also may is cause man beat ed.

狗 叫 人 打 了
dog cause man beat ed.

狗 或者 是 挨 了 打 了
dog perhaps is suffer ed beat ed.

狗 被 打 了
dog suffer beat ed.

狗 許 是 被 打 了
dog perhaps is suffer beat ed.

狗 被 人家 打 了
dog suffer person beat ed.

狗 許 打 了
dog perhaps beat ed.

狗 也 許 挨 過 打 了
dog also perhaps suffer ed beat ed.

Indicative.   Subjunctive.

Pluperfect.

The dog had been beaten. | *The dog might have been beaten.*
(As in the Perfect.) | (As in the Perfect.)

Future.

The dog will be beaten.

狗　要　挨　打
dog　will　suffer　beat.

狗　要　挨　打　了
dog　will　suffer　beat　ed.

狗　就　要　挨　打
dog　then　will　suffer　beat.

就　要　打　狗　了
then　will　beat　dog　lo.

就　打　狗
then　beat　dog.

狗　將來　要　打
dog　hereafter　will　beat.

Conditional.

The dog would be beaten. | *The dog would have been beaten.*
(As above.) |
  | 狗　就　挨　了　打　了
  | dog　then　suffer　ed　beat　ed.
  | 狗　就　要　叫　人　打　了
  | dog　then　will　cause　man　beat　ed.
  | 狗　就　挨　上　打　了
  | dog　then　suffer　beat　ed.

IMPERATIVE.

Let the dog be beaten.

就 叫 人 打 狗
then call man beat dog.

叫 狗 挨 打
cause dog suffer beat.

INFINITIVE.

To be beaten.

挨 打　　受 打　　被 打
suffer beat, suffer beat, suffer beat.

To have been beaten.

挨 了 打 了　　被 打 了　　受 打 了
suffer ed beat ed, suffer beat ed, suffer beat ed.

To be about to be beaten.

要 挨 打 了　　要 受 打
want suffer beat ed, want suffer beat.

PARTICIPLE.

Beaten.

打 了　　挨 打 了　　受 打 了　　被 打 了
beat ed, suffer beat ed, suffer beat ed, suffer beat ed.

One or other of the above forms, if correctly applied, will suffice to reproduce any mood or tense of the verb that is likely to present itself. If the student will keep these in mind, and will take note of the few hints that follow, he need not trouble himself for some time to come with the intricacies of Chinese grammar.

Note that the pronoun "it" is very seldom used. We could say, 把 他 拏 來, "bring it here," but in ninety-nine cases out of a hundred 拏 來 would be sufficient.

The conjunction "and" is not often required. In the sentence "you *and* I are invited," the Chinese would commonly say, 你 我 都 請 了, "you I all invited."

The equivalent for "and," when it is used, is 同, t'ung², "with"; 連, lien², "together with"; or, as above, 都, "all" or "both."

Degrees of comparison are worked with one or other of the following characters:—

比	多	更	最	頂	一點	些	強
pi³,	to¹,	kêng¹,	tsui⁴,	ting³,	i¹ tien³,	hsieh¹,	ch'iang².
compare,	many,	more,	most,	utmost,	a little,	some,	superior.

這 個 比 那 個 好 . . . This is better than that.
這 個 比 那 個 強 . . . This is better than that.
這 個 好 多 了 . . . . This is much better.
這 個 更 好 . . . . . This is better still.
這 個 最 好 . . . . . This is the best.
這 個 頂 好 . . . . . This is best of all (or, very good).
這 個 好 一 點 . . . . This is a little better.
這 個 好 些 . . . . . This is a little better.

The preposition "to" is expressed by 和, ho², or han⁴, "with," or 對, tui⁴, "to."

他 和 我 說 來 着 . . . He spoke to me about it.
你 對 他 說 了 沒 有 . . Did you speak to him about it?

The preposition "with" is expressed by 跟, ken¹, or 同, t'ung².

你 跟 我 來 . . . You come with me.
我 同 他 去 . . . I will go with him.

"For" is represented by 給, kei³, 替, t'i¹, or 代, tai⁴.

我 給 你 做 . . . I will do it for you.
你 替 我 說 . . . You say it for (on behalf of) me.

的, ti, often forms the adverbial termination "ly," but in a large number of cases where "ly" is compulsory in English it is unnecessary in Chinese. For instance, in the sentences, "the boy writes nicely," 孩子寫的好 (boy write ing nice), "he speaks distinctly," 他說的清楚 (he speak ing distinct), the Chinese would, like an uneducated English person, drop the "ly." But, "do it carefully," would be expressed by 好好的做.

IX.
Examples.

1. There is a small matter in which I want to ask your assistance. I know you are a very busy man, and I did not like troubling you, but there is really no help for it because, excepting yourself, there is no one who is able to manage it for me.

2. That's nothing. Although I am busy I would always make time to lend you a hand. We are old friends, and you have helped me often enough. I am only too pleased to take a little trouble for you.

Have one piece (*chien*) small affair want invite you Sir mutual help. You Sir is piece very busy one man I is knowing, originally not want trouble you Sir, I but really not have remedy, because excepted you Sir, not have man can give me manage.

That not (*mei*) what. I although busy, always want divide a little leisure give you Sir help a hurry. We are old friends, you Sir help ed me how many turn, I too pleased give you Sir put forth (*ch'u*) a little strength.

---

1. 件 chien⁴, a numerative of things, matters, &c.
1. 相 hsiang¹, mutual, reciprocal, like.
1. 幫 pang¹, help, assist.
1. 相幫 hsiang¹ pang¹ } render assistance.
1. 忙 mang², haste, hurry, busy.
1. 本 pên³, root, origin, in fact.
1. 本來 pên³ lai² } originally, as a matter of fact.
1. 勞 lao², toil, trouble.
1. 動 tung⁴, move, touch.
1. 勞動 lao² tung⁴ } give trouble to, put to trouble.
1. 法 fa³, a way, system, law,
1. 法子 fa² tzŭ } method, way, remedy.
1. 除了 ch'u² liao } excepting, taking out, deducting.

1. 辦 pan⁴, deal with, manage, arrange, transact.
2. 總 tsung³, all, the whole, general, always.
2. 勻 yün², divide, parcel out, set aside.
2. 空 k'ung¹, empty.
2. 空兒 k'ung¹ êrh } leisure.
2. 幫忙 pang¹ mang² } lend a hand.
2. 朋友 p'êng² yu³ } a friend.
2. 樂 lo⁴, joy, pleasure, delight, to laugh; yueh⁴, music.
2. 樂得的 lo⁴ tê² ti } only too pleased, glad to get the chance.
2. 力 li⁴, strength, force.

3. Whom were you talking to just now? That was an official; he was the man who went to England last year; don't you remember? You saw him at my house.
4. To be sure; directly you mentioned it I remembered. Immediately I saw him it seemed to me as if I knew him, but for the moment I had forgotten where it was that I saw him.
5. How much did he give you for doing that piece of business for him?
6. If any one else were to ask me that question I certainly should not tell him, but as you recommended me to him I will tell you. Only don't tell any one else.

You sir, just now with who speak talk. That is piece do officer one, just (chiu⁴) is go year to England go ing that piece man, you Sir not remember? At I home in see ed (kuo) one.

Not wrong. You Sir one mention, I then think begin ed. I one see him I good resemble see ed (kuo); one time, but forget ed at where see ed (kuo liao).

You give him arrange that piece affair he give you how much money lai cho.

If is another man ask me I certainly not tell; you since take me recommend give him, I then tell you. You but don't tell another man.

---

3. 剛 kang¹, just, just now.
3. 纔 ts'ai², then, just now.
3. 剛 kang¹ } just now.
   纔 ts'ai² }
3. 誰 shui², who.
3. 國 kuo², a country.
3. 英 ying¹ } England.
   國 kuo² }
4. 提 t'i², suggest, mention, pick up.
   提 t'i² }
4. 起 ch'i³ } mention.
   來 lai² }

4. 像 hsiang⁴, like, an image, picture, photograph.
4. 好 hao³ } seemed to; seem-
   像 hsiang⁴ } ingly.
6. 別 pieh², do not, other, another.
6, 既 chi⁴, since.
6. 薦 chien⁴, introduce, recommend.
6. 薦 chien⁴ } introduce to, re-
   給 kei³ } commend to.

7. When his father was alive he used often to do work for me, but he started a small business after his father died and he doesn't do carpenter's work now.

8. What o'clock is it? By that clock it is half past three, but it is slow. I'll go and fetch my watch from my bedroom. I know that's right, as I compared it with the church clock this morning.

He father exist (*tsai*) ing time he often give me do work. He father die ed, he then open ed piece small buy-sell; now not act as (*tang*) carpenter *lo*.

Now how many (*chi*) dot bell. According to that piece clock is three dot half bell, that piece clock but slow *lo*. Wait I to recline room in go take my watch bring come. I know that piece correct *lo*, because I to day early with church's clock compare ed one compare (*tui*).

---

7. 在 tsai⁴, exist, consist in (p. 37).
7. 常 ch'ang², constantly, often.
7. 活 huo², alive, a livelihood, work.
7. 死 ssŭ³, dead, to die.
7. 活着 huo² cho } living.
7. 做活 tso⁴ huo² } to work, to gain a livelihood.
7. 當 tang¹, act as, serve as, ought, at the time, when.
7. 木頭 mu⁴ t'ou² } wood.
7. 木匠 mu⁴ chiang⁴ } a carpenter; chiang, a mechanic.
8. 幾點鐘 chi³ tien³ chung¹ } what o'clock?

8. 鐘 chung¹, a bell, clock.
8. 按着 an⁴ cho } according to.
8. 臥 wo⁴, to lie down, recline.
8. 房 fang², a house, room.
8. 房子 fang² tzŭ } a house.
8. 表 piao³, a watch.
8. 準 chun³, correct, to permit.
8. 禮 li³, ceremony, courtesy.
8. 拜 pai⁴, to worship, visit.
8. 禮拜 li³ pai⁴ } Sunday, the days of the week, worship.
8. 堂 t'ang², a hall, a large room.
8. 禮拜堂 li³ pai⁴ t'ang² } a church.
8. 對 tui⁴, to compare, correct, opposite, a pair.

9. This is not as large as that. There's very little difference between them.
10. The night was so dark that I couldn't even see the road, and I very nearly fell into the river.
11. You cannot put as large a table as this into that small room.
12. That being the case, you can manage the thing as you like. You need not consult your friend.
13. I shall certainly arrive at a quarter to five. If by any chance I am delayed from any cause I will send a man with a message to you.

This piece not have that piece great. Two piece differ not much.
Heaven black ing, even road all look (*ch'iao*) not see ed. Differ a little, not fall at river in.
Thus (*ché-mo*) large 's table, thus (*na-mo*) small 's room place not down.
Since is thus, you like how manage then how manage. No use with your friend consult.
I four dot bell three quarter positive come. Ten thousand one, have what business take me delay ed, I then despatch one piece man give you send piece message.

---

9. 差 ch'a¹, to differ, error, mistake.
9. 差 ch'a¹ ⎫
   不 pu⁴ ⎬ nearly, almost.
   多 to¹ ⎭
10. 黑 hêi¹, black, dark.
10. 瞧 ch'iao², look, look at, see.
10. 瞧 ch'iao² ⎫ seen.
    見 chien⁴ ⎭
10. 掉 tiao⁴, to fall.
10. 掉 tiao⁴ ⎫
    下 hsia⁴ ⎬ to fall from above,
    來 lai² ⎭
10. 掉 tiao⁴ ⎫
    下 hsia⁴ ⎬ to fall down below.
    去 ch'u⁴ ⎭
10. 河 ho², a river.
11. 棹 cho¹ ⎫ a table.
    子 tzŭ ⎭
11. 屋 wu¹ ⎫ a room.
    子 tzŭ ⎭
12. 商 shang¹, to consult, a merchant.
12. 量 liang², to measure, estimate.
12. 商 shang¹ ⎫ discuss, consider
    量 liang⁴ ⎬ together, take
              ⎭ counsel.
13. 刻 k'o⁴, a quarter of an hour, to carve.
13. 萬 wan⁴ ⎫
    一 i¹   ⎬ if by any chance.
              ⎭
13. 耽 tan¹ ⎫
    悞 wu⁴ ⎬ to delay, hinder.
              ⎭
13. 發 fa¹, to put forth, break out.
13. 打 ta³ ⎫ send, despatch on an
    發 fa¹ ⎬ errand.
              ⎭
13. 送 sung⁴, give, send, escort.

14. My finger is dreadfully painful. I gave it a knock last night, and it pained me so all night that I could not get to sleep.
15. What are you pointing at?
16. Don't buy that bottle; it's got a flaw in it. A small flaw like that doesn't matter. Just see how beautifully those flowers are drawn, and the colours are very good. A jar like that, although it has a flaw in it, is worth a great deal more than he asks for it.

I finger pain ing dreadful. Yesterday evening I knock ed one time (*i hsia'rh*), pain ing I, one night sleep (*shui*) not succeed (*chao*) *lo*.
You point what.
Don't buy that piece bottle; have flaw. Like that piece fashion 's flaw not important. You look (*ch'iao*) that flower draw ing many as (*to mo*) good look (*k'an*). Colour also good. Like that fashion one jar, although have flaw, also compare he want ing that piece price worth many *lo*.

---

14. 指 chih³, point at, point out, indicate.
14. 指頭 chih² t'ou² } the finger, fingers.
14. 疼 t'êng², sore, painful, to be deeply attached to.
14. 利 li⁴, gain, profit, interest, acute.
14. 害 hai⁴, to injure, injury.
14. 利 li⁴ } dreadful, terrible, 害 hai⁴ } dangerous, severe.
14. 碰 p'êng⁴, to hit, knock, bump against.
14. 一下子 i¹ hsia⁴ tzŭ } a blow, a turn, a time.
14. 夜 yeh⁴, night.
14. 睡 shui⁴, to sleep.
14. 睡覺 shui⁴ chiao⁴ } to go to bed, to go to sleep, sleeping.
14. 睡着 shui⁴ chao² } to be asleep, to go off to sleep.

16. 瓶子 p'ing² tzŭ } a bottle, a vase.
16. 毛 mao², a hair, fur.
16. 毛病 mao² ping⁴ } a flaw, a fault, a defect in character.
16. 緊 chin³, tight, pressing, close.
16. 要緊 yao⁴ chin³ } important.
16. 花兒 hua¹ 'rh } a flower, flowers; hua¹, to spend.
16. 畫 hua⁴, to draw, paint.
16. 畫兒 hua⁴ 'rh } a picture, a painting.
16. 顏色 yen² sê⁴ } colour.
16. 比 pi³, to compare, compared with.
16. 價錢 chia⁴ ch'ien² } price, cost.
16. 值 chih², to be worth.

17. We two are friends of long standing. When he lived in the Capital we used to see each other constantly. The year before last he went to live in the country some fifty or more *li* from here, and now we don't often meet. I propose to go and see him next spring and to bring him back with me in the summer. When autumn comes, I shall see. If he won't spend the winter with me here, I shall go back with him. I won't be separated from him again.

We two piece man have many year's friendship. He at Capital city live ing time we is constantly see face ing. Before year he to country go live, distant from here have fifty more *li*; now we not great constantly meet. I next year spring day propose go see him, summer day take (*pa*) him bring (*tai*) return come. Arrive ed autumn day, see (*ch'iao*). He if not at I here pass winter, I then with (*t'ung*) him together return go. I again not separate from him.

---

17. 交 chiao¹, to deliver, hand over to, interchange.

17. 交 chiao¹ ⎫
　　情 ch'ing² ⎭ friendship.

17. 京 ching¹, a metropolis.

17. 城 ch'êng², a walled city or town, the wall of a city.

17. 京 ching¹ ⎫
　　城 ch'êng² ⎭ the capital.

17. 面 mien⁴, face, surface.

17. 離 li², to separate from, apart from, distant from.

17. 離 li² ⎫ to be apart, keep
　　開 k'ai¹ ⎭ apart, separate from, leave.

17. 里 li³, a Chinese mile; twenty Chinese *li* equal seven English miles.

17. 明 ming² ⎫
　　年 nien² ⎭ next year.

17. 春 ch'un¹ ⎫
　　天 ti'en¹ ⎭ spring.

17. 算 suan⁴, to count, reckon.

17. 打 ta³ ⎫ to propose, calcu-
　　算 suan⁴ ⎭ late.

17. 夏 hsia⁴ ⎫
　　天 t'ien¹ ⎭ summer.

17. 秋 ch'iu¹ ⎫
　　天 t'ien¹ ⎭ autumn.

17. 冬 tung¹ ⎫
　　天 t'ien¹ ⎭ winter.

17. 再 tsai⁴, again, a second time.

18. If you have any dealings with that man I advise you to be a little cautious. Outwardly he is very friendly, but at heart he is dangerous. I've run foul of him so I know his disposition.

19. Is that a quiet horse? If you ride him constantly and keep him short of corn, any one can ride him, but if you give him too much corn, or keep him in the stable for two or three days without riding him, he will show temper.

You if with that piece man have what affair, I advise you retain a little heart. Out face very harmonious, heart in but dangerous (*li hai*). I bump ed (*kuo*) his nail, therefore I know his disposition.

That piece horse quiet not quiet. You if constantly ride him, few feed him grain, what man all can ride. You if many feed him corn, or two three day put at stable in, not ride, he then will show temper.

18. 勸 ch'üan⁴, advise, urge, recommend, exhort.
18. 留 liu², retain, detain, keep.
18. 留下 liu² hsia⁴ } keep back, retain, detain, a remainder.
18. 心 hsin¹, the heart.
18. 留心 liu² hsin¹ } pay attention, take care.
18. 外面 wai⁴ mien⁴ } outwardly, the outer surface.
18. 和氣 ho² ch'i⁴ } friendly, harmonious, affable.
18. 釘子 ting⁴ tzŭ } a nail.
18. 碰釘子 p'êng⁴ ting⁴ tzŭ } to get a rap over the knuckles, get bitten, have an unpleasant experience.
18. 以 i³, according to, take, use.
18. 所以 so³ i³ } therefore; so³, that which, place.
18. 脾氣 p'i² ch'i⁴ } temper, disposition.

19. 老實 lao³ shih² } quiet, steady, honest, simple-minded.
19. 騎 ch'i², to ride.
19. 餧 wei⁴, to feed an animal, to feed an infant or invalid.
19. 糧食 liang² shih² } grain, corn, fodder, "feed"; shih², food, eat.
19. 號 hao⁴, mark, label, style.
19. 或 huo⁴, either, or.
19. 馬號 ma³ hao⁴ } a stable.
19. 圈 ch'üan⁴, a coop, pen, encircle; ch'üan¹, a circle.
19. 馬圈 ma³ ch'üan⁴ } a stable.
19. 鬧 nao⁴, to make a disturbance, scold, make a noise, show temper.
19. 鬧脾氣 nao⁴ p'i² ch'i⁴ } to show temper, get nasty, be disagreeable.

20. If the weather is fine on Saturday next I propose to take the forenoon train to Peking, spend the Sunday there, and come back on Monday afternoon.

Below Sunday six, weather if good *lo*, I propose sit upper half day's fire carriage to North Capital go. At there pass Sunday; Sunday one, lower half day, return come.

21. Where are you going to stop in Peking? I have a relative there. I wrote to him yesterday to ask him if he has a room disengaged. If he has room I shall stay at his house, but if he has not, the only thing I can do, I suppose, is to stop at the hotel.

At Peking what place live. I there have relative. I yesterday give him write ed one piece (*fêng*) letter ask him have disengaged room not have. He if have place, I then at his house live. He if not have place, only good at stranger inn in live *pa*.

22. Is there any news in this morning's paper? There is no particular news.

To-day early 's new hear paper have new hear not have. Not have what new hear.

---

20. 天氣 t'ien¹ ch'i⁴ } weather.
20. 火 huo³, fire.
20. 火車 huo³ ch'ê⁴ } railway carriage.
20. 北 pei³, north.
20. 北京 pei³ ching¹ } Peking.
21. 地 ti⁴, ground, land, the earth.
21. 地方 ti⁴ fang¹ } a place.
21. 方 fang¹, square.

21. 親戚 ch'in¹ ch'i⁴ } a relative, relatives.
21. 閒 hsien², unoccupied, at leisure, vacant.
21. 只 chih³, only.
21. 只好 chih³ hao³ } the only thing to do.
21. 客 k'o⁴, guest, stranger, visitor.
21. 店 tien⁴, inn, hotel.
22. 新 hsin¹, new.
22. 聞 wên², to hear, to smell.
22. 新聞紙 hsin¹ wên² chih³ } a newspaper.

23. What is the market rate of silver to-day? I have not yet heard, but I am passing the Bank this afternoon and I will go in and inquire.	To-day silver what market rate. I yet not hear say. After half day I by (*ta*) silver establishment pass. I then enter go inquire inquire.
24. If you are going to the Bank may I trouble you to change this Bank note for me?	You Sir if is to Bank go, trouble you Sir's chariot, take this silver note give me change cash.
25. What kind of money do you want? Taels or dollars?	You Sir want what kind one money. Is want silver, is want foreign (ocean) money.
26. What is the most convenient form of money to use here?	At here employ what kind one money convenient.

---

23. 銀 yin² / 子 tzŭ } silver.
23. 行 hang², a mercantile establishment, house of business.
23. 行 hang², another form of the foregoing.
23. 市 shih⁴, a market.
23. 行 hang² / 市 shih⁴ } the market rate.
23. 銀 yin² / 行 hang² } a bank.
23. 進 chin⁴, to advance, enter.
23. 進 chin⁴ / 去 ch'ü⁴ } to enter, go in.
23. 進 chin⁴ / 來 lai² } to come in, come in.
23. 打 ta³ / 聽 t'ing¹ } to inquire.

24. 勞 lao² / 駕 chia⁴ } (trouble chariot); may I trouble you? thank you.
24. 換 huan⁴, to change, exchange.
24. 票 p'iao⁴ / 子 tzŭ } a ticket, a bank note.
24. 銀 yin² / 票 p'iao⁴ } a bank note for silver.
25. 洋 yang², the ocean, foreign.
25. 塊 k'uai⁴, a bit, a piece.
25. 一 i¹ / 塊 k'uai⁴ / 洋 yang² / 錢 ch'ien² } a dollar.
26. 使 shih³, to use, employ, cause.
26. 便 pien⁴, convenient, handy.
26. 方 fang¹ / 便 pien⁴ } convenient.

27. Dollars of course are the most convenient. For buying odds and ends at the shops people always use dollars. Silver is mostly used for business transactions of a large kind.

Of course is foreign money convenient. At shop in buy odds and ends thing, people all is use foreign money. Silver, great half is do large buy sell use ing.

28. We are going for a two or three days' trip into the country the day after to-morrow, and we want to take some eatables with us. Tell the cook to get some provisions ready.
What sort of provisions do you want, Sir?

We after day to country go ramble two three day, want carry some eat ing. Order cook prepare several kind food (vegetables).

You Sir, want what kind 's food.

29. Tell him to boil a chicken or two, to roast a piece of beef and to make four or five bottles of soup. We shall also want some

Order him boil one two piece little chicken, roast one bit ox meat, make four five bottle soup. We also want eggs, some (*chi*) kind

---

27. 自 tzŭ⁴, self, from.
27. 自然 tzŭ / jan² } of course.
27. 自然 tzŭ⁴ / jan } spontaneous.
27. 舖 p'u⁴, shop (see 39).
27. 碎 sui⁴, bits, fragments.
27. 零碎 ling² / sui⁴ } fragmentary, odds and ends.
27. 人家 jên² / chia⁴ } people, one, some people.
28. 逛 kuang⁴, to ramble, sight-see.

28. 廚子 ch'u² / tzŭ } a cook.
28. 預備 yü⁴ / pei⁴ } to prepare.
28. 菜 t'sai⁴, vegetables, food generally.
29. 煮 chu³, to boil.
29. 小雞子 hsiao³ / chi¹ / tzŭ } a chicken, a fowl; chi tzŭ³ êrh, eggs.
29. 烤 k'ao³, to roast.
29. 牛 niu², an ox, cow.
29. 肉 jou⁴, flesh, meat.
29. 湯 t'ang¹, soup, broth, gravy.

G

eggs, an assortment of cakes, and so forth. Then there's tea, sugar and salt; these must all be got ready. Tell him to wrap them up in paper packets. We shall also want a tea-pot, a kettle for boiling water, tea cups, saucers, soup bowls, plates, knives, forks and spoons. Don't let him forget the milk either. We don't want fresh milk, as I am afraid it would be bad by the second day. He had better buy foreign milk. The kind that is kept in tins is the best.

cakes, what one. Still have tea leaf, sugar, salt; these piece all must prepare. Order him take paper wrap up parcel. We also want one piece tea pot, open water's open water pot, tea cup, saucer, soup bowl, plate, knife, fork, spoon. Still have that cow milk; don't let (*chiao*) him forget ed. We not want fresh (*hsien*) milk, fear arrive ed number two day then spoil ed. Still is buy that iron box in pour ing that out country (*wai kuo*) milk good.

29. 點心 tien³ hsin¹ } pudding, confectionery, light refreshment.
29. 甚麼的 shên² mo ti } and what not, &c., and so forth.
29. 茶 ch'a², tea.
29. 茶葉 ch'a² yeh⁴ } tea leaves.
29. 葉子 yeh⁴ tzŭ } a leaf, leaves.
29. 糖 t'ang², sugar.
29. 鹽 yen², salt.
29. 包上 pao¹ shang⁴ } to wrap up.
29. 包兒 pao¹ 'rh } a parcel, bundle.
29. 壺 hu², a pot.
29. 水 shui³, water.
29. 開水 k'ai¹ shui³ } boiling water.
29. 碗 wan³, a bowl.

29. 碟子 tieh² tzŭ } a saucer.
29. 盤子 p'an² tzŭ } a plate.
29. 刀子 tao¹ tzŭ } a knife.
29. 义子 ch'a¹ tzŭ } a fork.
29. 匙子 ch'ih² tzŭ } a spoon.
29. 牛奶 niu² nai³ } milk, cow's milk.
29. 鮮 hsien¹, fresh, new.
29. 壞了 huai⁴ liao } spoilt, destroyed.
29. 鐵 t'ieh³, iron.
29. 盒子 ho² tzŭ } a box with a cover that is not hinged.
29. 灌 kuan⁴, to fill with water, to pour fluid into, to force fluid into.

30. In hot weather like this, Sir, I should not take many eatables, for what you don't finish on the first day will be bad on the second. It would be better to buy things as you want them along the road.

31. I am thirsty. Bring me some soda water. Will you drink it plain, Sir, or mixed with wine? If there is any red wine I'll mix a little with it.

32. Bring me my tobacco pouch and my pipe. I want some matches too.

33. This tea is very weak; where was it bought? It wasn't bought; Mr. Shih sent it to you as a present, and asked you to try it and see if you like it.

Weather thus hot, mister (*lao yeh*) few carry eat ing good. Top one day not eat finish ed one, number two day then spoiled. Still is road on according want according buy, good.

I thirsty ed. Give me bring air water come. Mister is single drink, or is mix wine drink. If is have red wine I then mix a little.

Take my tobacco pouch tobacco pipe bring come. Also want self come fire.

This tea very weak; tea leaf is at where buy ing; tea leaf not is buy ing; is Shih *lao yeh* send you Sir ing, invite you Sir try a try, look look good not good.

---

30. 老 lao³ ⎫ sir, mister; a title or form of address to minor officials or gentry.
    爺 yeh² ⎭
30. 隨 sui², to follow, comply with, according to.
31. 渴 k'o³, thirsty.
31. 氣 ch'i⁴ ⎫ soda water.
    水 shui³ ⎭
31. 單 tan¹, single, singly, alone.
31. 單 tan¹ ⎫ a list, bill, memorandum.
    子 tzŭ ⎭
31. 喝 ho¹, to drink.
31. 紅 hung², red.
31. 對 tui⁴, to add, as an ingredient, to agree, a pair.

31. 酒 chiu³, wine.
32. 煙 yen¹, tobacco, smoke.
32. 荷 ho² ⎫ a pouch, purse, reticule.
    包 pao¹ ⎭
32. 煙 yen¹ ⎫ a tobacco pipe.
    袋 tai⁴ ⎭
32. 自 tzŭ⁴
    來 lai² ⎬ matches.
    火 huo³
33. 裡 and 裏 are interchangeable.
33. 淡 tan⁴, weak (of tea, &c.), pale (of colour).
33. 讓 jang,⁴ to permit, allow, yield, invite.
33. 試 shih⁴, to try test.

34. If you are going to the Post Office, may I trouble you while you are about it to buy me a dollar's worth of postage stamps?	You Sir if is to letter establishment go, trouble you Sir chariot, while about it (*chiu shou 'rh*) give me buy one piece money's letter ticket.
35. May I trouble you to mention that affair of mine when next you see him?	You Sir below turn see him's time, expend you Sir heart, take I that piece affair mention a mention.
36. Make your mind easy. I shan't forget it.	Let go heart. Forget cannot (*pu liao*).
37. I am so much obliged for all the trouble you have taken for me.	You Sir thus give me expend trouble, many thank's very.
38. What time do you go to the office every day? There's no certain time. If there is plenty to do I go early; if there is not much doing I go late. There is nobody to control me, and I can go when I like and leave when I like. I suit my own convenience.	You Sir day day what time to office go. Not have positive time. Affair many, early a little go; affair few, late a little go. Not have man control me. I like what time go, then what time go, like what time walk, then what time walk. All is follow (*sui*) my convenience (*pien*).

---

34. 局 chü², a depot, store, shop.
34. 票 p'iao⁴, a ticket, label.
34. 郵 yu² ⎫
    政 chêng⁴ ⎬ a government
    局 chu² ⎭ post office.
34. 手 shou³, the hand.
34. 就 chiu⁴ ⎫ ready to hand,
    手 shou³ ⎬ while about it.
    兒 'rh ⎭
34. 信 hsin⁴ ⎫ a postage stamp.
    票 p'iao⁴ ⎭
35. 費 fei⁴, to spend, lavish.
    費 fei⁴ ⎫ may I trouble you?
35. ⎬ thank you. Used
    ⎪ particularly of
    ⎪ acts requiring
    心 hsin¹ ⎭ mental effort.

36. 放 fang⁴, to place, let go.
36. 放 fang⁴ ⎫ to make the mind
    心 hsin¹ ⎭ easy.
37 事 shih⁴, trouble, business.
    費 fei⁴ ⎫ to take trouble,
37. ⎬ cause trouble,
    事 shih⁴ ⎭ troublesome.
37. 謝 hsieh⁴, to thank.
38. 衙 ya² ⎫ a government office
    門 mên² ⎭ of any kind.
    隨 sui² ⎫ according to con-
38. ⎬ venience, as you
    便 pien⁴ ⎭ please.

39. The manager of that shop used to be compradore in a foreign firm. Last year they dispensed with his services for some reason or other. He had a little capital, and so he started in business.

That shop in control till one formerly is foreign firm (*yang-hang*) in 's compradore. Last year, not know what cause, not want him ed. He have a little root money, then do commence buy-sell come ed.

40. It does not matter about the height, but the breadth is important. If it is too wide you won't be able to place it inside. If it is too narrow it will be loose.

High low not important, broad narrow but is important one. Too broad *lo*, then put not enter go; too narrow *lo*, then loose *lo*.

41. Why do you wear such thin clothes on a cold day like this? Aren't you afraid of catching cold?

Day thus cold you for what wear thus thin one clothes. You not fear catch cool?

---

39. 鋪 p'u¹, to spread out, spread.
39. 鋪子 p'u⁴ tzŭ } a shop (see 27).
39. 掌 chang³, the palm of the hand, to control.
39. 櫃 kuei⁴, a chest, safe, cupboard.
39. 掌櫃的 chang³ kuei⁴ ti } the proprietor or manager of a shop.
39. 從 ts'ung², from, to follow.
39. 從前 ts'ung² ch'ien² } formerly.
39. 買辦 mai³ pan⁴ } a compradore.
39. 緣 yüan², origin, cause, affinity.
39. 故 ku⁴, cause.

39. 緣故 yüan² ku⁴ } cause, reason.
39. 本錢 pên³ ch'ien² } capital, prime cost.
40. 高 kao¹, high, tall, eminent.
40. 矮 ai³, short, low.
40. 高矮 kao¹ ai³ } height.
40. 寬 k'uan¹, broad.
40. 窄 chai³, narrow, straitened.
40. 寬窄 k'uan¹ chai³ } width.
40. 鬆 sung¹, to loose, loose, slack.
40. 咯 lo, another form of the final *lo*.
41. 薄 pao², thin.
41. 涼 liang², cool.
41. 著涼 chao² liang² } to catch cold.

42. It is blowing from the north-west. I expect it will rain before dark.

Blow west north wind *lo*. Not arrive dark, expect want down rain.

43. That's not at all certain. With a north-west wind it doesn't often rain here. The rainy wind comes from the south-east.

That also not certain. Blow west north wind, here not great down rain. Carry rain's wind is east south wind.

44. Excuse me, Sir, can you tell me how far it is from here to the provincial capital?

Borrow rays. Please ask, from here to province city have many far.

45. It is not very far, but the main road is bad. If you follow this small road it is much nearer. Carts can also go that way.

Far, is not very far, only is big road not good walk. If following this small road walk, then near many *lo*; carts also walk succeed *liao*.

46. Let me introduce you two gentlemen to each other. This is His Excellency Kuan; this is Lo ta lao yeh. Happy to meet you, Sir.

I give you two gentlemen see a see. This is Kuan *ta jên*, this is Lo *ta lao yeh*. Long (*chiu*) look up to, long look up to.

---

42. 風 fêng¹, wind.
42. 颳 kua¹ } to blow, a breeze.
    風 fêng¹ }
42. 黑 hei¹ } at dark, after dark,
    下 hsia⁴ } darkness.
42. 天 t'ien¹ } night, dark.
    黑 hei¹ }
43. 南 nan², south.
44. 光 kuang¹, rays, brightness, light, bare, only.
44. 借 chieh⁴ } excuse me, allow me; can you inform me? (borrow light).
    光 kuang¹ }

44. 省 shêng³, a province, to save, economise.
44. 省 shêng³ } a provincial capi-
    城 ch'êng² } tal.
45. 順 shun⁴, fair (of wind, tide, &c.), to follow, docile.
45. 順 shun⁴ } following (a route,
    着 cho } doctrine, &c.).
45. 近 chin⁴, near.
46. 位 wei⁴, gentleman.
46. 久 chiu³, a long time.
46. 仰 yang³, to look up to.
46. 久 chiu³ } I have long looked up to you, happy to make your acquaintance.
    仰 yang³ }

47. You will save money if you buy coal by the cart-load.
48. With a fair wind and tide you will get there in a very short time.
49. Those two are brothers. The elder brother is called Ta Shun-tzŭ, and the younger one Hsiao Shun-tzŭ. There is one elder sister and two younger ones. The brothers come in the middle.
50. That wine glass is not clean. How often have I told you that after you have washed the glasses you must wipe them dry with a duster?

Coal if is complete cart 's buy, then save money.

Follow wind, follow water, short time then arrive ed.

That two piece men is brothers. Elder brother call Ta Shun-tzŭ, younger brother call Hsiao Shun-tzŭ. Still have one piece elder sister, two piece younger sister. Middle is they brothers two piece.

That wine cup not clean. I tell you how many turn, wash finish ed glass cup must take rub cloth rub dry ed.

---

47. 煤 mei², coal.
47. 成 ch'êng², complete, accomplish, a fraction, a tenth part.
47. 成車 ch'êng² ch'ê¹ } by the cart-load, by the full cart.
48. 一會兒 i¹ hui³ 'rh } a short time, in a short time.
49. 弟兄 ti⁴ hsiung¹ } brothers.
49. 兄弟 hsiung¹ ti⁴ } a younger brother.
49. 哥哥 ko¹ ko¹ } an elder brother.
49. 姐妹 chieh³ mei⁴ } sisters.

49. 姐姐 chieh³ chieh³ } an elder sister.
49. 妹妹 mei⁴ mei⁴ } a younger sister.
49. 中 chung¹, centre, middle, inside; chung⁴, to hit the mark.
49. 中間 chung¹ chien¹ } the middle, in the middle.
50. 杯 pei¹, a cup, tumbler, glass.
50. 乾 kan¹, dry.
50. 乾淨 kan¹ ching⁴ } clean.
50. 洗 hsi³, to wash.
50. 玻璃 po¹ li² } glass.
50. 擦 ts'a¹, to rub.
50. 布 pu⁴, cloth, a cloth.

51. My knife won't cut this thick string. Lend me yours, will you? The one I gave you on your last birthday. Don't talk about it! Unfortunately I've lost it. How did you manage that? I don't know, but I fancy I must have lost it when I went to the barber's shop on Wednesday to have my hair cut. I know positively that I had it on Wednesday morning, because I cut my thumb when I was using it to sharpen a pencil. The next time I wanted to use it I hadn't got it, and I have a sort of recollection that I took it out at the barber's to pare my nails and I fancy I left it

My knife cut not complete (*liao*) this fashion one big string. You take yours lend give me *pa*; just is you last year born day I give you ing that piece (*pa*) knife. Don't mention, unfortunately lose ed. You how lose ing. Not know, fear is Sunday three to shave head shop in go cut hair that one day lose ing. I positively know, Sunday three, upper half day have *lai cho*, because I employ ed pare pencil *lai cho*, take big thumb finger cut broke ed. Lower turn want use ing time not have ed. I good resemble remember I at shave head shop in bring out come, pare finger nail, fear leave behind ed. I

---

51. 剌 la², to cut.
51. 繩子 shêng² tzŭ } string, rope, cord.
51. 惜 hsi¹, pity.
51. 可 k'o³ 惜 hsi¹ } unfortunately, to be pitied, deserving of pity.
51. 可 k'o³ 惜 hsi¹ 了 liao³ 兒 'rh 的 ti } unfortunately.
51. 丟 tiu¹, to lose.

51. 剃 t'i⁴, to shave (the head).
51. 鉸 chiao³, to cut with scissors or shears.
51. 髮 fa³, the hair of the head.
51. 頭 t'ou² 髮 fa³ } the hair of the head.
51. 削 hsiao¹, to pare.
51. 筆 pi³, a chinese pencil, a pen.
51. 拇 mu³, the thumb.
51. 破 p'o⁴ 了 liao } broken, a cut or broken skin.
51. 指 chih² 甲 chia³ } the nails, nail of the finger or toe.

behind. I went back to the barber's to inquire if they had seen it, and they all declared they hadn't, but although they said so I expect one of the employés stole it.

52. Find me a piece of wood. It must be about five feet long and three inches thick. A short piece won't do.

53. That man is a very fair scholar, and his composition is passable, but his memory is bad and his hand-writing cannot be called first-class.

54. What book are you reading? I am reading a French book. Oh, do you understand French? I wouldn't

return to shave head shop in go, ask them see (*ch'iao*) ed not have, they all say not see. Although is thus speak, fear is they employés steal ed go *lo*.

You give me seek one piece wood come. Must above below five feet long, three inch thick. Short one not suit.

That piece man very have a little learning, pen ink on also passable (*pa-liao*), only is remember disposition not good; character writing also not reckon ten parts good.

You look ing is what book. I look French book. Ah, you still understand French talk? Not ven-

---

51. 落 la⁴ / 下 hsia⁴ } to leave out or behind; *lao⁴*, to perch, alight.
51. 夥 huo³ / 計 chi⁴ } a partner, mate, companion, employé.
51. 偷 t'ou¹, to steal.
52. 尺 ch'ih³, a foot, foot measure.
52. 上 shang⁴ / 下 hsia⁴ } about, more or less.
52. 寸 ts'un⁴, an inch.
52. 尺 ch'ih² / 寸 ts'un⁴ } linear measurement.
53. 學 hsüeh², to learn; hsiao², to imitate.
53. 學 hsueh² / 問 wên⁴ } learning, erudition.
53. 墨 mo⁴, ink.
53. 筆 pi³ / 墨 mo⁴ } composition.
53. 性 hsing⁴, disposition.
53. 記 chi⁴ / 性 hsing⁴ } memory.
53. 分 fên¹, a portion, a tenth part, to divide, a minute.
54. 書 shu¹, a book.
54. 看 k'an⁴ / 書 shu¹ } to read a book.
54. 法 fa⁴ / 國 kuo² } France, French.

venture to say that I understand French, I only know a little. Will you read a few sentences aloud to me? I should like to hear what it sounds like.

55. You have not been to see me for several months. What is the reason of that? Is it because I have offended you? Don't talk like that! How could you offend me? It's only because I am terribly busy and haven't even time to attend to my own domestic affairs. When I come back from the office I am so tired that I don't feel inclined even to eat, and what time, I ask you, have I got to look up my friends?

56. I say! where are you shoving to? You've trodden on

ture say understand French talk, also only is know a little. You take few sentence recite give me listen *pa*. I want listen listen that sound how fashion.

This good some piece month you not come see me, is what cause. Is I offend ed you *lo*? Don't speak that piece talk. You where offend ed me *lo*. Only is because I busy ing dreadfully, even I self home in 's affair all not have leisure manage. From yamên return come ing time I tire ing dreadful, even food all not think eat. Please ask, I where have leisure see (*ch'iao*) friend go.

Ai, this is towards where shove. Tread ed I foot finger *lo*.

---

54. 敢 kan³, to dare, venture.
54. 句 chü⁴, a sentence.
54. 念 nien⁴, to recite, read aloud, study.
54. 念書 nien⁴ shu¹ } to study.
54. 聲 shêng¹, sound, tone.
54. 音 yin¹, note, sound.
54. 聲音 shêng¹ yin¹ } sound, tone, note.
55. 罪 tsui⁴, fault, crime, sin, punishment, penalty.
55. 得罪 tê² tsui⁴ } to offend.
55. 自己 tzŭ⁴ chi³ } one's self.
55. 乏了 fa² liao } tired.
56. 唉 ai¹, an exclamation of regret or remonstrance.
56. 往 wang³, towards, to go.
56. 擠 chi³, to push, shove, crowd.
56. 趾 ts'ai³, to tread on.
56. 脚 chiao³, the foot.

my toe. I beg your pardon.

57. That child's case is very sad. His father and mother are dead, and he is living with a distant relation who doesn't like him very much, and doesn't treat him very well. He is now thirteen years old, and hasn't yet been to school. It seems to me that this is not as it should be, for the boy isn't living there for nothing. His father left a little property, and his relative is getting the interest, which is more

Have fault, have fault, not retain attention.

That child true pitiable. He father mother all dead ed, he at far relative home live. That relative not great pleased him, treat him also not good. He now (*ju chin*) thirteen years of age (*sui*) là, also not to learn. According to I look, this not correct; because that child not is gratis live. He father leave (*liu hsia*) ed a little property, interest all is he that relative take. That interest compare support him that

---

56. 脚 chiao³ ⎫
    指 chih² ⎬ the toe, toes.
    頭 t'ou ⎭

56. 神 shên², spirit, spirits, divine, spiritual.

56. 留 liu² ⎫ to pay attention,
    神 shên² ⎭ take heed.

57. 孩 hai² ⎫ a child.
    子 tzŭ ⎭

57. 眞 chên¹, true, truly.

57. 憐 lien², to pity, pity.

57. 可 k'o³ ⎫ pitiable.
    憐 lien² ⎭

57. 父 fu⁴ father ⎫ parents.
    母 mu³ mother ⎭

57. 死 ssŭ³, to die.

57. 喜 hsi³, happiness.

57. 歡 huan¹, satisfaction, pleasure.

57. 喜 hsi³ ⎫ to be pleased,
    歡 huan¹ ⎭ pleased with, glad, rejoice.

57. 待 tai⁴, to treat, behave towards, wait.

57. 如 ju², as, if.

57. 如 ju² ⎫ now.
    今 chin¹ ⎭

57. 歲 sui⁴, years of age.

57. 上 shang⁴ ⎫ to go to school.
    學 hsüeh² ⎭

57. 據 chu⁴, according to, evidence.

57. 白 pai², gratis, gratuitously, white.

57. 產 ch'an³ ⎫ property.
    業 yeh⁴ ⎭

57. 利 li⁴ ⎫ interest, profits.
    息 hsi² ⎭

57. 利 li⁴ ⎫ interest.
    錢 ch'ien² ⎭

than twice as much as the cost of the boy's keep.

58. The train starts at twenty minutes past three. The baggage must be ready by ten minutes to three, as the carriage will be at the door then, and it will take a quarter of an hour to drive to the station.

59. When you told him that joke what did he say? He didn't say anything: he only laughed.

60. Chinese is indeed difficult to learn. European languages are much easier.

piece money, more one fold *lo*.

That fire cart three dot one quarter five open. Baggage, three dot less ten minutes all must prepare good ed, because horse cart then is at that piece time arrive door mouth *lo*. Sit horse cart arrive cart station must one quarter's time (*kung fu*).

You tell him that piece smile talk, he say what. He not say what, he only laugh ed.

Chinese talk true difficult learn. West country talk easy many *lo*.

---

57. 養 yang³, to nourish, rear, raise.

57. 養 yang³ } to bring up, nourish, keep (as horses, a 活 huo² } family, &c.).

57. 一 i¹ } one fold, double. 倍 pei⁴

58. 火 huo³ } fire carriage, a railway carriage, 車 ch'ê¹ } railway train.

58. 開 k'ai¹, to start (as a train, steamer, &c.).

58. 李 li³, a plum.

58. 行 hsing² } baggage, luggage. 李 li³

58. 口 k'ou³, a mouth, gap.

58. 門 mên² } a doorway, threshold. 口 k'ou³

58. 站 chan⁴, to stand still, stationary.

58. 車 ch'ê¹ } a railway station. 站 chan⁴

58. 工 kung¹, work.

58. 夫 fu¹, a man, a labouring man.

58. 工 kung¹ } work, labour, 夫 fu¹ } leisure, time.

59. 笑 hsiao⁴, to smile.

59. 笑 hsiao⁴ } to chaff, make fun 話 hua⁴ } of.

59. 笑 hsiao⁴ 話 hua⁴ } a joke. 兒 'rh

59. 樂 lo⁴, to laugh, be pleased.

60. 難 nan², difficult.

60. 容 jung² } easy. 易 i⁴

61. You are the most difficult to manage of all the five children.
62. When I was passing his gate his dog ran out and bit me. After a few days my leg began to swell, and I sent for the doctor to look at it. He said it wasn't serious and told me to rub on some remedy which he gave me. Sure enough it didn't pain me on the second day, and on the fourth day it was quite well.

63. Take those thick clothes, pack them in a bag and carry them to the tailor. Tell him that the coat doesn't fit and he must

Five piece child most (*tsui*, or *ting*) difficult control one, then is you.
I by his door mouth pass, his dog run forth come ed, take I leg bite ed one time (*hsia'rh*). Pass ed two (*liang*) day, that leg then swell begin ed. Invite ed doctor come look a look (*ch'iao*), he say not important, order me take he give I ing a little medicine rub on. Sure enough, number two day then not pain ed, arrive ed number four day, then great well ed.

Take hold that thick clothes, pack at bag in side, carry to tailor there go. Tell him that coat not proper, must alter. That

---

61. 最 tsui⁴, very, most.
61. 頂 ting³, top, summit, very.
62. 跑 p'ao³, to run, gallop.
62. 腿 t'ui³, the leg.
62. 咬 yao³, to bite, bark.
62. 腫 chung³, to swell.
62. 腫了 chung³ liao } swollen.
62. 大夫 tai⁴ fu¹ } a doctor.
62. 藥 yao⁴, medicine, drugs.
62. 抹 mo³, to rub on, rub out.
62. 敢情 kan³ ch'ing² } sure enough.

63. 厚 hou⁴, thick.
63. 裝 chuang¹, to pack.
63. 口袋 k'ou³ tai⁴ } a sack, bag.
63. 裁 ts'ai², to cut out.
63. 縫 fêng², to sew.
63. 裁縫 ts'ai² fêng² } a tailor.
63. 褂子 kua⁴ tzŭ } a coat.
63. 合 ho², in harmony with.
63. 合式 ho² shih⁴ } to fit, suit, be in accordance with pattern.

alter it. The waistcoat and trousers, too, are not right; the trousers are too long and the waistcoat is too short. They must both be altered.

64. This is strange. You were quite well yesterday; how is it you are ill to-day? I don't know how I got ill. I expect I must have caught cold last night. It was very hot in the afternoon and so when I went out I put on thin clothes. At eight o'clock in the evening it suddenly turned chilly. I felt a little uncomfortable at the time, but I didn't think much of it, and this morning when I woke my throat was sore

waistcoat, trousers, also not correct. Trousers too long, waistcoat too short. Two piece all must alter.

This strange *lo*. You yesterday good good ly (*ti*), to-day how then ill ed. I not know how obtain ing. Fear is yesterday evening catch ed cool ed. After half day very hot, go out door's time then wear ed thin clothes *lo*. Arrive ed evening eight dot bell, suddenly then cool commence ed. At (*tang*) time then have a little not comfortable, but not great pay heed. To-day early sleep awake ed, throat then sore, full body put

---

63. 改 kai³, to alter.
63. 砍 k'an³, to cut, as with a sword.
63. 肩 chien¹, the shoulder.
63. 砍肩 k'an³ chien¹ } a waistcoat.
63. 褲子 k'u⁴ tzŭ } trousers.
64. 奇怪 ch'i² kuai⁴ } strange.
64. 忽然 hu¹ jan² } suddenly.
64. 當時 tang¹ shih² } at the time.

64. 舒坦 shu¹ t'an³ } comfortable.
64. 理 li³, to heed, notice.
64. 理會 li³ hui⁴ } to pay attention.
64. 醒 hsing³, to awake.
64. 醒了 hsing³ liao } awake.
64. 睡醒了 shui⁴ hsing³ liao } to awake from sleep.
64. 嗓子 sang³ tzŭ } the throat.
64. 滿 man³, full.

and I felt burning all over. I think I'll lie down for a bit with a quilt over me and I shall probably be better by the evening. If I am not, I'll take a dose of medicine.

65. Mr. Li was formerly a military official, but he was obliged to give up in consequence of failing eyesight. He now lives in a village not far from the south gate of Peking.

66. The Emperor goes out of the palace to-morrow, and the shop-keepers on both sides of the streets through which he passes have to close their shops.

forth (*fa*) burn. I propose lie down a lie down, cover on counterpane, late half day probably well ed *pa*. If still not well, I eat one dose medicine that's it.

Li lao-yeh formerly do military officer *lai cho*. Because eye not good ed, not have remedy, then not do officer. He now distant from north Capital south gate not far ly one piece village in live.

Emperor to-morrow forth Imperial palace. Pass ing that street two side 's shop all must close door.

---

64. 身子 shên¹, or shên-tzŭ, the body.
64. 燒 shao¹, to burn.
64. 發燒 fa¹ shao⁴ } to feel burning, to be feverish.
64. 躺 t'ang³, to lie down.
64. 蓋 kai⁴, to cover, to build.
64. 蓋上 kai⁴ shang⁴ } to cover.
64. 蓋子 kai⁴ tzŭ } a cover.
64. 被 pei⁴, to suffer, endure.
64. 窩 wo¹, a nest, lair.
64. 被窩 pei⁴ wo¹ } a quilt, the upper covering of a bed.
64. 概 kai⁴, all, the whole.
64. 大概 ta⁴ kai⁴ } probably, the general outline.
64. 劑 chi¹, a dose.
64. 劑一藥 chi⁴ i¹ yao⁴ } a dose of medicine.

65. 武 wu³, military.
65. 武官 wu³ kuan¹ } a military officer.
65. 眼睛 yen³ ching¹ } eye.
65. 村子 ts'un¹ tzŭ } a village.
65. 村庄 ts'un¹ chuang¹ } a village.
66. 皇上 huang² shang⁴ } the Emperor, an emperor.
66. 皇宮 huang² kung¹ } an Imperial Palace.
66. 街 chieh¹, a street.
66. 旁 p'ang², side, lateral.
66. 邊 pien¹, edge, side, margin.
66. 旁邊 p'ang pien¹ } the side, at the side.
66. 兩旁 liang³ p'ang² } both sides.

67. He doesn't like spending money. If any one goes out on an excursion with him, when it comes to paying he always tries to make the other man pay.

He not like spend money. He if is with (*t'ung*) people go out ramble go, arrive ed give money 's time, he always want think remedy call that piece man give money.

68. I am going out in the carriage this afternoon to pay visits. Tell the servant that he must come with me and bring my visiting cards with him. Is he to walk, or follow you on horseback, Sir? He can walk by the side of the carriage. I'm not going very far.

I to-day after half day sit cart salute stranger go. Tell servant he must follow ing me go, and (*hai²*) must carry name slip. He is walk, *ah*, still is ride horse follow ing (*cho*) you Sir go. He can at cart side walk. I go ing not far.

69. The sun is very hot, don't sit in the sun. There is shade under the tree; why don't you sit there?

Sun very hot; don't at sun ground in sit. Tree below have shade. Why not at there sit.

---

67 花 hua¹ } to spend money.
    錢 ch'ien²

67. 溜 liu¹ } to stroll; ta¹, to add.
    搭 ta¹

67. 想 hsiang³ } to devise a way,
    法 fa²   or remedy,
    子 tzŭ   think of a plan.

68. 拜 pai⁴ } to pay a formal call.
    會 hui⁴

68. 拜 pai⁴ } to pay calls.
    客 k'o⁴

68. 班 pan¹, a troupe, row, order.

68. 跟 kên¹ }
    班 pan¹ } a servant.
    的 ti

68. 名 ming² } a name.
    子 tzŭ

68. 片 p'ien⁴, a strip, slip.

68. 名 ming² } a visiting card.
    片 p'ien⁴

68. 呢 ni, an interrogative final particle.

68. 可 k'o³ } can, will do.
    以 i³

69. 太 t'ai⁴ } the sun.
    陽 yang²

69. 太 t'ai⁴ }
    陽 yang² }
    地 ti⁴ } in the sunshine.
    裏 li³

69. 樹 shu⁴, a tree.

69. 底 ti³ } below, underneath.
    下 hsia⁴

69. 底 ti³, the bottom.

69. 陰 yin¹ }
    涼 liang² } shade.
    兒 'rh

70. I seem to have seen that gentleman before, but I can't remember where I saw him.	That one gentleman good resemble formerly see ed (*kuo*), but not remember is at where see ed (*kuo*) one.
71. Don't move; a wasp has settled on your collar. Wait till I drive him away. Ah! I'm more frightened of wasps than anything. If they sting one it's no joke.	Don't move. Have one piece wasp settle at your collar on Wait I take him drive away. Ai, I most fear ing is wasp. Sting ed, not is play ing.

---

70. 位 wei⁴, position, place, the "numerative" of gentlemen, &c. (see 45).

71. 螞 ma³ } a wasp.
    蜂 fêng¹ }

71. 落 lao⁴, to settle, perch (see 51).

71. 領 ling³ } a collar; ling³, to
    子 tzŭ } lead, guide.

71. 閧 hung¹ } drive away, frighten away.
    開 k'ai¹ }

71. 螫 chê², to sting.

71. 玩 wan², to play.

Mention has been made at the close of Section VII. of the value of the observance of conventionalities when conversing with Chinese. The student, if he is in China, will at this stage no doubt wish to try the effect of what he has learnt upon the native, but if he fires off a prepared sentence abruptly upon a stranger the chances are that his remark will be greeted with a stare of bewilderment. In nine cases out of ten the Chinese addressed will not give the speaker the credit of being able to speak the language and will, on the spur of the moment, take it for granted that the remark addressed to him is in the language of the foreigner and therefore must be unintelligible. If, however, the remark is introduced by a ceremonial bow, or if a question is prefaced with 借光 *chieh*⁴ *kuang*¹, "borrow light;" 請問 *ch'ing*³ *wen*⁴, "may I be permitted to ask," or 勞駕 *lao*² *chia*¹, "trouble your chariot," etc., the effect will be very different, for the person addressed will have his attention arrested, he will realize that the foreigner knows the laws of politeness, and the remark that follows will almost always be understood.

The undesirability of the indiscriminate use of 你 you, instead of 您, or 您納, you sir, has already been called attention to. A few other hints on etiquette may profitably be added.

Always rise to receive a visitor of any but markedly lower standing, and never sit down again until your visitor has been invited to sit and has taken his seat.

Never precede a visitor into or out of a room, and when greeting him, or taking leave of him, or when asking a question of a stranger, any one who is wearing spectacles should remove them.

When meeting a friend, if you are riding or are seated in a carriage, etiquette demands that you should get down, but in order to save your friend the trouble of doing the same thing it is desirable to pretend not to see him. This is the law of Chinese etiquette, but it is now often relaxed where foreigners are concerned. It is, however, a breach of manners to remain on one's horse or in one's carriage when addressing a friend or a stranger unless the latter is of the "coolie" class.

A man's wife should be referred to with reserve, and when she is mentioned she should be called 令夫人 $ling^4 fu^1 jên^2$, your honourable wife, or 寶眷 $pao^3 chüan^4$, your precious family. Never, as the tyro would be apt to call her, must she be referred to as 你的媳婦 $ni^3 ti hsi^2 fu^4$, your wife.

The word 令 $ling^4$, should precede any reference to the relatives of the person addressed, as 令愛 $ling^4 ai^4$, your daughter, 令尊 $ling^4 tsun^1$, your father, 令弟 $ling^4 ti^4$, your younger brother.

If your host or visitor rises from his chair you must not fail to rise also. When your host, after a certain interval, asks you to drink tea it may be taken as a sign that he wishes the visit to close.

Tea should not be drunk by the visitor at the beginning of a visit without the invitation of the host, and when the host himself rises to place a cup of tea before his guest the latter should rise and receive it with both hands.

One of the most common of Chinese greetings is 吃了飯了 $ch'ih^1 liao fan^4 liao$, "have you had your meal." The answer which should be given is 偏過了 $pi'en^1 kuo^4 liao$, or 偏了您納 "I have been selfish enough to do so"; the implication being that you ought to have waited for the other person to join you.

When a host escorts a visitor to the door, as it is his duty to do, the visitor should request him to 留步 *liu² pu⁴*, restrain his steps, to which the answer might be given 禮當 *li³ tang¹*, politeness requires.

To a complimentary remark, or to a complimentary action, 不敢當 *pu¹ kan³ tang¹*, I am unworthy, is the ordinary reply.

When asking a person his name, do not say 你姓甚麼 *ni³ hsing⁴ shêmmo*,² unless to a person of the coolie class, but, 貴姓, honourable name, or 您貴姓, you, sir, honourable name.

By an observance of these few rules credit will be obtained for at least an elementary knowledge of the laws of politeness from a Chinese point of view.

X.

Examples.

1. Put those old linen clothes in the bath and wash them. You need not wash them with soap, just put them in hot water to soak for an hour or two, then wring them out dry and hang them out in the sun. When they are dried, fold them up and put them in the cupboard. | Take hold that old linen clothes put at bathe basin in wash a wash. Not use employ soap wash, only put at hot water in soak one two hour's time. Return come, twist dry ed, hang at sun ground in dry a dry. Dry good ed, then fold up, place at cupboard in side.
2. When are you going to pay me back the money I lent you? Whenever I've got any ready money I'll pay you. At the moment I've not got a single cash. | I borrow give you ing that piece money you when repay me. I when have now money, I when repay. At the moment even one piece great cash all not have.

---

1. 舊 chiu⁴, old.
1. 洗 hsi³ } to bathe.
   澡 tsao³ }
1. 盆 p'ên², a basin, tub.
1. 胰 i² } soap.
   子 tzŭ }
1. 泡 p'ao⁴, to soak.
1. 擰 ning², to twist, squeeze, wring.
1. 挂 kua⁴, to hang up.
1. 挂 kua⁴ }
   起 ch'i³ } to hang up.
   來 lai }
1. 曬 shai⁴, to dry in the sun, warm in the sun.

1. 疊 tieh² }
   起 ch'i³ } to fold up.
   來 lai }
1. 櫃 kuei⁴ } cupboard.
   子 tzŭ }
2. 多 to¹ } when.
   暫 tsan¹ }
2. 還 huan², to pay back, repay.
2. 現 hsien⁴ } ready money.
   錢 ch'ien² }
2. 目 mu⁴, the eye (seldom used colloquially).
2. 目 mu⁴ } at the moment.
   下 hsia⁴ }

3. When he wakes tell him I'm waiting for him in the courtyard, and that breakfast is laid. Directly he comes we will have it, and the earlier the better.
4. Don't be offended if I say that you are wrong and he is in the right. He was sitting there quite quietly not speaking to any one at all, and you without rhyme or reason crossed over and abused him. Of course he got angry and swore back at you. Any one, no matter who, would object to being abused for nothing, and it seems to me that you ought to make him an apology.

He sleep wake ed 's time you tell he I at courtyard in wait he. Early food all spread out good ed. He one come ed we then eat. The more early the more good.
You don't take offence I say, you wrong ed, he have reason. He quietly (good good ly) sitting, not at all with who speak talk, you without cause (*wu yuan wu ku ti*) cross go curse he. He of course is beget anger. What man, no matter (not discuss) is who, not willing call people white curse he. According to I look, you ought give he make good piece fault (*pu shih*).

3. 院子 yuan⁴ tzŭ } a court, courtyard, inclosure.
3. 擺 pai³, to spread out, lay out.
3. 越 yüeh⁴, the more, to overstep.
4. 怪 kuai⁴, to resent, take offence.
4. 理 li³, right, reason, principle, to arrange.
4. 並不 ping⁴ pu⁴ } not at all, by no means.
4. 無 wu², not; used colloquially in a few combinations only.
4. 無緣無故的 wu² yuan² wu² ku⁴ ti } without cause, without rhyme or reason.
4. 罵 ma⁴, to curse, swear.

4. 論 lun⁴, to discuss, argue.
4. 不論 pu⁴ lun⁴ } no matter, of no consequence, never mind, irrespective of.
4. 願意 yüan⁴ i⁴ } to be willing.
4. 白 pai², for nothing, for no cause.
4. 應該 ying¹ kai¹ } ought.
4. 應當 ying¹ tang¹ } ought, should.
4. 賠 p'ei², to forfeit, make good.
4. 賠不是 p'ei² pu⁴ shih⁴ } to make an apology.

5. Strictly speaking, I am not bound to do this business, but as he is ill and cannot come to the office to-day, if I don't do it for him your affairs will be delayed.

Discuss principle, this not is I ought arrange ing affair. Because he to-day ill ed, not can to Yamên, if not is I go instead of he arrange, you Sir's affair then delayed.

6. He was very pleased when he heard you were going with him to call upon His Excellency Li. He always was timid, and when he sees a person for the first time he can't say a single word.

He heard say you Sir with (*t'ung*) him go visit Li great man, he very pleased. He originally gall small, top one occasion (*hui²*) see man, even one sentence talk all speak not out come.

7. I can't find my spectacles. I don't remember where I put them. I've looked everywhere for them; under the table, under the chairs, even in the coal box, and I can't find them anywhere.

My spectacles seek not find. Not remember put at where. I each place seek ed, at table below, chair below, even coal box in all seek ed. Where all seek not succeed.

8. The weight of that box is too great for one man to carry on his shoulder. I fancy

That piece box's weight too heavy; one piece man carry on shoulder not move.

---

5. 替 t'i⁴, for, a substitute for, instead of.
6. 膽 tan³ } the gall, courage.
   子 tzŭ
6. 次 tz'ŭ⁴, a time, an occasion, inferior.
7. 眼 yên³
   鏡 ching⁴ } spectacles.
   子 tzŭ
7. 各 ko⁴, each, every.
7. 各 ko⁴ } every one, each
   各 ko⁴ } singly.
7. 處 ch'u⁴, a place.

7. 匣 hsia² } a box, casket.
   子 tzŭ
8. 箱 hsiang¹ } a box, trunk.
   子 tzŭ
8. 分 fên¹, to divide, a division.
8. 量 liang⁴, capacity, measure, to consider; liang², to measure.
8. 分 fên¹ } weight.
   量 liang⁴
8. 重 chung⁴, heavy, severe.
8. 扛 k'ang², to carry on the shoulders.

it will require two men to carry it between them. It seems heavy, but in reality it is very light. It only contains straw hats.

9. He has really no luck. Last year he built a house and spent a lot of money over it. Just as it was finished, it was burnt down. He hadn't insured it either.

10. Those two men were fighting in the street yesterday. The policeman saw them and dragged them off to the police court. The official never inquired who was right and who was wrong, but ordered each of them to receive fifty blows with the bamboo.

11. I did this myself. If you don't believe what I say

Fear must two piece men carry on pole. Look ing is heavy, the true is very light. Pack ing not ex-ceed is straw hat.

He true not luck. Go year he build ed piece house, spend ed how much money. Just build finish ed, call fire burn spoil ed. He also not guarantee danger.

That two piece man yesterday at street on fight *lai cho* Watch street one saw ed, then take them drag to officer yamen go. That officer not at all (*ping pu*) ask who is, who not is, only call each man beat fifty boards.

This is I myself do ing. You if not believe my talk then

---

8. 抬 t'ai², to carry between two people, to lift up.
8. 其 ch'i², he, she, it, the; seldom used colloquially.
8. 其實 ch'i² shih² } the truth is, in reality, in fact.
8. 輕 ch'ing¹, light.
8. 草 ts'ao⁴, grass.
8. 帽子 mao⁴ tzŭ } a hat, cap.
9. 眞 chên¹ true, truly.
9. 運氣 yun⁴ ch'i⁴ } fortune, luck.
9. 蓋房子 kai⁴ fang² tzŭ } to build a house.

9. 保 pao³, to guarantee.
9. 險 hsien³, dangerous, danger.
9. 保險 pao³ hsien³ } to insure against accident.
10. 架 chia⁴, a frame, stand.
10. 打架 ta³ chia⁴ } to fight, quarrel, come to blows.
10. 看街的 k'an¹ chieh¹ ti } a policeman, a street watchman.
10. 拉 la¹, to drag, draw.
10. 各人 ko² jên² } both, each person.
11. 我各人 wo³ ko² jên² } I myself.

ask my brother. You know he won't tell you a lie.

12. When you get on board the steamer count your baggage and see if the number of things is complete. I think a bundle of rugs has been left behind. If it has, send me a telegram when you get to Shanghai, and I will go to the hotel and inquire whether they have it or not. If they have, I will send it on to you.

13. How did you get on with your sport yesterday? Did you get anything? No, I had bad luck. When I got to the wood on the other side of the hill I had not gone many paces when I saw a pheasant.

ask my younger brother. He not lie, you is knowing.

You on steamer 's time, take hold your baggage count a count number, look look correct not correct. I fear leave out ed one bundle blanket. If leave out ed, arrive ed Shanghai you give me issue piece telegram, I then to food inn go, inquire inquire they have not have. If have ed, I then send to you there go.

You yesterday go shooting, how fashion, obtain ed what not have. Not have luck. Arrive ed hill that side that tree grove in, not walk ed few pace then saw (ch'iao chien) ed piece wild chicken, lift up gun

---

11. 撒 sa¹, to let go, let loose.
11. 謊 huang³, a lie, falsehood.
11. 撒 sa¹ } to tell a lie.
    謊 huang³ }
11. 謊 huang³ } lies.
    話 hua⁴ }
11. 輪 lun², a wheel (not of a cart wheel).
11. 船 ch'uan², a ship, vessel, boat.
11. 輪 lun² } a steamship.
    船 ch'uan² }
12. 落 la⁴ } to leave out, or behind.
    下 hsia⁴ }

12. 毡 chan¹ } a blanket, felt, rug.
    子 tzǔ }
12. 海 hai³, the sea.
12. 電 tien⁴, electricity.
12. 報 pao⁴, to report, requite.
12. 電 tien⁴ } a telegram.
    報 pao⁴ }
13. 圍 wei², to surround, enclose.
13. 打 ta³ } to go shooting, hunting.
    圍 wei² }
13. 林 lin² } a grove, wood, forest.
    子 tzǔ }
13. 步 pu⁴, a step, pace.
13. 野 yeh³, wild, savage, rude.

I put up my gun to fire at him, but it was empty; I had forgotten to load it. I had not gone much farther when I caught my foot in the root of a tree, fell down and broke my gun in two.

14. Light the lamp and put it on the small table. Move the table out a little. If you put it close to the curtains I am afraid they may catch fire.

15. Where did you buy that cotton cloth? I bought it at the foreign goods shop. What did you buy it for? I thought of making shirts with it. That kind of cloth won't do to make shirts of; it is too coarse, you want finer

come, want beat, that gun is empty one, forgot ed pack *lo*. Walk ed not far, cause tree root trip up ed foot *lo*, take hold me tumble lie down ed, my gun also snap ed.

Take hold lamp light up, place at that small table on. Take hold table remove a little, don't next curtain place (*fang*), fear curtain want catch (*chao*) *lo*.

That cloth you at where buy ing. At foreign goods shop in buy ing. Buy that piece do what. I propose make shirts use. That fashion 's cloth make shirt not suit, too coarse *lo*. Make shirt must fine a little 's material. Not important;

---

13. 舉 chu³, to lift up.
13. 鎗 ch'iang¹, a shot-gun, rifle.
13. 根子 kên¹ tzŭ } a root.
13. 絆 pan⁴, to trip up.
13. 跌 tieh¹ tsai¹ } to fall down.
13. 折 shê² chê² } to break, snap.
14. 燈 têng¹, a lamp.
14. 點燈 tien³ têng¹ } to light a lamp.
14. 放 fang⁴, to put, place down (see IX. 36).
14. 挪 no², to move, remove.
14. 挪開 no² k'ai¹ } to move away.
14. 挨着 ai¹ cho } next to, near to.
14. 帳子 chang¹ tzŭ } curtains.
15. 貨 huo⁴, goods, wares.
15. 汗 han⁴, sweat, perspiration.
15. 出汗 ch'u¹ han⁴ } to sweat, perspire.
15. 汗衫 han⁴ shan¹ } a shirt.
15. 粗 ts'u¹, coarse.
15. 細 hsi⁴, fine.

material than that for shirts. Never mind, it will come in useful. We haven't enough dusters; I'll make dusters of it.

16. I am looking for a servant. Do you know of a good one? What is the servant to do? I want him to act as cook. If you are not very particular I know of a man who is disengaged at present. He can cook ordinary dishes fairly well, and he is clean, quiet, and willing to work. The only thing is he is a little deaf, and occasionally he likes to take a drop of drink, but I never saw him drunk. What wages does he want? He is asking twenty-five dollars a

have use place. Rub cloth not enough, make rub cloth use *pa*.

I look for piece below man; you Sir know have good one not know. That below man is want do what one. I want him serve as cook. You Sir if not very particular, I know have one piece man; he now unoccupied. Ordinary one vegetables do ing still passable (*pa liao*), man clean, also (*yu*) quiet (*lao shih*), also (*yeh*) willing use effort. Only is have one kind; he ear have a little deaf, now and again (*ou êrh*) he also like drink glass wine, I but not seen (*ch'iao chien*)

---

15. 材 t'sai² / 料 liao⁴ } materials, material.
16. 當 tang¹, to act as (see IX. 7).
16. 講 chiang³ / 究 chiu¹ } particular, exacting, fastidious.
16. 講 chiang³, to explain, expound.
16. 平 p'ing², level, even.
16. 常 ch'ang,² constantly, frequently, often.
16. 平 p'ing² / 常 ch'ang² } common, ordinary.
16. 又 yu⁴, again, also, moreover.

16. 肯 k'ên³, to be willing.
16, 功 kung¹, work, effort, meritorious service.
16. 耳 êrh³ / 朵 to³ } the ear.
16. 聾 lung², deaf.
16. 偶 ou³ / 爾 êrh³ } occasionally, once in a way.
16. 醉 tsui⁴ / 了 liao } drunk.
16. 工 kung¹ / 錢 ch'ien² } wages.

month, but you need not pay him as much as that; I think twenty will be enough. Could you tell him to come and see me to-night after dinner? Yes, I can, but I think you had better tell him to come for a month on trial and see whether he will suit or not. Thank you so much, I'm afraid I am giving you a lot of trouble; I will come round in a day or two and repeat my thanks. You do me too much honour.

him drink drunk ed. He want how much labour money. Want ing is twenty-five dollars one piece month, you Sir but not use give him thus some piece. I think twenty bits enough *lo*. You Sir call he to-day late food after come see me, suit not suit. Suit *lo*. I think you Sir still is call he come one piece month try a try, suit not suit. Trouble chariot ing very, cause you Sir expend heart; pass two day I to you Sir there go, again give you Sir offer (*tao*) thanks. How dare, how dare.

17. I have not seen you for ages. Have you been all right all this time? Thanks to your good fortune, I've been well. Are you well at home? Thanks for

Long not met, long not met; you Sir this one period well *lo*. Beholden to prosperity, all good *lo*; you Sir palace on all well. Thanks for inquiries, all

16. 彀 kou⁴, enough.
16. 道 tao⁴ } to offer thanks,
    謝 hsieh⁴ } express thanks.
16. 豈 ch'i³, how? used in only a few combinations.
16. 豈 ch'i³ } how dare I? I am
    敢 kan³ } not worthy of the honour (a polite expression).
17. 違 wei², to oppose, disregard.
17. 久 chiu³ } we have not met
    遠 wei² } for a long time.

17. 一 i
    程 ch'êng² } an interval,
    子 tzŭ } while, time.
17. 托 t'o¹, to be beholden to.
17. 福 fu², happiness.
17. 托 to² } thanks to your prosperity, thanks to
    福 fu² } you.
17. 府 fu³, a prefectural city, prefectural residence, palace, your house.

your kind inquiries we are well, except my wife, who was ill for a couple of months. I hope she is quite well now. It is good of you to think of her, she is almost well now. I seem to remember that the last time we saw each other you were considering your daughter's betrothal. Has it been settled? Yes, long ago, and she is now married. We married her to the eldest son of Li ta lao yeh. Which Li ta lao yeh is that? The Prefect of Foochow? No it is not that Li family. This Li ta lao yeh is not a civil official, he is a military officer. He is unemployed at present, and holds no office.

well, only is our inside man ill ed two piece months. Now large well ed *pa*. Cause you Sir anxiety ing, differ not much, well ed. I good like remember we upper turn see face 's time you Sir consider your (plural) thousand gold fix relative 's business. Fix ed not have. Early already fix ed, now out door *lo*. Give ing is Li ta lao yeh 's big son. Which one gentleman Li ta lao yeh; is Foochow Chih Fu? Not is that Li family. This one gentleman Li ta lao yeh not is civil official, is piece military official. Now disengage ed, not do officer *lo*.

17. 承 ch'êng², to be the recipient of.
17. 承問 ch'êng² wên⁴ } thanks for kind inquiries.
17. 內 nei⁴, within, inner.
17. 內人 nei⁴ jên² } the inner person, my wife, his wife.
17. 惦記 tien⁴ chi⁴ } to be anxious, solicitous.
17. 千金 ch'ien¹ chin } your daughter, another person's daughter.
17. 定親 ting⁴ ch'in¹ } to betroth.

17. 早已 tsao³ i³ } long ago.
17. 出門子 ch'u¹ mên² tzŭ } to be married.
17. 州 chou¹, a division, department, sub-prefecture.
17. 知府 chih¹ fu³ } a prefect.
17. 文 wên², literature; civil as opposed to military.
17. 文官 wên² kuan¹ } a civil official.

18. What is your honourable name, Sir? My name is Ch'un, I've not the honour of knowing yours. My name is Tung—the *tung* of east and west. What may your lofty age be? I am young; just forty-eight. Ah, you are two years older than I am. How many sons have you, Sir? I've two sons and a daughter; how many have you? I've no good fortune, I've only one girl.

19. This pair of boots of mine is too tight. Did you buy them ready made, or were they made to order? The shoemaker took my mea-

You Sir honourable name. Common name Spring, not receive instruction. I name East, East West 's East. You Sir lofty longevity. I small *na*, just forty-eight. Ah, compare me great two year (*sui*). You Sir in front of how many gentlemen honourable youth. I have two piece son, one piece girl; you Sir in front of how many gentlemen. Not good fortune, only have one piece lass.

I this pair boots too tight *lo*. Buy ing is ready made ing or is fix make ing. Is fix make ing; that leather workman take feet inches

---

18. 敎 chiao⁴, to teach, instruct, a creed, faith, or sect.
18. 領 ling³ / 敎 chiao⁴ } to receive instruction, I am indebted to you for your information.
18. 壽 shou¹, longevity.
18. 哪 na¹, a final particle.
18. 跟 kên¹ / 前 ch'ien² } behind and before, a following; used with reference to the number of children or servants a person has.
18. 令 ling⁴, honourable, your.
18. 郎 lang², a youth, a son.

18. 令 ling¹ / 郎 lang² } your son.
18. 姑 ku¹ / 娘 niang² } an unmarried girl.
18. 妞 niu¹ / 兒 'rh } a girl, a daughter.
19. 雙 shuang¹, a pair (of boots).
19. 靴 hsueh¹ / 子 tzŭ } boots.
19. 緊 chin³, tight, pressing.
19. 現 hsien⁴ / 成 ch'êng² } ready made.
19. 定 ting⁴ / 做 tso⁴ } made to order.
19. 皮 p'i², skin, fur, leather.
19. 皮 p'i² / 匠 chiang⁴ } a worker in leather.

sure, and I can't think how he made them too small. Have you worn them? No, I can't wear them; they hurt my feet. Why don't you send them back? If they were mine I certainly should. If you haven't paid for them, and you refuse to take them, the shoemaker can't help himself.

20. What do you charge for the hire of a cart by the day? That all depends upon where you want to go; if it is a long journey it will be dearer; if you don't go outside the city of course it will be less. Couldn't we reckon it by the number of *li*? Yes, we can do that. What do you propose to give per *li*, Sir? You name a price and I will tell you whether or no it fits in with my idea. What do you say, Sir, to a hundred cash a

measure good ed, not know he how make little ed. You wear ed (*kuo*) not wear ed. Not wear ed, not can wear; wear ed, foot hurt. You why not reject return go; if is mine, I positively want reject return go. You Sir it is not give money, reject return, not receive, that make boots one not have remedy.

If hire cart, according to day (*jih tzŭ*), reckon must how many cash one day (*t'ien*). That all look you Sir want to where go. If road far, money then many *lo*. If not go out (*ch'u*) city, of course money less *lo*. We according to *li* number reckon, suit not suit. Suit *lo*; you Sir propose give how many cash. You before say piece price, I tell you agree my idea not agree my idea. You Sir regard one hundred cash one *li* how fashion.

---

19. 尺 ch'ih² ⎱ length of, measurement of (see IX. 52).
    寸 ts'un⁴ ⎰

19. 退 t'ui⁴, to reject, retire.

19. 退 t'ui⁴ ⎱ to reject, send back,
    回 hui² ⎰ decline to take.

19. 收 shou⁴, to accept, gather, receive.

19. 皮 p'i² ⎱ leather, skins.
    子 tzŭ ⎰

20. 雇 ku⁴, hire.

20. 合 ho² ⎱ meet with one's wishes
    意 i⁴ ⎰ or ideas, commend itself.

li? Of course the driver's food will be extra, and there's his tip besides. How much will the tip be? That's as you like, Sir; you give him what you please. How much does a hundred cash represent in foreign money? That all depends upon the market rate, but speaking generally, one dollar can be reckoned at one string of cash. All right, we will settle it so and call it a bargain.

That carter's food money of course at outside; adtional still have that wine money. That wine money must how many. That is following you Sir's convenience; like give how much, then give how much. One hundred cash reckon foreign (ocean) money how much. That look market rate; probably (*ta kai*) say, one piece foreign money can reckon one *tiao* cash. Then thus *pa*; this then reckon fix ed.

21. I told the carter to drive quickly or we should not catch you up, but the mule went so slowly that by the time we reached the city gate you had already gone.

I tell that drive cart one quick drive, otherwise we catch not up you *lo*. That mule walking thus slow, by the time reached (pursue, arrive ed) city gate's time you already walk ed.

22. I have no change, could you change this ten *tiao* note for me? Let me see what is the cash bank of issue.

I not have fractional cash, this ten *tiao* cash's note you can for me change *pa*. You Sir permit me look

---

20. 趕 kan³, to drive, drive away, when.
20. 趕車的 kan³ ch'ê¹ ti } a coachman, carter.
20. 另外 ling⁴ wai⁴ } besides, over and above, in addition.
20. 吊 tiao⁴, a string of one thousand copper cash.

21. 不然 pu⁴ jan² } otherwise, or.
21. 趕上 kan³ shang⁴ } to catch up.
21. 騾子 lo² tzŭ } a mule.
21. 趕到 kan³ tao⁴ } when.

Oh! it's the Fu-shun Bank. That Bank is right enough. Do you want notes, Sir, or do you want cash? You might give me one five *tiào* note, two one *tiao* notes and the balance in cash.

look is which piece cash shop's note. Ah, is Fu-shun cash shop; that piece cash shop not wrong. You Sir is want notes, is want cash. You give me one piece five *tiao* cash's note, two piece one *tiao* cash's, remainder ing give cash *pa*.

23. Would you make a little room for us to pass, Sir? Please pass, Sir. Thank you.

You Sir yield a little place *pa*, we good cross go. You Sir please *pa*. Borrow light *lo*.

24. I've come to-day to thank you, Sir. If you had not come forward as an intermediary that man would certainly have brought an action against me in the Court.

I to-day come give you Sir offer (*tao*) thanks. You Sir if not forth come mediate, that piece man positively want at *Yamên* in accuse me.

25. I went out for a stroll after the rain had stopped, and as long as I followed the high road there was not much mud, but when I left the road and crossed through the fields my boots got wet, and my

Down finish ed rain, I then forth go stroll stroll. Follow ing (*shun*) great road walk, not have how many mud. One separate great road, by grass ground pass, boots all damp ed, together with socks also damp ed. To-

---

22. 賸 shêng¹, residue, balance, remainder.
22. 賸 shêng⁴ ⎱ what remains, the
    下 hsia⁴ ⎰ balance.
22. 下 hsia⁴ ⎱ another form of
    賸 shêng⁴ ⎰ the above.

24. 說 shuo¹ ⎱
    合 ho² ⎰ to arrange, mediate.
24. 告 kao⁴, to accuse, bring an action against.
25. 泥 ni², mud.
25. 濕 shih¹, damp, wet.

socks too. When I wanted to wear them this morning my boots were as hard as boards, and I couldn't get them on. What am I to do? I'm afraid they are spoilt. They can't be spoilt; get some grease, smear them over with it, and rub it in hard; after that put them by the side of the fire, not too near, and warm them. The grease will soon melt and then they will be soft.

day morning want wearing's time that boots hard 's like boards, not can wear. How good; fear spoil ed. Spoil cannot (*pu liao*). Take oil, rub (*mo*) on, employ muscle, towards in rub (*ts'a*) then (return come) put at fire side, but don't too near *lo*; roast ed a roast, one short space of time (*i-hui 'rh*) that oil melt ed, boots then soft ed.

26. My razor is blunt and I can't shave with it. I must send it to the ironmonger's and have it ground.

My scrape face knife not sharp, not can scrape face. I must send to iron mechanic shop in go call them grind a grind.

27. I called you ever so many times. Why didn't you answer?

I call ed you good some turn. You why not answer.

28. Time's up. I ought to be off. If I arrive late he won't like it.

Is time *lo*. I ought walk *lo*. I if is arrive late ed, he not approve me.

29. What answer did he make when you asked him about

You ask him that piece affair he how reply ing. He say

---

25. 襪子 wa¹ tzŭ } stockings, socks.
25. 硬 ying⁴, hard.
25. 似 ssŭ⁴, shih⁴, like.
25. 相似 hsiang¹ ssŭ⁴, shih⁴ } like, resembling.
25. 油 yu², oil, grease.
25. 勁 chin⁴, muscle.
25. 化 hua⁴, to melt, transform.
25. 輭 juan³, soft.

26. 刮 kua¹, to scrape.
26. 臉 lien³, the face.
26. 快 k'uai⁴, sharp.
26. 磨 mo², to grind, rub, as ink on an ink stone.
27. 答 ta¹, to comply, consent, reply.
27. 答應 ta¹ ying¹ } to answer, assent to, approve.
29. 回答 hui² ta¹ } to reply.

I

that business? He said he was willing to undertake it, but he was afraid his master wouldn't agree. The last time some one asked him to lend a hand his master wouldn't allow him to go.

30. The water is deep here; if you go up a little higher it is shallower. It's up to your neck here; there it doesn't come up to your ankle.

31. I say, carter, there's nothing wrong about that mule of yours. What did you give for him? Ah, you've good eyes, Sir, and can spot a good animal. When this mule was bought my master didn't tell me the price, but I reckon he must have cost seventy or eighty taels; and he's worth it.

he willing arrange, only fear he master not assent. Above turn, person invite he help piece busy, he master not permit he go.

Here, water deep *lo*; towards above go a little, then shallow *lo*. Here, have neck thus deep; there, not reach ankle bone.

Carter, you that piece mule after all not wrong; is how much money buying. Ai, lao yeh 's eye strength good, seeing able out (*ch'iao tê ch'u*) good animal come. This piece mule buying time our lao yeh not tell me price, at I calculate must seven eight ten taels silver *na*.

---

29. 東家 tung¹ chia¹ } a master, employer.
30. 深 shên¹, deep.
30. 淺 ch'ien³, shallow.
30. 脖子 po² tzŭ } the neck.
30. 踝子骨 huai² tzŭ ku³ } the ankle, ankle bone.
30. 骨頭 ku² t'ou² } a bone, bones.

31. 倒 tao³, yet, after all, on the contrary, to pour, upset, fall.
31. 牲 shêng¹, cattle; not used alone.
31. 牲口 shêng¹ k'ou³ } a domestic animal, cattle, horse.
31. 估 ku¹, to reckon, estimate; not used alone.
31. 摸 mo¹, to feel, touch.
31. 估摸 ku¹ mo¹ } to estimate, value, appraise.

He's not more than seven years old by mark of mouth, has never been lame, and takes kindly to his food. Just look how sleek he is, Sir; when he came into my hands he was as thin as anything, but he's put on flesh now, and it's all because I am careful of him and don't overwork him. The first time I got into the cart he lifted his heels and tried to kick me, but he's all right now. Probably he's shy of strangers. It's not that way, Sir. Although that mule's a dumb animal he's got some sense, and he knows

Also worth; he not exceed seven year mouth, not lame ed (*kuo*), eat ing very fragrant. You Sir look, he how much sleek. He reach ed my hands in time, emaciate ing what like, now upon ed plump; all is I fond of (*hsin t'êng*) him, not fatigue him 's cause.

I top turn on cart's time he lift heels *lai cho*, want kick me; now good ed. Probably is recognise raw *pa*. Ai, my lao yeh, not is thus. That mule although is piece dumb animal, heart in but intelligent; also recognise man. He

31. 歲 sui⁴ } the age of an
    口 k'ou³ } animal.
31. 瘸 ch'üeh², lame, lameness.
31. 香 hsiang¹, fragrant, fragrance, scent, incense.
31. 漂 p'iao¹, to float, a float.
31. 亮 liang¹, bright, clear.
31. 漂 p'iao¹ } sleek, glossy.
    亮 liang⁴ }
31. 瘦 shou⁴, thin, lean, emaciated.
31. 臕 piao¹, fat (of animals).
31. 累 lei⁴, to trouble, fatigue, overwork, tired, embarrassed.
31. 撩 liao¹, to lift up, as petticoats, &c.

31. 蹶 chüeh³, a horse's hoof (colloquial, t'i⁴ tzŭ⁴).
31. 撩 liao¹ } to lift the hoofs,
    蹶 chüeh³ } to kick.
    子 tzŭ }
31. 踢 t'i⁴, to kick.
31. 認 jên⁴ } to recognise one
        } to be a stranger,
        } to be shy of
    生 shêng¹ } strangers.
31. 啞 ya³ } dumb, a dumb man.
    吧 pa¹ }
31. 畜 ch'u¹, an animal; not used alone.
31. 畜 ch'u¹ } an animal, brute,
    生 shêng¹ } brute beast.

people. The first time he saw you, Sir, he didn't know what sort of a person you were, but after you had ridden two or three times in the cart he found that you were a quiet gentleman and didn't want to press him, so of course he doesn't kick. I won't deceive you, Sir. What this mule of mine most dislikes is ladies, and of all ladies he dislikes my mistress the most. Directly he sees her coming to get into the cart he knows he is in for a bad time, and so he kicks. What for? Why, my mistress doesn't think about the mule; all she wants is to go fast, and directly she gets up, "Carter," she says, "you go fast." She don't mind whether the road is good or is not, whether it's hot or isn't hot; she's always top one turn see you Sir, he not know is what kind 's man; you, Sir, sit two three turn cart he know you Sir is quiet (*lao shih*) man, not want urge him; he of course then not kicked. Not deceive you Sir, say, I this mule most (*tsui*) dislike ing is ladies (*t'ai t'ai mên*); ladies inside most of all (*ting*) dislike ing is our lady. One see he come want get on (*shang*) cart, he then know want suffer punishment *lo*; then lift heels. How say *na*; our lady not care mule how fashion, only like quick walk. One get on cart *ah*, then say— carter, you quickly walk. She not care road good walk not good walk, day hot not hot, constantly call me beat mule, cause him quick run. I if is not diligent beat him, she

---

31. 瞅 ch'ou³, to look, see.
31. 瞅見 ch'ou³ chien⁴ } seen.
31. 催 ts'ui¹, to press, urge on, hurry.
31. 瞞 man², to deceive, impose upon.
31. 嫌 hsien², to dislike, have an aversion to, prejudice.

31. 受罪 shou⁴ tsui⁴ } to have a bad time, to suffer.
31. 竟 ching⁴, only, then, just.
31. 勤 ch'in², diligent.
31. 類 lei⁴, a class, category, species.
31. 一類 i¹ lei⁴ } of one class, the same, similar.

telling me to beat the mule and make him go fast, and if I don't keep on thrashing him she calls me a lazy beast like the mule, and sometimes she takes her umbrella and prods the mule with it. By the time we get back the mule is all of a sweat and won't eat his food, no matter what you give him.

Now, Sir, I ask you to bear in mind that I depend upon my mule for my living, and if he is driven like that and made sick by it, what am I going to say to the master? I keep on telling this to the mistress, but she don't care; she says I always spare the mule. She's

say I with mule one class one idle beast. Have times hold umbrella take mule poke one time. By (*kan*) return coming 's time that mule one body sweat; what food feed him all not eat.

Lao-yeh, you Sir reflect; I this mule I rely ing him pass days; then thus drive ing him, if is drive come sickness out, I how can confront our lao yeh. I constantly with lady say ed (*kuo*) this talk. She not care; she say I ever protect ing mule. Now, our lady to north side avoid heat

---

31. 懶 lan³, idle.
31. 傘 san³, an umbrella.
31. 搯 ch'o¹, to poke, poke at, prod.
31. 仗 chang⁴, to depend, rely upon, fight.
31. 仗 chang⁴ ⎫ relying on, depending on.
     着 cho ⎭
31. 對 tui⁴ ⎫
     得 tê² ⎬ to be able to face, to have a good answer to make, to be able to render an account of stewardship.
     起 ch'i³ ⎭

對 tui⁴ ⎫
31. 不 pu⁴ ⎬ not to be able to render a good account of one's self, not to be able to face a person.
     起 ch'i³ ⎭
31. 護 hu⁴, to protect, screen, guard.
31. 護 hu⁴ ⎫ protecting.
     着 cho ⎭
31. 避 pi⁴, to avoid.

gone north now to get out of the heat, and she won't be back for more than two months, so for that while the mule will have a comfortable time and my mind will be at rest.

32. Whenever I meet him he passes by with his head in the air and won't take any notice of me. In former times when he was poor we were thick enough, but now that he has become a high official he puts on airs. Well, the proverb rightly says, "One pace upwards and old neighbours get cut."

33. What are you two men quarrelling about? If you've

go ed, must two piece more month then (*ts'ai*) return come. This piece interval (*kung fu*) mule also comfortable, I also let go ed heart *lo*.

Every occasion meet him 's time he lift ing head pass go, not like heed me. He formerly poor 's time we two piece man how intimate; now do great officer *lo*, then wear tall hat *lo*. *Ai*, proverb say ing well— one step mount high not recognize old country connections *lo*.

You two piece man wrangle bawl what. Have talk, good

---

31. 暑 shu³, heat, torrid heat.
32. 每 mei³, every, each, constantly.
32. 逢 fêng², to meet, encounter.
32. 每 mei³ ⎫ whenever, on every
    逢 fêng² ⎭ occasion.
32. 遇 yü⁴, to meet, meet with.
32. 遇 yu⁴ ⎫ to meet, meet
    見 chien⁴ ⎭ with, occur.
32. 窮 ch'iung², poor, to exhaust.
32. 親 ch'in¹ ⎫ intimate, close intimacy, on very
    熱 jo⁴ ⎭ intimate terms.
32. 戴 tai⁴, to wear on the head.
32. 俗 su², common, vulgar.
32. 語 yü³, sayings, words.

32. 俗 su² ⎫ a common saying, a
    語 yü³ ⎭ proverb.
32. 俗 su² ⎫
    話 hua⁴ ⎭ colloquial.
32. 登 têng¹, to ascend, mount, climb.
32. 登 têng¹ ⎫ to ascend high, to
    高 kao¹ ⎭ go up in the world!
32. 鄉 hsiang¹ ⎫ a country neighbour, a home
    親 ch'in¹ ⎭ aquaintance, a friend of old days.
33. 吵 ch'ao³, to wrangle, make an uproar, clamour for.

got anything to say say it quietly; what do you want to shout for? I don't want to shout, but he is treating me most unfairly. We went into partnership over a small business on the distinct understanding that each party was to take half the profits, and he wont give me my share. What do you say to that?

good ly say; why want bawl. Not is I want bawl; only (*pu kuo*) is he treat me too not fair. We two piece man unite ing partner do little buy-sell, say clearly ed, gain ed money, each man divide one half. My division he not give me; you say this can (*kʻo*) how fashion good.

34. Just look how dirty this floor is! It looks as if you couldn't have swept it for several days. You be quick and sweep it. If this happens again you needn't think of applying to me for your wages at the end of the month.

You look this ground board have how much dirty *lo*. Seemingly (*kʻan chʻi lai*) positively is you this some days not sweep. You quick quick give me sweep clean ed *pa*. Again thus fashion, by the time arrive ed month bottom, not use think from me want wages.

35. You're too fond of boasting altogether. You don't mean to say that only your

You this piece man only like speak mouth. Difficult say only is you one piece

---

33. 嚷 jang³, to bawl, shout, shout at each other.
33. 吵 chʻao³ } to quarrel noisily, 嚷 jang³ } an altercation.
33. 公 kung¹, public, just, male species.
33. 公 kung¹ } just, fair, equit- 道 tao⁴ } able.
33. 賺 chuan⁴, to earn money by trade, &c., make a profit.
33. 賺 chuan⁴ } to make money. 錢 chien² }

33. 合 ho² } to join in partner- 夥 huo³ } ship, enter into partnership.
34. 骯 ang¹ } dirty. 髒 tsang¹ }
34. 掃 sao³, to sweep.
35. 嘴 tsui³, the mouth.
35. 說 shuo¹ } to boast, brag. 嘴 tsui³ }
35. 難 nan² } you don't mean to 道 tao⁴ } say. 說 shuo¹ }

things are good and that nobody else's are? You would do well to be a little modest.

36. I have invited some friends to dine to-morrow and go to the theatre, and have arranged for dinner at the T'ung Ho Lou restaurant at four o'clock sharp.

We two don't stand on ceremony with each other, so I have not sent you a written invitation, and we will reckon this a verbal invitation.

I shall be most happy to come. What theatre do you propose to go to?

man's good, other man's all not good? You modest a little, then is.

I to-morrow invite ed some gentlemen friend eat food, listen theatricals. I engage ed them at city outside T'ung Ho Lou restaurant, precisely (*chun*) four o'clock eat food.

We two piece man not grasp mud, therefore I not give you down invitation card. I now then reckon is mouth invite ed.

Obey command, obey command; you Sir propose to what theatre go.

35. 謙 ch'iên¹, humble, yielding, respectful.
35. 遜 hsün⁴, humble, complaisant.
35. 謙 ch'ien¹ / 遜 hsun⁴ } humble, modest.
36. 戲 hsi⁴, theatricals, a play.
36. 聽 t'ing¹ / 戲 hsi⁴ } to go to the theatre.
36. 約 yo¹, a contract, to invite, make an engagement, to contract.
36. 樓 lou², an upper story, a house with an upper story.
36. 館 kuan³, an inn, hall, eating-house.
36. 飯 fan⁴ / 館 kuan³ / 子 tzŭ } a restaurant.

36. 拘 chu¹, to lay hold of, restrain.
36. 不 pu⁴ / 拘 chü¹ / 泥 ni² } don't (or not to) stand on ceremony.
36. 帖 t'ieh¹, to stick to, attach to, a ticket, label.
36. 請 ch'ing³ / 帖 t'ieh¹ } a card or letter of invitation.
36. 口 k'ou³ / 請 ch'ing³ } a verbal invitation.
36. 遵 tsun¹, honoured, eminent, to venerate, obey, obedience.
36. 命 ming⁴, fate, lot, destiny, a command.
36. 遵 tsun¹ / 命 ming⁴ } to obey a command.
36. 園 yüan² / 子 tzŭ } a garden.

I was going to ask you about that, because I don't often go to the theatre and don't know which company is the best.

This I is want request instructions you Sir ing, because I not constantly to theatre go, not know which troupe good.

37. There are going to be festivities at our neighbours' on the fifth of next month, and I hear it will be a very gay affair.

'Our neighbour below month first (ch'u) five day want manage happiness business. Heard say want very gay.

What festivities are there going to be? A birthday or a wedding?

Want manage what happiness business? (ni), is manage birthday, is marry wife ah.

They are going to marry off their second son.

Is give their two young gentleman marry wife.

Are you going?

You sir go not go.

Why, of course. They are friends of long standing, and I must go.

How not go ni. Many year 's friendship, must positively go.

38. You've come at a most opportune moment. I was just going to send somebody to ask you to come across.

You sir come ing truly opportune. I just (chêng) want send man invite you cross come.

---

36. 戲 hsi⁴ } 園 yuan² } a theatre. 子 tzŭ }

36. 請 ch'ing³ } may I ask? kind- 教 chiao⁴ } ly inform me.

36. 戲 hsi⁴ } 班 pan¹ } a theatrical troupe. 子 tzŭ }

37. 坊 fang¹, a street, ward, factory.

37. 街 chieh¹ } a neighbour, 坊 fang¹ } neighbourhood.

37. 初 ch'u¹, commencement, beginning.

37 初 ch'u¹ } 次 tz'ŭ⁴ } the first time.

37. 熱 jo⁴ } gay, bustling, 鬧 nao⁴ } lively.

37. 少 shao⁴ } the son of a person 爺 yeh² } of rank or position.

37. 呢 ni¹, interrogative particle.

37. 娶 ch'u³, to marry a wife.

37. 媳 hsi² } 婦 fu⁴ } a wife.

37. 娶 ch'u³ } 媳 hsi² } to marry a wife. 婦 fu⁴ }

37. 必 pi⁴, must, certainly.

37. 必 pi⁴ } 得 tei³ } positively must.

38. 巧 ch'iao³, lucky, opportune, clever, cunning.

38. 正 chêng⁴, on the point of, straight, just.

39. Are you taking enough money with you on your journey south to-morrow? Quite enough. I have a hundred taels of ready money in hand and that cheque for five hundred taels which you gave me. These two amounts added together will certainly be sufficient. I propose to cash the cheque on arrival, but there's one point: the cheque is drawn on this bank and ought to be cashed locally. I don't know whether they will levy a discount or not at the branch bank.

I expect they will levy a discount, but it won't be

You to-morrow to south side go take ing money enough not enough. Fully enough *lo*, I hand in have one hundred- tael 's ready money, yet have you Sir give me ing that five hundred tael silver .?s. cheque. This two items money collect at together certain is enough *lo*. I propose, arrive there take silver certificate draw money. But have one point. This silver certificate is at this bank open ing, ought at original place draw money. I not know at division establishment deduct not deduct.

Deduct, expect is want deduct; that has limit, probably is

---

39. 足 tsu², enough, the foot, complete.
39. 足 tsu² / 彀 kou⁴ } ample.
39. 銀 yin² / 單 tan¹ } a cheque.
39. 一 i¹ / 筆 pi³ / 錢 ch'ien² } a sum of money, an item.
39. 湊 ts'ou⁴, to assemble, collect.
39. 取 ch'u³, to draw, as money—receive, take.
39. 層 ts'êng², a word indicating past action, a point.
39. 一 i¹ / 層 ts'êng² } one point, a consideration.

39. 本 pên³ / 處 ch'u⁴ } the place of origin.
39. 分 fên¹ / 行 hang² } a branch establishment.
39. 扣 k'ou⁴, to deduct, discount, knock.
39. 限 hsien⁴, a limit, to limit.
39. 有 yu³ / 限 hsien⁴ } inconsiderable, limited.
39. 景 ching³, condition, appearance.
39. 光 kuang¹ / 景 ching³ } probabilities, circumstances.
39. 抽 ch'ou¹, to pull out, take out, per-centage.

much—probably one li per tael.

40. From the tone of his remarks he is not willing to undertake this business.

It is the rule of their firm that employés are not permitted to do outside business. He couldn't very well tell you outright of the existence of this regulation, so he gave you a vague answer.

41. What do you keep on bothering me for? I tell you straight out that it doesn't matter how much you beg, I will positively not consent.

one tael silver deduct one thousandth (*li*) *pa*.

Listen his mouth breath, is not willing undertake this piece business.

Their establishment in 's custom not permit their counter on man transact outside 's business; this piece regulation he not good intention straight tell you, therefore he indefinite ly reply ed.

You persistently worry me do what. I decisive ly tell you, you even if (na^3 $p‘a$) how solicit, I positive not consent.

---

39. 厘 li^2, the thousandth part of a tael.
40. 口 $k‘ou^3$ ⎫ the tone of a per-
     氣 $ch‘i^4$ ⎭ son's conversation.
40. 規 $kuei^1$ ⎫ custom, usage, con-
     矩 $chü^4$ ⎭ duct, decorum.
40. 櫃 $kuei^4$ ⎫ employés in a
     上 $shang^4$ ⎬ business estab-
     人 $jên^2$ ⎭ lishment.
40. 章 $chang^1$ ⎫ regulations.
     程 $ch‘êng^2$ ⎭
40. 直 $chih^2$, straight out, straight, upright, proper.
40. 含 han^2 ⎫ reserved, reticent,
     糊 hu^2 ⎭ ambiguous.
41. 僅 $chin^3$, only, barely.
41. 僅 $chin^3$ ⎫ persistently.
     自 $tzŭ^4$ ⎭

41. 囉 lo^2 ⎫ to bother, pester, importune, bothersome, complicated,
     唆 so^1 ⎭ fidgetting.
41. 幹 kan^4, to do, manage.
41. 幹 kan^4 ⎫ what are you do-
     甚 $shên^2$ ⎬ ing? why?
     麼 mo ⎭
41. 簡 $chien^3$, concise, to retrench.
41. 簡 $chien^3$ ⎫ concisely, and plainly, short and straight,
     直 $chih^2$ ⎭ plainly.
41. 那 na^3 ⎫ it doesn't matter how, no matter how, if it must come to that, I will
     怕 $p‘a^4$ ⎭ even go so far as.
41. 求 $ch‘iu^2$, to beg, entreat, solicit, seek after.
41. 決 $chüeh^2$, positively, decidedly.

42. It's too cold to go now, we'll talk about it when the weather is warm.

This time go, weather too cold. Wait day warm again speak *pa*.

43. These children are fidgetty, sure enough. They are always wanting to play, and if I was not a patient individual I positively couldn't stand it.

These children truly fidgetty, only covet play. I if not is endure heart bother 's man, I positively (*chien chih ti*) suffer not able (*pu tê*) *lo*.

44. Why do you cut that horse's tail?

That horse tail you why give shear short.

For appearance sake, that's all.

For is (*wei-ti-shih*) good look, that's all.

You think of appearances, but have no sympathy for the horse. Just think, on a hot day like this the flies are so annoying that you are never without a fly-brush in your hand. The horse's tail is a fly-

You think ing good look, but not sympathize that horse. You think, thus kind one hot day, that fly worry (*nao*) ing you that fly-brush ever not separate hand. Horse tail also is piece fly-brush, you cut

---

42. 暖 nuan³ } warm.
    和 ho²

43. 淘 t'ao² } fidgetty, mischievous.
    氣 ch'i⁴

43. 貪 t'an¹, to covet, be always wanting to, covetous.

43. 貪 t'an¹ } fond of play, wanting to play.
    玩 wan²

43. 耐 nai⁴, to bear, endure, patient.

43. 煩 fan², trouble, to trouble, troublesome.

43. 耐 nai⁴ } to bear patiently, to put up with annoyance.
    煩 fan²

43. 耐 nai⁴
    心 hsin¹ } patient.
    煩 fan²

44. 尾 i³ } a tail; also read *wei*³.
    巴 pa¹

44. 體 t'i³, the body.

44. 諒 liang⁴, to believe, consider, think about.

44. 體 t'i³ } to be thoughtful or considerate for, to sympathize with.
    諒 liang⁴

44. 蒼 ts'ang¹ } a fly.
    蠅 ying¹

44. 刷 shua¹, to brush.

brush too, and if you cut it short he can't whisk off the flies and suffers in consequence.

45. How much altogether was that fruit you bought?
I haven't reckoned it up yet; it wasn't all bought at one place. Wait till I get the bills they made out and reckon it up.

46. You stupid! Why are you such a fool? A brainless, lazy lout like you isn't fit to serve in a respectable family. Out you get, sharp.

short ed, he how able drive away fly, then want suffer punishment *lo*.

You buying that fruit altogether how much money.
I yet not reckon up; not is one piece place buy ing. Wait I take them open ing bills bring come reckon a reckon.

You this stupid thing. How thus idiotic. Like you thus not have brains, also lazy, also loutish, serve (*chung*) what use *ah*. Not fitted at respectable man home do affair. You quick give me roll out go *pa*.

- 44. 刷 shua¹ 子 tzŭ } a brush (there is also another character for fly brush).
- 45. 菓 kuo³ 子 tzŭ } fruit.
- 45. 通 t'ung¹, to pass through, to penetrate.
- 45. 共 kung⁴, all.
- 45. 通 t'ung¹ 共 kung⁴ } altogether, the whole.
- 45. 合 ho² 算 suan⁴ } to reckon up, add up a sum.
- 45. 賬 chang⁴, a bill, account.
- 45. 開 k'ai¹ 賬 chang⁴ } to make out a bill, to open an account.
- 46. 糊 hu² 塗 t'u² } stupid.
- 46. 混 hun⁴, muddy, dull.
- 46. 混 hun⁴ 賬 chang⁴ } stupid, doltish.
- 46. 腦 nao³ 子 tzŭ } brains.
- 46. 笨 pên⁴, clumsy, awkward, stupid, thick-headed.
- 46. 中 chung¹ 用 yung⁴ } to be of use, capable of use.
- 46. 配 p'ei⁴, to match, pair.
- 46. 不 pu⁴ 配 p'ei⁴ } not fit, not worthy.
- 46. 經 ching¹, past, the warp of textile fabric.
- 46. 正 chêng⁴ 經 ching¹ } honest, respectable, straightforward.
- 46. 滾 kun³, to roll (a strong term of abuse, to be used sparingly), boiling (of water).

47. Where are you off to? I am going to the garden to see if the seeds sown there have come up or not. The man that is looking after the garden now is not very satisfactory, and I am not sure that he has sown them properly. He has been my coolie hitherto, and was not a gardener, but for the last few months he has been frequently with the gardener and now understands a little about it. The gardener has applied for two months' leave, and he is taking his place.
48. Both these roads go to Peking. The west one, although a little nearer, is not good going. A little further on you reach a

You this is towards where go. I to flower garden go, look look garden in sow ing seeds come out ed not have. Now that piece care garden's man not great satisfactory. I not know he sow ing correct not correct. Hitherto he is give me serve as coolie; originally not is gardener. This few piece month constantly with gardener at together, now then understand a little. Because that gardener ask ed two piece month's leave, he then give him serve substitute work. This two strip road all is towards Peking go ing. West side one, although near a little, but not good walk; walk ed not far then is stone

---

47. 往 wang³, to go towards, towards, past and gone.
47. 種 chung⁴, to plant, sow.
47. 子 tzŭ³ } seeds.
　　 粒 li⁴
47. 妥 t'o³, secure, satisfactory.
47. 妥 t'o³ } satisfactory.
　　 當 tang¹
47. 向 hsiang¹, towards, facing.
47. 向 hsiang¹ } hitherto, heretofore.
　　 來 lai²
47. 苦 k'u³, bitter, unpleasant, distressing.
47. 苦 k'u³ } a coolie.
　　 力 li⁴

47. 花 hua¹
　　 兒 'rh } a gardener.
　　 匠 chiang⁴
47. 假 chia⁴, leave of absence; chia³, false.
47. 告 kao⁴ } to ask for leave of absence, to be on leave.
　　 假 chia⁴
47. 替 t'i⁴ } a substitute.
　　 工 kung¹
48. 條 t'iao², a strip; the numerative of roads, dogs, trowsers, towels, &c.
48. 路 lu⁴, a road, way.

stone road which has not been repaired for a good many years, and is full of holes. The other road, although it makes a bit of a detour, is the more expeditious in the end.

49. You gave me seven tiao, didn't you? I spent altogether nine tiao eight hundred cash on the things I bought for you, so you have got to give me two tiao eight hundred cash and we shall be quits.

I've no change, but you can deduct your two tiao eight hundred cash from this dollar and give me the balance of seven tiao. That won't do. The dollar changes now for nine tiao, and by that reckoning I should lose.

road. That stone road good some years not repair, only is some holes. That one strip road although wind a little far, after all compare this piece expeditious many *lo*.

You not is give me seven tiao cash? I give you buy ing those things altogether spend ed nine tiao eight hundred cash. You yet must give me make good two tiao eight hundred cash, we two piece man then reckon not affair *lo*.

I not fraction money. You take this one dollar take out your two tiao eight hundred cash; remainder seven tiao find give me *pa*.

That not suit. Now foreign money exchange nine tiao cash. Thus reckon, I then eat loss *lo*.

---

48. 石 shih², stone.
48. 石頭 shih² t'ou² } stone, of stone.
48. 修 hsiu¹, to mend, repair.
48. 坑 k'êng¹, a pit, hole.
48. 繞 jao⁴, to wind, go round, make a detour.
48. 到底 tao⁴ ti³ } after all; ti³ hsia⁴, below, hereafter.
48. 簡便 chien³ pien⁴ } expeditious, saving of time, simpler.
49. 共總 kung⁴ tsung³ } altogether.

49. 補 pu³, to patch, fill up, repair.
49. 找補 chao³ pu³ } to make up a deficiency, to make good, pay over a deficit.
49. 刨 p'ao², to dig, hoe.
49. 刨出 p'ao² ch'u¹ } to deduct, take out.
49. 虧 k'uei¹, a deficiency, loss, to lose.
49. 吃虧 ch'ih¹ k'uei¹ } to be a loser, to lose by a transaction.

50. This fan isn't very good. I'll go to the shop to-morrow and choose another one.

Dear me, this picking and choosing is not good form; a person makes you a present with the kindest intentions and you go and turn up your nose at it. If he knows you have been to change it he will most surely send you no more presents.

51. What's your hurry? Sit down and rest a bit. Please excuse me from joining you, but there's a man waiting for me over there, and if I don't go as soon as possible, I am afraid his business will be delayed.

52. Don't be impatient. As he made you a promise, he will arrange it for you sooner or later.

This piece (*pa*) fan not great good. To-morrow I to that shop in go again choose one piece *pa*.

Ai, you thus choose five choose six ing is what fashion. Person good intention send you ing things, you still turn nose up at. He if is know you go change go, below posifively not again send you things *lo*.

Hurry what ing. Sit down rest a rest *pa*. You Sir please *pa*. There have man wait me; if is not hurrying go, fear delay ed his business.

Don't get impatient; he since promise ed you, early late he must give you manage.

---

50. 扇 shan⁴, a fan, a leaf of a folding door.
50. 扇子 shan⁴ tzǔ } a fan.
50. 挑 t'iao¹, to choose, pick out.
50. 挑五挑六 t'iao¹ wu³ t'iao¹ liu⁴ } to be fastidious.
50. 挑眼 t'iao¹ yên³ } to look down upon, to be supercilious, to turn one's nose up at.
51. 歇 hsieh¹, to rest

51. 趕 kan³ } to hurry up, as quickly as possible.
51. 快 k'uai⁴
51. 悞事 wu⁴ shih⁴ } to delay business.
52. 急 chi², urgent, urgently, anxious, impetuous, excited.
52. 着急 chao² chi² } to be impatient, get excited, anxious, irritated.
52. 許 hsü³, to allow, promise, perhaps, much.
52. 應許 ying¹ hsü³ } to promise.

53. Aren't you very dull sitting here all by yourself? Why don't you make a trip to the Western hills? The scenery there is very fine, and there are temples all over the place; wouldn't it be nice to stop there for three or four days?
54. Yes, it would be nice, but there isn't much fun for me going alone; if I could find a companion it would be all right. Can't you go with me? I should like to very much, but for the moment I can't get away. If you could wait a few days I will try and see if I can ask for a few days' leave.
That would be excellent.

You at here one piece man sitting not dull? You why not to West hill go tour a tour. There 's scenery very good, each place all have temple, at there live piece three five day not good?

Good, is good, only is I one piece man go not interest (*i-ssŭ*); can find piece man do companion, then good. You with me go, suit not suit. I very willing go, only is temporarily not can put off body. You if can wait few day I then think plan ask few days leave.

That good extreme *lo*.

---

53. 悶 mên⁴, dull, melancholy, sad, oppressive.
53. 慌 huang¹, agitated, confused, dreadfully.
53. 悶 mên⁴ } very much bored, dull.
    得 tê
    慌 huang¹
53. 山 shan¹, hills, mountains.
53. 山 shan¹ } scenery.
    水 shui³
53. 廟 miao⁴, a temple.
54. 伴 pan⁴, a companion.
54. 做 tso⁴ } to be a companion.
    伴 pan⁴
54. 情 ch'ing² } perfectly willing, only too pleased.
    願 yuan⁴
    意 i⁴

54. 暫 chan⁴, temporary, a short time.
54. 且 ch'ieh³, moreover, besides, for the time being, a while.
54. 暫 chan⁴ } temporarily.
    且 ch'ieh³
54. 脫 t'o¹, to put off, as clothes; to retire, escape.
54. 脫 t'o¹ } to get away, to get away from.
    身 shên¹
54. 待 tai⁴, to wait (see IX. 57).
54. 極 chi², the utmost, extreme.
54. 好 hao³ } excellent, capital.
    極 chi²

K

55. His grandfather is seriously ill, and I heard from his people that there is no hope. From his condition it would appear to be a matter of only three or four days.
56. This coat of mine is torn. Get a needle and thread and sew it up.
57. The rent is too big; sewing won't do, it will have to be patched. This coat of yours is not new, and if I only sew it up I'm afraid the stitches won't hold. If I do it neatly the patch won't show.

He grandfather ill ing very heavy. I heard their home in ' s man say not have hope. Look he that piece fashion also then at this three four day *lo*.

I this piece coat torn, take needle thread give me sew up.

Tear ing rent too big; only sew up not suit. According I look, positively must patch on one piece patch then can substantial. You sir this piece coat not is new one, only take thread sew up, fear that thread eat not hold *lo*. Hand work if is fine a little, that patch then show not out come.

---

55. 爺 yeh² / 爺 yeh² } a grandfather.
55. 望 wang⁴, to hope, look towards, towards.
55. 指 chih³ / 望 wang⁴ } hope.
56. 撕 ssŭ¹, to tear.
56. 針 chên¹, a needle.
56. 線 hsien⁴, thread.
57. 口 k'ou³, the mouth, an opening (see IX. 58).
57. 口 k'ou³ / 子 tzŭ } a rent.
57. 縫 fêng² / 上 shang⁴ } to sew up.
57. 補 pu³ / 釘 ting⁴ } a patch.

57. 打 ta³ / 補 pu³ / 釘 ting⁴ } to put on a patch.
57. 結 chieh¹, to tie; chieh², to finish.
57. 結 chieh¹ / 實 shih² } firm, strong, hardy.
57. 吃 ch'ih¹ / 不 pu⁴ / 住 chu⁴ } won't hold, cannot endure.
57. 手 shou³ / 工 kung¹ } handiwork, work, handicraft.
57. 顯 hsien³, apparent, manifest, visible, conspicuous.
57. 顯 hsien³ / 出 ch'u¹ / 來 lai² } to be apparent, to show.

58. Then, according to you, if I want to go into the interior I must have a passport. From whom do I get it?

You get it from the Consulate.

Must I go and get it myself?
59. You needn't. You can write to the Consul and tell him where you want to go. He will fill in a blank passport form and send it to the local official with a request that he will put his seal on it, that's sufficient.
60. In the compilation of the above sentences only eight hundred characters odd have been employed altogether. If the reader can commit these to memory he may be considered to know a little Chinese.

Thus, according to you thus speak, I want to interior go tour go, must have passport. This passport from (*kên*) who receive (*ling*) na.

From (*ta*) Consul office receive.

Must I own (*ko*) man go receive?
Not must. You give Consul write a piece letter, say want towards what place go. He then take one piece empty white passport add on character, send give place official request him affix seal, then finished.

Above make ing these character sentences inside altogether use ing not exceed is eight hundred more character. Look officer if can take this eight hundred character all record at stomach in, also can reckon is know a little Chinese talk *lo*.

---

58. 照 chao⁴, to reflect, according to.
58. 按 an⁴ } according to.
    照 chao⁴ }
58. 內 nei⁴ } the interior, away
    地 ti⁴ } from the coast.
58. 執 chih² } a passport.
    照 chao⁴ }
58. 領 ling³ }
    事 shih⁴ } a consul.
    官 kuan¹ }
59. 空 k'ung¹ } a blank, in blank.
    白 pai² }
59. 添 t'ien¹, to add.
59. 印 yin⁴, a seal, to print.

59. 蓋 kai⁴ } to affix a seal, to
    印 yin⁴ } seal.
60. 以 i³ } foregoing, in
    上 shang⁴ } excess of, upwards of.
60. 字 tzŭ⁴ } sentences.
    句 chü¹ }
    看 k'an⁴ } reader, the reader;
60.   a form of
             address used
    官 kuan¹ } only in novels.
    肚 tu⁴ } the stomach, the seat
60.   of intelligence, the
    子 tzŭ } mind.
60. 可 k'o¹ } can.
    以 i³ }

XI.

In the following three stories the paraphrase, of which the student is by this time doubtless thoroughly weary, has been dispensed with. It is obviously impossible to translate literally from one language to another, but an endeavour has been made in the English version to follow the Chinese text as closely as is consistent with a due regard for readable English. If the student wishes to criticise the translation, he is recommended to paraphrase the Chinese text for himself as in the foregoing exercises, and after doing so he can correct the English translation to suit his own taste. The notes will indicate new characters and will explain fresh combinations.

An apology is perhaps needed for the juvenile character of these stories. Experience has proved to the writer that, if simplicity of style is aimed at, the nearer one can get to the style in which one would tell a story to a child, the easier will the language be to understand. It is so difficult to find purely Chinese stories for Chinese children, that in two of the stories he has gone back to the memories of childhood for inspiration, with the result, no doubt, that these stories have suffered much mutilation in the process of reconstruction. But he ventures to claim for them the merit of being fair specimens of simple colloquial Chinese.

XI.[1]

A Story of the Recompense of Virtue and Wickedness.

Once upon a time there was a widow, and this widow had two daughters. These sisters were very unlike in appearance; the elder one being the ditto of her mother, not only plain, but also of a very bad disposition, while the younger sister was very handsome and was of a very kindly nature. As the elder sister had the same temperament as her mother, the latter was very fond of her. This is a natural principle, and she could not be blamed for that, but what she was to be blamed for was the way in which she treated the younger sister. The elder sister was well fed and well dressed, while the younger sister did all the coarse work of the house. Not only did she prepare the food every day for her mother and her elder sister, but her duties even comprised the cleaning out of the rooms, the washing of the floor and the drawing of water from the well. She fed on the leavings of the other two, and she wore the old clothes that her sister had discarded. One day the younger sister went as usual to the well to draw water, and when she got to the mouth of the well she saw an old lady sitting there. Directly the old lady saw the girl approach she stood up and said, "Kind-hearted girl, have pity upon an old woman who is suffering from thirst, and bestow on me a bowl of cold water to drink." The girl promptly drew a bucket of water from the well, ladled out a bowlful, and gave it to the old lady to drink. When the old lady had finished drinking it she thanked the girl and said, "As you have shown sympathy for an aged person, and have most kindly waited upon a stranger from afar whom you do not know, I will bestow a benefit upon you. Hereafter, every time you speak, a pearl shall drop from your mouth." As she spoke, she turned into a cloud and floated away. When the girl saw the old lady suddenly change into a cloud and drift away with the wind she was very much surprised, and when she had finished drawing the water she carried it away on a carrying-pole, wondering to herself as she went. When she returned to the house her mother abused her, and said, "You idle drab, why have you delayed all this time upon the road? I know, you have been gossiping on the way with some good-for-nothing dissolute youth." Now this girl was naturally a very bashful person, and directly she heard her mother use this unseemly kind of language her heart began to flutter, and she said, "I never did so." Directly she had said this sentence of four words, four pearls dropped from her mouth. As soon as her mother saw these bright glossy things drop from her daughter's mouth she hastily picked them up and looked at them. Sure enough they were four real pearls. "What's all this about?" she promptly inquired.

Gentle reader, just reflect: if pearls drop out from the mouth whenever a person speaks, and these are picked up by somebody else, although the latter may gain the advantage, the individual himself cannot help being somewhat embarrassed, for if directly one speaks he is to spit out precious stones, a loquacious person would in a very short time spit out so many that the ground would be covered with them, and in the course of a year, if they were all picked up by people, precious stones would become common articles and no one would want them. The fairy (the old lady was a fairy) had also foreseen this point, and so, although she bestowed the power of spitting out pearls upon the girl, she left her free to use or not to use this power as she liked, and so the girl suited her own convenience about spitting them out or not. But this is a digression. To return meanwhile to our story. Her mother closely cross-questioned her daughter, and got out of her all that she said to the old lady from first to last, how the old lady replied, and how she acted; and when she had heard everything she called the elder sister to come, and said, "What do you think of the pearls your sister has spit out?" handing to her as she spoke the pearls for her to see. She also told her all the details of the business from first to last. Now the elder sister was a greedy person, one who thought of ten when she had got five, so she said to her younger sister, "Spit out some more pearls. I want to see with my own eyes." Her younger sister was unwilling to do so, and so she would not spit out any; whereupon the mother and elder sister lost their tempers and drove the young girl out of the room, telling her to make haste and get the dinner ready, after which the mother said to her elder daughter, "You think this business of spitting out pearls is not real, but I saw her spit them out with my own eyes, and so I know she can spit them out; the reason she does not do so is all because of her obstinacy. She does not want to let us gain a little advantage. Never mind, the benefits she has obtained you can also obtain. You have only got to go to the well and bale out a bowl of water for an old woman, and the thing is done." "I won't demean myself," replied the elder sister, "by drawing water for people. I am not a servant. Why should I wait upon an ugly old woman? I won't go." Her mother urged her for a long time, and at last she consented, and went strutting and swaggering off to the well holding a well-bucket in her hand. On arriving at the mouth of the well she looked all round, but there was no one, so she sat down with a pout on her lips and grumbled at her mother. "This is fooling people," she said; "there is no one here, and isn't this making me come for nothing? Wait till I get back, and if I don't take that lying little baggage and give her a jolly good hiding I'm not a 'thing.'" When she had said thus far she suddenly heard the sound of a person walking. She lifted her head and saw a nice-looking old lady standing there in front of her. "Good maid," said the lady, "I am thirsty. Won't you give me a little water to drink?" When the elder sister heard the two words "ya t'ou" (maid) her face flushed, and she said, "What maid? I am a young lady of an honourable family. If you want water to drink, draw it for yourself." "I beg your pardon," replied the old lady, "I beg your pardon; I have made a mistake. I thought you were a kind-hearted person, and so I asked you to draw me a little water to drink. You go back, and when you get home give my compliments to your mamma and see what jumps out of your mouth when you speak." When the elder sister heard this remark about things jumping out of her mouth she thought to herself, "This surely must be the fairy"; and she was just about to return her a polite reply, when suddenly the lady disappeared. The elder sister gave her eyes a rub and looked again—sure enough, there was not a vestige of the lady. "This is strange," thought she; "just now there certainly was a lady standing there. How can she have disappeared?" Then she slowly walked home, pondering as she went, found her mother and began to tell her the strange story. She had just opened her lips and said the two words "Ma ma," when out jumped two frogs from her mouth. "Ai-ya!" cried her mother, and asked, "How's this?" The elder daughter replied, "I don't"—two more frogs—whereupon she daren't say any more. When her mother saw these frogs jump from her daughter's mouth she got into a furious rage, and said, "This is surely your younger sister's doing; she is determined to injure you. Wait till I get hold of her and beat her to death." As she spoke she looked round for a big stick with the intention of beating her second girl to death.

When the young girl heard through the kitchen wall her mother say that she would beat her to death, she didn't wait, but rushed out bareheaded and ran wildly away. After she had run for some time she reached a wood and hid there, not venturing to return home. After she had waited a long time in the wood and did not see her mother come she became a little more composed in mind. "Since I cannot return home," thought she, "I must think of some way of finding some other person's home in which to live. Unfortunately I am a girl. If I was a man, that could be easily managed. All that I can do is to find some family and exchange my ability to cook for food and clothing." So she got up and walked into the wood, proposing to find some road that passed through the wood. She walked a long time, but the farther she walked the denser became the wood. By this time the girl was not only tired but was also both hungry and thirsty and could not walk any farther, so she sat down and began to cry. Who would have thought that just at the time she was crying there a young gentleman heard the sound of her crying? He hastily bored his way through the thick foliage and there saw an extremely beautiful girl sitting on the ground crying.

Gentle reader, would you guess who this young gentleman was? He was none other than the eldest son of the Prince of that place, who was hunting in the forest, and most opportunely came across the young girl. This young nobleman was both dignified and handsome, and was moreover of the most compassionate disposition. The thing he could least endure was the sight of anyone suffering hardship or calamity and so directly he saw the girl crying there his heart was touched, and he hastily asked, "Why are you crying so, young lady? Is it that you have lost your way, or is it that you have suffered some wrong?" When the young girl heard the sound of a human voice she was really like a dead person come to life again, and hastily replied, "Ah! good sir, my deliverer, you have arrived most opportunely; I was waiting here to die." What did she think at this crisis about spitting out pearls or not? And so, as she spoke, pearls went dropping from her mouth. The young nobleman was very much surprised, and promptly asked the reason, whereupon the girl told him the particulars of the story that has been narrated above. The subsequent story need not be told in detail. The same principle holds good all over the world. A good-looking young nobleman, an elegant and handsome girl; have we not here to hand an appropriate match? Of course the young gentleman helped the girl to rise and slowly conducted her to his palace, where his mother carefully nursed her, and in a few days the girl was quite well again. The Prince was just looking for a satisfactory person to give his son to wife and this girl exactly suited his ideas; moreover, she had the capacity of spitting out pearls. So it was not a month before the wedding took place and a virtuous and handsome nobleman and an elegant young lady became husband and wife.

If you ask what subsequently became of the elder sister who spit out frogs, this will not take many words to tell. When the elder sister saw that every time she talked, frogs jumped from her mouth, she was afraid to speak and in course of years she became dumb, while her mother became ill from vexation and died.

---

1. 善 shan⁴, goodness, virtuous, virtue.
2. 報 pao⁴, to requite ⎫ reward, recompense, requital.
   應 ying¹, to reward ⎭
3. 傳 chuan⁴, a record, story. ch'uan², to transmit, hand down.
4. 前 ch'ien², before ⎫ formerly, before.
   者 chê³, here, -ly, sometimes ing. ⎭
5. 寡 kua³, few, solitary ⎫ a widow.
   婦 fu⁴, woman, wife ⎭
6. 容 jung², face ⎫ appearance, facial appearance.
   貌 mao⁴, manner, air ⎭

7. 相 hsiang¹, mutual ⎫ similar.
   同 t'ung², same ⎭
8. 對 tui⁴, a pair, a match.
9. 長 chang³, to grow ⎫
   的 ti ⎬ was good looking.
   好 hao³ ⎪
   看 k'an⁴ ⎭
10. 不 pu⁴ ⎫ not only.
    但 tan⁴, only, but ⎭
11. 美 mei³, handsome, beautiful.
12. 疼 t'êng², to be fond of.
13. 難 nan², difficult ⎫ cannot object, find fault with.
    怪 kuai⁴, to object ⎭
14. 所 so³ ⎫ that which was objected to.
    怪 kuai⁴ ⎭

15. 連 lien², even.
16. 打 ta³, verb of action } to sweep, to sweep out.
    掃 sao³, to sweep
17. 打 ta³, verb of action } to draw water.
    水 shui³, water
18. 井 ching³, a well.
19. 照 chao⁴, according to } as was her wont.
    樣 yang⁴, fashion
20. 老 lao³, old } an old woman, lao³-p'o, a wife.
    婆 p'o², woman
    子 tzŭ
21. 賞 shang³, to bestow, reward, gaze upon.
22. 趕 kan³ } promptly, forthwith.
    緊 chin³
23. 筲 t'ung³ } a bucket, barrel.
    子 tzŭ
24. 舀 k'uai³ or yao³, to dip, bale, ladle out.
25. 伺 tz'ŭ⁴ } to wait upon.
    候 hou⁴
26. 好 hao³ } benefits, advantages.
    處 ch'u⁴
27. 顆 k'o¹, a bead; the numerative of beads, precious stones.
28. 寶 pao³, precious } a pearl, chu¹-tzŭ, pearls or beads.
    珠 chu¹, pearl
29. 變 pien⁴, to change } changed into.
    成 ch'êng², to become
30. 雲 yün², cloud } clouds.
    彩 ts'ai³, variegated
31. 飄 p'iao¹, whirled by the wind, floating in the air.
32. 詫 ch'a⁴, originally to brag } to be surprised, astonished.
    異 i⁴, strange

33. 一 i¹ } at one and the same time.
    邊 pien⁴, side
34. 納 na⁴ } to be puzzled.
    悶 mên⁴
35. 了 ya¹, forked } a female servant, a serving maid.
    頭 t'ou², head
36. 半 pan⁴ } a long time.
    天 t'ien¹
37. 不 pu⁴ } to serve no purpose, useless.
    中 chung⁴
    用 yung⁴
38. 浪 lang⁴, a wave, dissipated, profligate.
39. 小 hsiao³ } a youth, youngster.
    子 tzŭ
40. 閒 hsien² } idle gossip.
    話 hua⁴
41. 恬 mien³ } shy, bashful.
    惉 t'ien³
42. 醜 ch'ou³, ugly, offensive, disgraceful.
43. 跳 t'iao⁴, to jump.
44. 並 ping⁴ } (ping⁴ intensifies the negative) never did.
    沒 mei²
45. 顆 k'o¹ { a bead; the numerative of beads, precious stones, trees, &c.
46. 光 kuang¹ } bright, shining, lustrous.
    亮 liang⁴
47. 撿 chien³ } to pick up.
    起 ch'i³
    來 lai²
48. 這 chê⁴ } what's this all about? what's the meaning of this?
    是 shih⁴
    怎 tsên³
    麽 mo
    的 ti
    事 shih⁴

49. 看官 k'an⁴ kuan¹ } reader, gentle reader.
50. 得便宜 te² p'ien² i² } to score, gain an advantage.
51. 本人 pên³ jên² } the individual, the man himself.
52. 免 mien³, to avoid, dispense with.
53. 累贅 lei⁴ chui⁴ } embarrassment.
54. 吐 t'u³, ⁴, to spit out, vomit.
55. 成 ch'êng², to become.
56. 物 wu⁴, things, articles.
57. 神仙 shên², spirit hsien¹, fairy, genii } a fairy.
58. 想到 hsiang³ tao⁴ } to think of, foresee.
59. 這一層 chê⁴ i¹ ts'êng² } this point, or particular.
60. 權 ch'uan², power, authority.
61. 自由 tzŭ⁴, self yu² from, by } to proceed from one's self, of one's own accord, as one pleases.
62. 另外的 ling⁴ wai⁴ ti } separate, outside, something extra. Here with hua, a digression.
63. 且 ch'ieh³, for the time being, moreover.
64. 問長問短 wên⁴ ch'ang² wên⁴ tuan³ } to ask the long and short, to cross-question closely.
65. 至 chih⁴, to reach, arrive at. Rad. 38.
66. 尾 wei³, the tail, end.
67. 行 hsing², to do, act.

68. 問出來 wên⁴ ch'u¹ lai² } to get out by questioning.
69. 說着 shuo¹, speak cho, ing } as she spoke.
70. 遞給 ti⁴ kei³ } to hand to.
71. 原委 yuan⁹, origin wei³, to depute. } from beginning to end, the whole story.
72. 一五一十的 i¹ wu³ i¹ shih² ti } in detail, the full particulars.
73. 貪心不足 t'an¹, covetous hsin¹, heart pu¹, not tsu², enough } greedy, avaricious.
74. 親眼瞧 ch'in¹ yen³ ch'iao² } to see with one's own eyes.
75. 著急 chao² chi² } to get impatient, to lose one's temper.
76. 趕出去 kan³ ch'u¹ ch'u⁴ } to drive out.
77. 回頭 hui², turn t'ou², head } afterwards, by-and-bye.
78. 以為 i³, to take wei², to be } to take, to be, consider, regard as.
79. 牛心 niu², ox hsin¹, heart } obstinate, perverse.
80. 犯不上 fan⁴, to offend pu⁴ shang⁴ } it's not worth my while.
81. 到了兒 tao⁴, arrive liao³, end êrh } in the end, at last.

82. 搖 yao², to shake } strutting,
    擺 pai³, to spread } swaggering.
83. 提 t'i¹ } to hold by the handle.
    溜 liu¹
84. 柳 liu³, willow } a well bucket
    罐 kuan⁴, jar, } made of
    mug, canister } withes.
85. 四 ssŭ⁴
    可 hsia⁴ } in every direction.
    裏 li³
86. 噘 chüeh¹, to pout out the lips } to pout, purse the lips.
    着 cho
    嘴 tsui³, the mouth
87. 抱 pao⁴, to cherish } to grumble, complain.
    怨 yuan⁴ resentment
88. 胡 hu², how, blindly, recklessly } to make a fool of, deceive.
    弄 nung⁴, to do, make
89. 傢 chia¹ } household utensils, furniture, a "baggage."
    伙 huo³
90. 一 i⁴ } a turn, time (used of a meal, a beating, &c.).
    頓 tun⁴
91. 不 pu⁴
    是 shih⁴ } a good-for-nothing, a useless person.
    東 tung¹
    西 hsi¹
92. 聲 sheng¹, sound, noise } sound of any kind.
    音 yin¹, sound, tone, notes. Rad. 180.
93. 體 t'i³, the body } respectable.
    面 mien⁴, the face
94. 替 t'i⁴, for } on my behalf.
    我 wo³, me
95. 媽 ma¹, nurse, mother } mama.
    媽 ma¹
96. 問 wên⁴ } to ask after a person's health, to greet.
    好 hao³

97. 必 pi⁴ } must be.
    是 shih⁴
98. 影 ying³, shadow, vestige.
99. 一 i¹ } at one and the same thinking, thinking as she walked.
    面 mien⁴
    想 hsiang³
100. 蝦 ha² } a frog.
     螺 ma¹
101. 唉 ai¹ or 噯 ai¹ } an exclamation of pleasure, pain, or surprise.
102. 有 yu³ } intentionally, designedly.
     意 i⁴
103. 棍 kun⁴ } a stick.
     子 tzŭ
104. 隔 ko², separated } separated by the wall, on the other side of the wall.
     着 cho
     牆 ch'iang²,
     wall
105. 光 kuang¹
     着 cho } bareheaded.
     頭 t'ou²
106. 混 hun⁴, wildly, confusedly.
107. 藏 ts'ang², to hide, conceal.
108. 好 hao³ } a good while, long time.
     久 chiu³
109. 心 hsin¹ } ease or quietude of mind.
     定 ting⁴
110. 爺 yeh² } men, a man.
     們 mên
111. 以 i³, to take.
112. 本 pên³ } ability, capacity.
     事 shih⁴
113. 深 shên,¹ deep, thick } dense.
     密 mi⁴, thick, close
114. 餓 o⁴, hungry.
115. 走 tsou³ } could not walk, could not walk farther.
     不 pu⁴
     動 tung⁴

116. 哭 k'u¹, to cry, weep.
117. 相公 hsiang¹ kung¹ } a youth, young gentleman.
118. 鑽 tsuan¹, to bore, pierce, a gimlet.
119. 猜 ts'ai¹, to guess.
120. 本處 pên³ ch'u⁴ } of that place.
121. 王爺 wang² yeh² } a prince.
122. 公子 kung¹ tzŭ³ } a nobleman's son.
123. 恰巧 ch'ia¹, timely ch'iao³, lucky } fortunately.
124. 碰見 p'êng⁴, bump against chien⁴, see } to come across.
125. 性情 hsing⁴ ch'ing² } disposition, temperament.
126. 慈悲 tz'ŭ², kind, kindness, mercy pei¹, pity, sympathy, sad } compassionate, merciful.
127. 忍 jên³, to endure.
128. 苦難 k'u³, bitter nan⁴, trouble, misfortune } trouble, sorrow, misfortune.
129. 迷了道 mi², puzzled, bewildered liao tao⁴ } lost the way.
130. 委屈 wei³, to send, depute, bend down ch'u¹, bent, injustice } injustice, wrong.
131. 呢 ni¹, an interrogative particle, a final particle.
132. 而 êrh², and, and yet. Rad. 126.

133. 救命 chiu⁴, to rescue ming⁴, life } to save life.
134. 隨着說 sui², to follow cho shuo¹ } as she spoke, following her speech.
135. 以上 i³ shang⁴ } foregoing
136. 故事兒 ku⁴ shih⁴ êrh } a story.
137. 秀 hsiu⁴, elegant, accomplished.
138. 佳耦 chia¹, good, excellent ou³, a pair } a good or happy match.
139. 扶起來 fu,² to assist, hold ch'i³ lai² } helped up her up.
140. 撫養 fu³, to soothe, pacify yang³, to nourish } to nurse, take gentle care of.
141. 妥當 t'o³ tang¹ } satisfactory.
142. 能爲 nêng³ wei² } ability, capacity.
143. 秀流 hsiu¹, elegant liu², to flow, glide } graceful, elegant.
144. 夫婦 fu¹ fu⁴ } husband and wife.
145. 年深日久 nien² shên jih⁴ chiu³ } in course of time, after a long time.
146. 啞巴 ya³ pa¹ } dumb, a dumb person.
147. 因 yin¹, because of.

XI².

THE STORY OF THE MAGIC BEAN.

CHAPTER I.

A GREAT many hundred years ago, I cannot precisely remember how many years it was, there was a widow. This widow was very poor, and when her husband died he did not leave her any property except one small house, two acres of ground and a cow. This widow had only one son and the two of them depended entirely for their subsistence upon the milk which this cow gave. Unfortunately the son was not a good son; he did not help his mother in the least to look after the household and all he thought of was playing with his little friends in the street. So, after several years had passed, as the income did not equal the expenditure, the widow owed a considerable number of debts and the proprietors of the shops in the village would not sell her anything. "You owe us a considerable amount of money," said they, "you do not pay us the money you owe us and still come to us here to demand things. That won't do; we also have wives and children, and if we give you things for nothing how are we going to live?" So it came to pass that one day the widow's son (I forgot to say that his name was Chieh-ko) came home in the evening and wanted some food to eat. "My son," said his mother, "I have really no help for it; there is no money in the house, none of the shopkeepers will give me credit and we must go to bed hungry." On getting up the next day the widow said to Chieh-ko, "My son, I have been thinking all the night, and there is really no other way, we must sell the cow; so you take it and lead it to the market and sell it." So Chieh-ko, with an empty stomach, took the cow and led it away. He had not walked very far when he met a butcher. The butcher asked him, "Where are you driving this cow of yours to?" "I am driving her to market to sell," replied Chieh-ko, and as he spoke he gazed at some things that the butcher held in his hand;

they were neither round nor square, neither blue nor green. "What are those things that you are holding in your hand?" asked he. "These are very rare things and are worth a great deal of money," the butcher told him. "If you want them I will exchange this bagful of them for your cow." Now Chieh-ko had always been a simple child and he did not know that the things which the butcher was carrying were only beans; but the butcher did not know that amongst these beans there was a magic bean. If you ask what is a magic bean, read on farther and you will know. Chieh-ko took what the butcher was saying to be the truth, so he took the cow and exchanged her for the beans. He returned home in high spirits and told his mother how he had come across the butcher, and how the butcher had in the kindness of his heart given him these pretty beans, and how he had given the cow to the butcher. Directly his mother heard this story she began to cry, and said, "You good-for-nothing boy, will not this cause us to die of hunger?" and as she spoke she took the beans and threw them into the garden, the mother and son going hungry to bed.

The next morning early when Chieh-ko got up he went to the window and looked out, when he saw a big tree. "This is strange," thought he to himself, "yesterday there was no tree in the garden; how could a big tree like this have grown up in one night?" He hastily went down to look, and sure enough there was a big tree which grew so high that when he looked up he could not see the top. Chieh-ko did not wait to say anything to his mother, but climbed up. He climbed for several hours before he reached the top, and when he looked round on all sides from the top of the tree there was no sky, all was ground. By this time Chieh-ko had not only come out all over perspiration but he was also very tired, so he got down on to the ground from the top of the tree and directly he lay down he fell asleep. How long he slept before he waked I do not know, but by this time, as Chieh-ko had not eaten anything for two days, he was naturally insufferably hungry and all he thought about was finding something to eat. He looked all round him, but there were no houses and no people, so he walked forwards, thinking that perhaps he might find a house and demand a little food from the people in the house to appease his hunger. He walked for several miles and crossed over a small hill, when he saw right in front of him a large house. When Chieh-ko saw this house he was much rejoiced in heart, and quickly ran to the front door and rang the bell. The bell sounded loudly, and in a short time a woman came out. Directly she saw Chieh-ko, "Ai-ya!" said she, "what have you come for? Run away quickly, otherwise you cannot live two days." "I do not know what the meaning of your remarks is," said Chieh-ko, "but I do know that if you don't give me something to eat I cannot live even a single day," and as he spoke he fell down to the ground and lay there just like a dead person.

Now the woman was a kindly person at heart, and as soon as she saw Chieh-ko's condition she picked him up in her arms and carried him into the house. If you want to know what happened afterwards, kindly read the next chapter.

CHAPTER II.

Now the house that Chieh-ko had come to was not the house of an ordinary individual. The master of it was a very cruel giant, whose chief delight was the devouring of small children whom he went out every day to look for. As the residents of that neighbourhood had had a considerable number of their children eaten by the giant they had all run away, and this was the reason why Chieh-ko had not come across anyone on the road.

I will now resume the story of Chieh-ko's affairs. When the woman carried him into the house the giant was not at home, having gone out to look for small children. After a time Chieh-ko came to again and the woman gave him food and drink; and when Chieh-ko had finished his meal he felt very much better, whereupon he asked the woman, "What did you mean when you said just now that I could not live two days here? I don't understand." "You do not know," said the woman, "that my husband is a very dreadful giant and is particularly fond of eating small boys. Directly he hears you are here he will take you and eat you." When Chieh-ko heard this he began to be afraid, and was just going to run away when he heard the loud voice of a man calling outside. The woman hurriedly took Chieh-ko and put him into a big iron stove (there was no fire in the stove) and told him to hide in there and not to make the slightest sound, otherwise her husband would certainly eat him. As she spoke she went out to open the door for her husband. The giant had been unsuccessful in his search for small children and having returned empty-handed he was naturally full of rage. Directly he came into the room he lifted up his head, gave a sniff, and said, "I smell the smell of a small child." "What are you talking about?" replied his wife, "there are no small children here, this is dream talk." The giant gave a grunt and sat down, telling his wife to make haste and bring the supper, whereupon the old woman brought in a whole pig from the kitchen and the giant ate it all, besides drinking several large jars of wine, after which his anger gradually subsided. Then said he, "Bring the hen"; and his wife brought in a big hen and put it on the table. "Lay a golden egg," said the giant; and the hen laid a large golden egg. "Lay another," said the giant; and the hen laid another. So it went on, the hen laying five or six large golden eggs in succession as the giant gave the order. At this time, as there was not much air in the stove, Chieh-ko had gently pushed open the door a little, and looking out through the crack in the door he saw the hen laying the golden eggs. Thought he to himself: "If we could have a magic fowl in our house like that we should never suffer hunger all our lives," and the more he thought about it the more he coveted the fowl. After a while the giant, having drunk too much wine, became sleepy. First he nodded and afterwards went to sleep. Chieh-ko waited till he was sound asleep and then, creeping stealthily out of the stove, made a grab at the magic fowl and ran off. If the fowl had not cried out nothing would have happened, but it gave several squawks in succession and the giant woke up with a start. Directly he opened his eyes and saw Chieh-ko running off with the fowl under his arm he gave chase and, my word! the race was a terrible one. If the giant had caught up Chieh-ko there would be no occasion to proceed farther with this story, but where the advantage came in was this: Chieh-ko was young and the giant was both old and fat; Chieh-ko was the first to get to the top of the tree, and although he was panting so that he could hardly breathe, he did not wait, but hastily climbed down, the giant climbing down after him. Chieh-ko got down to the ground first and looking up he saw the tree waving backwards and forwards, so he knew the giant was coming down after him. He saw an axe on the ground, and picking it up he hacked at the trunk of the tree with all his

L

might. In a short time the trunk of the tree snapped and down fell the giant, bumped on the ground, and died.

The sequel does not require much telling. The magic fowl laid golden eggs for Chieh-ko every day, and so he soon became very rich. Afterwards he married the daughter of a high official and had five sons. These five sons also married when they grew up and each one of them also had five sons besides a number of daughters, and the three generations all lived happily together in one large enclosure. After the fowl had laid a good many tens of thousands of golden eggs it died. Chieh-ko was very fond of the fowl and was unwilling to bury it in the ground, so he skinned it, stuffed the skin with straw and put it into a glass case, which is still kept in the house of Chieh-ko's descendants. If anyone does not believe it he can go to the house and see.

Possibly there may be people who assert that Chieh-ko was not a Chinaman. I venture to ask, how do they know?

---

1. 豆 tou⁴, a bean. Rad. 151.
2. 畝 mu³, a Chinese acre.
3. 牛 niu², an ox. Rad. 93.
4. 擠 chi³, to squeeze } to milk.
   奶 nai³, milk
5. 過 kuo⁴, to pass }
   日 jih⁴, day   } to live, get a living.
   于 tzŭ
6. 賒 shê¹, to buy or sell on credit.
7. 屠 t'u², to butcher }
   户 hu⁴, door, family } a butcher.
8. 圓 yüan², round.
9. 藍 lan², blue.
10. 綠 lu⁴, green.
11. 希 hsi¹, rare, seldom }
    罕 han³, rare, seldom } rare.
12. 傻 sha³, foolish, simple.
13. 高 kao¹, high } the repetition
    興 hsing⁴,   } intensifies the spirits meaning.
14. 沒 mei²   } that brings
    有 yu³   } in no in-
    出 ch'u¹, to bring } terest;
        forth,   } therefore
        produce.   } worthless,
    息 hsi², interest } good for
        on money   } nothing.
15. 扔 jêng¹, to throw, throw away.
16. 窗 ch'uang¹, a win- }
        dow   } a window.
    户 hu⁴, a door   }
17. 頂 ting³ }
    兒 êrh   } the top.
18. 爬 p'a², to climb, crawl.
19. 或 huo⁴ }
    者 chê³ } perhaps.

20. 解 chieh³, to explain, undo, get rid of.
21. 里 li³, a Chinese mile. Rad. 166.
22. 鈴 ling², a small bell } a small bell, a house bell.
    鐺 tang¹, a pedlar's gong
23. 響 hsiang³, to sound.
23a. 響 hsiang³ 聲 shêng¹ 兒 êrh } sound.
24. 噯 ai¹ 呀 ya¹ } ai-ya!
25. 摔 shuai¹, to tumble 倒 tao³, to upset } tumbled over.
26. 回 hui², a chapter of a novel.
27. 兇 hsiung¹, malevolent, cruel.
28. 大 ta⁴ 個 ko⁴ 兒 êrh } a giant.
29. 醒 hsing³ 過 kuo⁴ 來 lai² } to come to after a fainting fit.
30. 覺 chueh², to perceive 着 cho } felt, felt himself.
31. 害 hai⁴ 起 ch'i³, to begin 怕 p'a⁴ 來 lai² } began to be afraid.
32. 爐 lu² 子 tzŭ } a stove.
33. 不 pu⁴ 做 tso⁴ 聲 shêng¹ } not to make a sound.
34. 聞 wên², to smell or sniff.
34a. 味 wei⁴, taste or smell.
35. 夢 mêng⁴, a dream.
35a. 做 tso⁴ 夢 mêng⁴ } to dream.

36. 哼 hêng¹, to grunt 了 liao 一 i¹ 聲 shêng¹ } gave a grunt.
37. 整 chêng³, complete, whole, entire.
38. 猪 chu¹, a pig.
39. 罎 t'an² 子 tzŭ } an earthenware jar.
40. 消 hsiao¹, to melt, dissolve.
41. 金 chin¹, gold. Rad. 167.
42. 推 t'ui¹, to push.
43. 縫 fêng⁴ 兒 êrh } a crack, fissure.
44. 一 i¹ 輩 pei⁴ 子 tzŭ } a generation, all one's life.
45. 困 k'un⁴ 了 liao } sleepy.
46. 打 ta³, verb of action 頓 tun³, to nod with sleep 兒 êrh } to nod with sleep.
47. 睡 shui⁴, sleep 熟 shu², mature 了 lo } sound asleep.
48. 偷 t'ou¹, to steal 偷 t'ou¹ 兒 êrh 的 ti } stealthily.
49. 抓 chua¹, to grab, clutch, scratch.
50. 叫 chiao⁴, to call 喊 han³, to cry aloud } to call or cry out.
51. 連 lien², successively.
52. 嘎 ka¹, to cackle.
53. 驚 ching¹, alarm, terror 醒 hsing³, awake 了 lo } to wake with a start.

54. 挾 chia¹, to carry under the arm.
55. 追 chui¹, to pursue.
56. 哎 ai¹ } ai-yo! hai-ya! an
    哟 yueh¹ } ejaculation.
57. 好 hao³, good } but the advantage lay
    可 k'o³, but } in this; but
    在 tsai⁴, at } there was
    這 chê⁴, this } this advantage.
    上 shang⁴, upon
    頭 t'ou
58. 胖 p'ang⁴, fat, corpulent.
59. 喘 ch'uan³, to gasp for breath.
60. 斧 fu³ } an axe.
    子 tzŭ
61. 樹 shu⁴ }
    桿 kan⁴ } the trunk of a tree.
    子 tzŭ
62. 發 fa¹, to put forth } to get rich.
    財 ts'ai², wealth
63. 埋 mai², to bury.
64. 剝 pao¹, to flay }
    了 liao } skinned.
    去 ch'u

XI³.

The Dog that repaid a Kindness.

In the district city of Wu-hu, on the Yangtsze River, there was a merchant named Wang who had been in business there for twenty odd years and had made a fortune of a lakh and more of taels. As he was over fifty years of age, he relinquished his business and made up his mind to return to his place of domicile, there to rest and foster his old age. As soon as he had come to this decision he hired a junk, placed his baggage on board and selected an auspicious day upon which to set sail on his return to his home. Just as the junk was about to get under way old Mr. Wang saw from the deck a man tying up a dog on the river's bank, with the evident intention of killing it to eat. Old Mr. Wang, observing the pitiful appearance of the dog, thereupon went ashore, gave the man a few cash and ransomed the dog's life. Directly the dog was released Mr. Wang returned on board the junk and ordered the skipper to get under way. The dog followed him on to the junk and would not leave his side; but Mr. Wang did not take much notice of the dog, only casually throwing him scraps to eat at meal-times. Now, this skipper and his mates were not respectable people. On the contrary, they were river pirates of many years' standing; and when they saw that their passenger had brought with him by no means an inconsiderable amount of baggage they conceived the idea of murdering him and distributing his effects amongst themselves. They accordingly proceeded to pole the junk to a solitary spot and took out their swords with the intention of killing old Mr. Wang. When Mr. Wang saw their savage demeanour he realised that his end had come; so he said to them, "Since you want to do me to death, all I ask is that you will do me the favour of leaving me with an unmutilated body." This request seemed reasonable to the pirates, so, after consulting amongst themselves for a short time, they proceeded to thrust Mr. Wang into a sack and having tied up the mouth of the sack with cord they threw both sack and man into the river. Directly the dog saw the sack which contained his benefactor thrown into the river, he jumped after it, took it into his mouth and floated down the stream with it. After floating for some time he reached a spot where the water was shallow and his four feet found ground. The dog then waded through the water, and having dragged the sack to the river's edge, proceeded to gnaw the cord with which the sack was tied, with the intention of releasing his benefactor. He gnawed for some time but failed to undo it, so he ran to a house that overhung the river and howled loudly in front of the door. The inmates came out; and when they saw the dog howling and at the same time running towards the river's bank they followed him to the bank and there they saw the sack. They undid it, and inside they saw a man half dead and half alive. They hastily carried him between them to the house, took off his clothes and after lustily rubbing him for some time he came to and proceeded to tell them the foregoing episode. Although these men were simple country folk they were none the less possessed of consciences, so they nursed him for several days and then placed him upon one of their small boats and sent him to a neighbouring market town. As luck would have it, an old friend of Mr. Wang's lived in this market town, so he went to look up this friend, borrowed money from him, rewarded the countrymen and sent them back to their home. After this he stayed a few days in the friend's house waiting for a convenient vessel upon which to return to his home. One day old Mr. Wang and his friend were walking on the river's edge, the dog following as usual, when the dog suddenly ran on board a junk that was lying alongside the shore, seized a man on board the junk by the leg and held him fast. Mr. Wang hastily jumped on board the junk with the intention of driving the dog off. He gave a look—the man that the dog had hold of was none other than the chief of the pirates! Old Mr. Wang thereupon cried out, some bystanders ran up, and Mr. Wang told them the whole story of how the skipper of this junk had tried to murder him. The men thereupon bound the skipper of the junk and afterwards searched his vessel, in the hold of which Mr. Wang's baggage was still stowed. There were the pirates and there was the booty. Wasn't this sufficient evidence? If it be asked how, for the moment, old Mr. Wang had not recognised the junk and the skipper of the junk, it was all due to the fact that the pirates had painted the junk a different colour and had changed all the clothes they originally wore.

Dear! dear! A dog who thus repays a favour can surely afford an example to those who forget benefits and are ungrateful for kindness shown!

---

1. 報 pao⁴, to requite ⎫ to requite
   恩 ên¹, grace, favour, kindness ⎭ a kindness.

2. 長 ch'ang², long ⎫ the Yang-
   江 chiang¹, a river ⎭ tsze River.

3. 蕪 wu², abundant (not used colloquially) ⎫ the port of Wu-hu on the Yangtsze.
   湖 hu², a lake ⎭

4. 縣 hsien⁴, a departmental district.

4a. 知 chih¹ ⎫ a district magis-
    縣 hsien⁴ ⎭ trate.

5. 商 shang¹ ⎫ a merchant, trader.
   人 jên² ⎭

6. 擱 ko¹, put ⎫ to relinquish,
   下 hsia⁴, down ⎭ lay down.

7. 定 ting⁴ ⎫ made up his mind,
   主 chu³ ⎬ came to the de-
   意 i⁴ ⎭ termination.

8. 本 pen³, original, personal
   籍 chi², a register of population; hence place of domicile ⎬ his own place of domicile.

9. 養 yang³, to cherish, nurture ⎫ to foster his old age.
   老 lao³, old ⎭

10. 隻 chih¹, classifier of ships, birds, &c.

11. 好 hao³ ⎫ an auspicious day
    日 jih⁴ ⎬ according to the
    子 tzŭ ⎭ calendar.

12. 開 k'ai¹ ⎫ to start on a
    船 ch'uan² ⎭ voyage.

13. 老 lao³, old ⎫ the manager
    板 pan³, board ⎭ of a shop, &c.

14. 河 ho², river ⎫ the river's
    沿 yen², bank, edge ⎭ edge.

15. 綁 pang³, to bind, tie up.

16. 一 i¹, a ⎫
    條 t'iao², the classifier ⎬ [of dogs] a dog.
    狗 kou³, dog ⎭

17. 宰 tsai³, to slaughter animals.

18. 慘 ts'an³, pitiable, pitiful, cruel.

19. 上 shang⁴, to go ⎫ went ashore.
    岸 an⁴, shore ⎭

20. 贖 shu², to ransom, redeem ⎫ to ransom
    命 ming⁴, life ⎭ his life.

21. 寸 ts'un⁴, inch ⎫
    步 pu⁴, pace ⎬ never left his
    不 pu⁴, not ⎬ side.
    離 li², separate ⎭

22. 正 cheng¹, correct ⎫ respect-
    經 ching¹, past ⎭ able.

23. 賊 tsei², a thief, robber.

24. 搭 ta¹, to add ⎫ a passenger.
    客 k'o⁴, stranger ⎭

25. 起 ch'i³, to raise ⎫ raised the idea, it occurred to
    意 i⁴, idea ⎭ them.

26. 均 chun¹, equal, uniform ⎫ to divide
    分 fên¹, to divide ⎭ equally.

27. 隨 sui², according } they ac-
    就 chiu⁴, then } cordingly proceeded.
28. 撐 ch'êng¹, to pole, push off.
29. 僻 pi⁴, secluded } se-
    靜 ching⁴, quiet, still } cluded.
30. 刀 tao¹, a sword.
30a. 刀子 tao¹ tzŭ } a knife.
31. 殺 sha¹, to kill.
32. 弄 nung⁴, make, do } to do to
    死 ssŭ³, die } death.
33. 全 ch'uan², all, whole, complete } a whole body.
    身 shên¹, body.
34. 彼 pi³, that } mutually, mutual, amongst each other.
    此 tz'ŭ³, this }
35. 捆 k'un³, to bind } to bind up.
    上 shang⁴, up }
36. 啣 hsien², to hold in the mouth } to hold fast in the mouth.
    住 chu⁴, fast, tight }
37. 順 shun⁴, follow } with the current.
    着 cho
    溜 liu⁴, current }
38. 浮 fou², to float.
38a. 浮 fu² } to swim.
     水 shui³ }
39. 得 tê², to obtain } found ground.
    了 liao
    地 ti⁴, ground }
40. 趟 t'ang¹, to wade.
41. 啃 k'ên³, to gnaw.
42. 解 chieh³, loosen } could not undo.
    不 pu⁴, not
    開 k'ai¹, open }
43. 臨 lin², to approach, neighbouring.
44. 嚎 hao², to howl, wail } to howl.
    叫 chiao⁴, to call }
45. 脫 t'o¹, to take off, [shed] } to take off one's clothes.
    表 i¹
    裳 shang¹ }
46. 愚 yu², simple } simple folk.
    民 min², subjects, people }
47. 良 liang², good } conscience.
    必 hsin¹, heart }
48. 還 hai², still } they were still possessed of.
    在 tsai⁴, remain, exist }
49. 附 fu⁴, near } adjoining, in the neighbourhood.
    近 chin⁴, near }
50. 鎮 chên⁴, a market town } a market town.
    店 tien⁴, an inn }
51. 便 pien⁴, convenient } a convenient vessel.
    船 ch'uan², vessel }
52. 攏 lung³, to drag, lay alongside } lay alongside the shore.
    岸 an⁴, the shore }
53. 搜 sou¹, to search.
54. 艙 ts'ang¹, the hold of a ship.
55. 賊 tsang¹, booty.
56. 據 chu⁴, evidence.
57. 上 shang⁴ } to put on paint, to paint.
    顏 yen²
    色 sê⁴ }
58. 如 ju², as } thus.
    此 tz'ŭ³, this }
59. 世 shih⁴, the world, a generation } in the world.
    上 shang⁴, on }
60. 負 fu⁴, to be ungrateful for.
61. 義 i⁴, kindness, public spirit, high character.
62. 榜 pang³, list of names } an example.
    樣 yang⁴, fashion }

換了唉、一
條狗能如[58]
此報恩、
實在的實
可以給世[59]
上忘恩負[60]
義的人做[61]
個榜樣、[62]

就找這個朋友去了、跟他借了錢賞那些鄉下人、打發他們回去、後來就在那朋友家住了幾天等著便船回家去、有一天王老板同他的朋友在河邊上走著狗還是照樣兒跟著他們、這狗忽然跑到一隻攏岸的船上[51]、把船上一個人的腿咬住了不放王老板快跳到船上去、要把狗鬪開[52]、瞧咬的那個人不是別人、就是那河賊的頭兒咯、王老板就叫喊起來了、旁邊站著的人跑上來了、王老板就把這管船的要害死他的事情都告訴他們了、那些人就把管船的捆上、後來把船搜了、王老板的行李還在艙裏擱著[53]、賊贓[54]全在這不是實據麼[55]若問王老板怎麼一時沒認出船跟管船的來、都是因為那些賊、是把船上了別的顏色[56]、也把他們原衣裳都[57]

溜兒浮了去了浮了半天就到了一個水淺的地方四腳得了地了[39]那狗就趁著水把口袋拉到河邊上啃那細口袋的繩子要把他的恩人放了[41]啃了半天還是解不開他就跑到臨水的一個房子在門前大聲兒嚎叫[44]那房裏的人出來了看見狗一面嚎叫一面往河沿上跑去他們就跟著他上河邊在那裏看見這口袋了解開了看裏頭有一個半死半活的人、他們忙忙的抬他到房子裏去把他衣裳脫了使勁擦了他半天他就醒過來了、隨後就把以上的事都告訴他們了這些人雖然是鄉下的愚民[46]良心還在他們就養了他幾天後來把他擱在他們的一個小船上送到附近的一個鎮店去了恰巧有王老板的一個老朋友在這鎮店裏住他叫管船的開船狗也跟著他上船寸步不離他[21]、王老闆不大理會這狗、不過吃飯的時候隨便扔給他一點吃的就是了、原來這管船的同他的夥計們不是正經人倒是多年的河賊他們看見搭客帶的行李不少就起[22][23][24][25]意把他害死把他的東西均分隨就把船撐到一個僻靜地方拿出刀來[26][27][28][29][30]了、要把王老闆殺了王老闆看他們這兒樣子就知道是不能活的了所[31]以就跟他們說你們既要把我弄死只求賞一個全身就是了那些賊聽[32][33]見這話有理彼此商量了一會隨後就把王老闆裝在一個粗布口袋裏[34]頭、把口袋嘴拿繩子綑上連口袋帶人都扔在河裏頭了、那狗一看見裝[35]他恩人的口袋扔在河裏也就跟著跳在河裏去了、把口袋啣住了、順著[36][37]

XI.[3]
THE DOG THAT REPAID A KINDNESS.
CHINESE TEXT.

報[1]恩狗

長[2]江蕪湖縣地方[4]有個商人姓王[5]、在那裏做了二十幾年的買賣賺了十幾萬銀子因為年紀過了五十歲就把買賣擱[6]下了、定了主意[7]回到本籍去歇一歇養老主意一定[8]了、他就雇了一隻船把行李裝上了、挑[9]了好日子開船回家裏去船剛要開的時候[10]王老板打船面上看見了河沿[11]上有一個人在那裏縍著一條狗[12]明明的要宰他吃[13]、王老板看這狗的樣子怪慘的就上岸去[14]把幾個錢給了那個[15]人、贖[16]了那一條狗的命狗一放了王老板就回到船上去、鷄下了好幾萬金蛋之後、就死了、借哥因為他愛這個鷄不肯把他埋在地裏所以他把那鷄皮剝了去拿乾草裝在那空皮裏頭擱在玻璃匣子裏頭今還在借哥後輩家裏存著誰不信、誰可以上那房子去看、或者有人說借哥不是中國人、敢問他們怎麼知道、大個兒把借哥趕上了、這個話不用我往下說好可在這上頭借哥年輕、[57]大個兒又老又胖借哥是先到了樹頂子了雖然喘的不能出氣也沒等[58][9]忙忙往下爬了、大個兒也跟著往下爬借哥先到了地往上瞧就看見那個樹來囬的搖所以他知道大個兒是跟著他下去、他看見地上有一個斧子就抓起使勁砍那樹榦子不大的工夫那樹榦子折了大個兒就掉[60][61]在地下碰在地上死了以後的話不用細說、那神雞天天給借哥下了金蛋、所以借哥就快發了大財後來娶了一個大官的姑娘、生了五個兒子[62]那五個兒子長大了也娶了媳婦每一個兒子又生了五個兒子另外還有好些個姑娘、他們三輩子都是喜喜歡歡的、在一個大院子裏住、那個在棹子上、大個兒就說、下金蛋罷、那個鷄就下了一個金蛋、大個兒說、再下一個、那鷄又下了一個、這麼著大個兒一說鷄就連下了五六個大金蛋、這個時候借哥因爲爐子裏頭沒有多少氣就把門輕輕的推開一點[42]、打門縫兒往外瞧、就看見了那個鷄下金蛋心裏想著我們家裏若能有那個樣的一個神鷄我們一輩子就不挨餓了越想越貪那個鷄過了一會兒、大個兒因爲多喝了酒就困了先是打盹兒後來就睡著了、借哥等他睡熟了[47]、就偷偷兒的打爐子裏爬出來了、把那神鷄一抓就跑了、那個鷄若是沒有叫喊就沒有事了、他可連嘎了[51]幾聲[52]把大個兒驚醒了[53]、一開眼睛、就看見借哥挾著鷄跑、他也追他跑、哎喲、這個跑可了不得了、若是吃了借哥聽見這話就害起怕來了剛要跑的時候聽見外頭有人叫的[31]大聲兒那個娘兒們就忙忙的把借哥擱在一個大鐵火爐子裏頭爐子[32]裏沒有火叫他在那裏藏著一點不做聲不然他的男人一定要吃他說[33]著就出去給他男人開門那大個兒出去找小孩子沒找著空手回來了、自然是滿肚子氣一進屋子裏來抬了頭間一間說我聞見有小孩子味[34]兒他媳婦說這是甚麼話這裏沒有小孩子你說的是夢話那大個兒就[35]哼了一聲坐下叫他的老婆快拿晚飯來那老婆就把一個整猪打廚房[36][37][38]裏抬進來了大個兒把猪都吃了也喝了幾大罈子酒他的氣這就慢慢[39]的消了後來他說把母雞拿來他媳婦兒就把一個大母雞帶進來了擱[40]

第二回

原來借哥到這個房子、不是平常人的房子、那房主是一個很兒[27]的大個[28]兒、他最愛吃小孩子、天天出去找去那個地方住家的、因為大個兒吃了他們的孩子不少了、就都跑了、是因為這個緣故、借哥在道兒上沒碰見甚麼人、現在我再說借哥的事情、那個娘們把他抱進房子裏的時候、大個兒沒在家、找小孩子去了、過了一會兒、借哥醒[29]過來了、那個娘們就給他吃的喝的、借哥吃完了、自己覺著好多了、就問那娘兒們說、你剛纔[30]說我在這裏活不了兩天、是甚麼意思、我不懂得、那個娘兒們說、你不知道、我的男人是個很利害的人、他愛吃小孩子、他一聽你在這裏、他要把你快的就跑到大門拉鈴鐺那鈴鐺就大聲兒響[32]、了、不大的工夫有一個娘兒們出來了、一看見借哥就說噯[24]呀你做甚麼來了、快跑罷不然你活不了兩天了、借哥說我不懂得你這話的意思、我可知道你若是不給我吃的我連一天都活不了、說著就摔倒[25]在地下、在那裏躺著像死人一個樣那個娘兒們本來是個心好的人一看借哥這個樣子、就把他抱起來、拿到大房子裏頭去了、若要知道後來怎麼樣、請看下回[26]、這個奇怪了昨天園子裏沒有樹怎麼會一夜就長出這樣的一顆大樹來、他忙忙的下去看不錯是一顆大樹長的那麼高往上瞧就瞧不出頂[17]兒來、借哥沒等跟他媽媽說甚麼話就往上爬了幾點鐘纔到了樹頂兒上了打樹頂兒上四邊看不是天都是地這個時候借哥不但出了一身汗也很乏了就打樹頂下地上去一躺下就睡著了睡了不知道多大工夫就醒了這個時候借哥因為兩天沒吃甚麼東西自然就餓的難受了竟想著找吃的四面瞧沒有房子也沒有人他就往前走想著或者[19]可以找一個房子跟房子裏頭的人要一點飯解餓[20]他走了幾里過了一[21]個山面前就看見了一個大房子借哥看見了這個房子心裏很喜歡快甚麼東西屠戶告訴他、這是很希罕的東西、很直錢、你若要、我就把這一口袋東西換你那個牛借哥本來是一個儍[12]孩子、他不知道屠戶裏拿著的東西、不過是豆子屠戶可不知道這豆子裏頭有一個是神豆子、你若問甚麼是神豆子、往下看就知道了借哥以為屠戶所說的是真話、所以把牛換了豆子、[13]高高興興的回家去了告訴他母親他怎麼碰見屠戶、屠戶怎麼好心好意的把這好看的豆子給他、他怎麼把牛給了屠戶了、他母親一聽了這個話、就哭起來了說你這個沒出息的孩子、這不是叫我們餓死了麼、說著就把豆子往園子裏扔了、[14]母兒兩個、就餓著睡覺去了、第二天早起、借哥起來的時候、往窗[15]外瞧、就看見了一個大樹、他心裏想該我們的錢還上我們這裏來要東西、那是不行、我們也有老婆孩子若是白給你東西我們怎麼活著呢這麼著有一天那寡婦的兒子我忘了說他名字叫借哥、晚上囘家來了要飯吃他母親說我的兒我實在沒法子家裏沒有錢舖子掌櫃的都不給我賒賬、我們得餓著睡覺罷第二天起來的時候那寡婦就跟借哥說了我的兒我想了一夜實在沒有別的法子我們得把那個牛賣了你就把他拉到市上去那借哥就空著肚子把牛拉了走了他沒走很遠就碰見了一個屠戶[7]那屠戶問你這個牛是往那裏趕借哥答說我趕到市上去賣他一面說一面就聽著那屠戶手裏拿著些東西不圓不方[8]不藍不綠[9]就問他[10]你手裏拿的是

XI.[2]
THE STORY OF THE MAGIC BEAN.
CHINESE TEXT.

神豆傳[1] 第一回

好幾百年前我不準記得是多少年、有一個寡婦、這個寡婦是很窮他男人死的時候也沒留下別的產業只有一個小房子二[2]畝地一個牛這寡婦就生了一個兒子他們兩個人就仗著賣這牛搳[4]的奶過[5]日子可惜了兒的這個兒子不是個好兒子一點不幫著他的媽媽管家只想跟著小朋友們在街上玩這麼著過了幾年因為進的錢沒有出的錢多、那寡婦該的賬不少那鄉材裏舖子的掌櫃的就不賣給他東西、他們說你該我們的錢不少、你不還珠、所以他隨著說寶珠隨著打嘴裏往下掉、那公子很詫異、忙問緣故、姑娘[131]就把以上所說的故事兒細細的告訴他了、往下的話不用細說了、天下都[135]是一個理、一個好看的相公、一個秀美的小姐這不是現成的佳耦麼、那[136]相公自然把小姐扶起來了、慢慢的領到他府上去了公子的母親好好[139]的撫養他了、沒有幾天那姑娘就好了、那王爺正找一個妥當人給他兒[140][137][138]子做媳婦、這個姑娘正合他的意又有吐寶珠的能爲沒有一個月喜事[141]就辦完了、善美公子秀流小姐就成了夫婦了、若問那吐蝦蟆的大姐後[143][144][142]來怎麼樣這用不了多少話大姐一看每逢說話的時候打嘴裏跳出蝦[145]蟆來、他就不敢說話了、年深日久、就成了啞吧了、母親因急成病而死了、[146][147]

越走樹就越深密了、這個時候、小姑娘不但乏了、又餓又渴也走不動了、[113][114][115]就坐下哭起來了、誰想他正在那裏哭的時候、有一位相公聽見他哭的[116][117]聲音忙鑽進密樹裏頭、就瞧見一個極美的姑娘在地上坐著哭、看官您[118]猜這一位相公是誰、不是別人是本處王爺的大公子、在樹林子裏打圍、[119][120][121][122]恰巧就碰見這小姑娘了、這一位公子長的又體面又好看、性情也是極[123][124][125]慈悲的、最不忍看人家受甚麼苦難、所以一看那姑娘在那裏哭、心就動[126][127][128]了、忙問姑娘爲甚麼這麼哭、是走迷了道兒麼、還是受甚麼委屈呢、小姑[129][130][131]娘聽了人聲寳寳在在的像死而再生的人、忙答道、唉、救命的好相公、你[132][133]來的眞巧、我在這裏等著死呢、這個時候他那裏想甚麼吐寳珠不吐寳大姐囘答、我不○○又是兩個蝦蟆、他就不敢往下說咯、他母親看這蝦蟆打他姑娘嘴裏跳出來就大生氣說、這準是你妹妹弄的事有意要害你、等我把他打死了、說著就找一根大棍子要把他二姑娘打死了小姑娘在厨房裏隔著牆聽見他媽媽說要把他打死的話、也沒等就光著頭往外混跑、跑了半天就到了一個樹林子、在樹林子裏藏著、不敢囘家去、他在樹林子裏等了好久、不見他媽媽來、心就定了一點、想我旣不敢囘家去、我得想法子找甚麼別的人家住、可惜我是姑娘、我若是一個爺們那就好辦、我只能找甚麼人家、以做菜的本事換吃的穿的就是了這麼著、他就起來了往樹林子裏走、打筧找一條過樹林子的道兒走了半天、臉說甚麼了頭我是體[93]面人家的姑娘你要水喝自已打罷那老太太就說我錯了我錯了我錯看了人了我以為你是一個心好的人所以我請你給我打一點水喝你囘去罷、到了家裏替我給你媽媽[94]問好看看你說話的時候打嘴裏跳出甚麼來、大姐聽見打嘴裏跳出東西這一句話、心[95]裏想這必[97]是那神仙了、剛要拿好話囘答那老太太忽然沒有了大姐擦[96]了一擦眼睛再瞧不錯那一位老太太沒有影兒了、他心裏想這可奇怪[98]咯、剛繞明明有一位老太太在這裏站著怎麼會沒有了、一面想一面慢[99]慢的走囘家去了找他媽媽把這奇事告訴他、他剛開口說了媽媽兩個[100]字、打他嘴裏就跳出兩個蝦蟆來了、他母親噯呀了一聲問這是怎麼著、[101]

都是他那牛心、不願意叫我們得一點便宜、不要緊他得的好處、你也可[79]以得不過要上井裏去給一個老婆子盛一碗水就完了、姐姐說、我犯不[80]上給人家打水、我不是底下人伺候一個醜老婆子做甚麼、我不去他母[81]親勸了他半天、到了兒他答應了、搖搖擺擺的、提溜著柳罐上井那裏[82]去[83]了、到了井口、四下裏看、沒有人、他就噘著嘴坐下、抱怨他母親說、這是胡[84][85][86][87][88]弄人的事、沒有人在這裏、這不是白叫我來、等我囘去的時候、我若是[89]不把那說謊的小傢伙好好的打一頓、我就不是個東西、說到這裏、忽然[90][91]聽見人走的聲音、抬頭看、面前有一個好看的老太太、在那裏站著、那老[92]太太說、好丫頭、我渴了、給我一點水喝罷、那大姐聽見了頭兩個字、紅了用這個權、不用這個權、都是讓他自由[61]、這麼著、這姑娘吐珠不吐都是隨便、這可是另外的話[62]、且說他母親問長問短[63]的、就把他女孩子[64]和那老太太從頭至尾[65]的怎麼說的、老太太怎麼答怎麼行[66]的都問出來了[67]、聽完了[68]、就把大姐叫來了、說你看你妹妹吐出來的寶珠怎麼樣、說者就把那寶珠遞給他看[70]、並把這事情的原委[71]一五一十的告訴他、那大姐是一個貪心不足的人、得了五個就想十個[72]、所以就對他妹妹說再吐寶珠罷我要親眼瞧一瞧[74]、他妹妹不願意、就不吐咯、母姐兩個著了急[75]、把小姑娘趕出[76]屋子去了[77]、叫他快預備飯、回頭母親就對他大女孩兒說、你以為吐寶珠[78]的事不是真的、我可是親眼看見他吐、所以我知道他會吐不吐的緣故、道你是和甚麽不中用的浪小子、在道兒上說開話、這姑娘本來是一個[37]恓惶人、一聽他媽媽說這個樣的醜話心裏就跳起來了說、我並沒有[38][39][40][41][42][43][44]一說了這四個字的一句話、打嘴裏就掉下四顆寶珠來了他母親一看這光亮東西、打他女孩兒嘴裏掉下去、忙忙的撿起來瞧了不[45][46][47]錯、是四顆眞珠、忙忙的問、這是怎麽的事、看官您想說話打嘴裏掉寶珠、[48][49]若是叫別人撿起來、他們雖然得便宜、本人不免累贅一點、若是一說話[50][51][52][53]的時候嘴裏吐出寶石、愛說話的人不大的工夫、就要吐得滿地都是寶[54]石、一年的工夫、若叫人都撿起來、寶石就成了賤物了、沒有人要、那神仙[55][56][57]老太太是神仙也想到這一層、所以他雖然把吐寶珠的權賞給那姑娘、[58][59][60]

姐姐不要的舊衣裳、有一天、那妹妹照樣兒上井裏去打水、到了井口就看見了一個老太太在那裏坐著、那老太太一看那姑娘來就站起來說、心好的姑娘可憐一個挨渴的老婆子賞我一碗涼水喝、那姑娘趕緊的打井裏打了一桶子水、舀[23]了一碗給老太太喝了、老太太喝完了給那姑娘道謝說、你旣是體諒年老的、和和氣氣的伺候[25]不認得的遠客、我就賞你一個好處[26]、以後你每逢說話的時候打嘴裏就要掉下一顆寶珠來、說著就變成雲彩[30]飄[31]了去、小姑娘看見那老太太忽然變成雲彩順著風飄了去、心裏很詫[32]異打完了水、一邊挑著走、一邊納悶、囘到家裏的時候、他母親就罵他說、你這個懶了[35]頭、爲甚麼在道兒上耽悞了這半天、我知

XI.[1]
A STORY OF THE RECOMPENSE OF VIRTUE AND WICKEDNESS.

Chinese Text.

善惡報應傳[1][2][3]

前者[4]有一個寡婦[5]這寡婦有兩個女孩子、他們姐妹的容[6]貌大不相同[7]那大的就和他母親是一對兒長的不但[8]不[9]好看、脾氣也是很壞的、小的長的很美[11]又是很和氣、那大[10]姐既是和他母親一個樣的脾氣他母親很疼他這是自[12]然的理、也難怪他、所怪的是他待那小妹妹的樣子姐姐[13][14]吃好的、穿好的、妹妹就做家裏的粗活不但天天給他母[15]親姐姐做茶、連打掃屋子洗一洗地板打井裏的水都是[16][17][18]他一個人的事、吃的是他們兩個人賸下的飯穿的是他

M

衙門領。領得我各人去領麼59不必、你給領事官寫封信說要往甚麼地方去、他就把一個空白執照添上字送給地方官、請他們蓋印就得了60以上做的這些字句裏頭通共用的不過是八百多字、看官若能把這八百字都記在肚子裏也可以算是知道一點兒中國話了坐着不悶得慌麼、你爲甚麼不上西山去逛一逛、那裏的山水很好、各處都有廟、在那裏住個三五天不好麼．54好、是好、就是我一個人去沒意思、能找個人做伴纔好、你同我去行不行、我情願去、就是暫且不能脫身、你若能彀待幾天我就想法子告幾天假、那好極了．55他爺爺病的很重、我聽見他們家裏的人說沒有指望了、看他那個樣子、也就在這三四天了。56我這個袖子撕了拿針線給我縫上57撕的口子太大竟縫上不行、據我瞧總得補上一塊補靪纔能結實您這個袖子不是新的竟拿線縫上、怕那線吃不住了手工若是細一點那補靪就顯不出來、58那麼着按照你那麼說我要上內地去逛去得有執照、這執照跟誰領哪。打領事官年沒修、竟是些坑、那一條路雖然繞一點遠到底比這個簡便多了 49 你不是給我七吊錢麼、我給你買的那些東西共總花了九吊八百錢、你還得給我找補兩吊八百錢、我們兩個人就算沒事了。我沒零錢你拿這一塊洋錢、刨出你的兩吊八百錢下賸七吊錢找給我罷。那不行現在洋錢換九吊錢、這麼筭、我就吃虧了 50 這把扇子不大好、明天我上那鋪子裏去、再挑一把罷。唉、你這麼挑五挑六的、是甚麼樣子人家好意送你的東西、你還挑眼、他若是知道你去換去底下他決不再送你東西了。51 忙甚麼的、坐下歇一歇罷。您請罷、那裏有人等我、若是不趕快的去怕悞了他的事了 52 別著急、他既應許了你、早晚他必給你辦 53 你在這裏一個人個蒼蠅刷、你鈹短了、他怎麼會鬧蒼蠅、就要受罪了 45 你買的那菓子、通共多少錢。我還沒合算起來、不是一個地方買的、等我把他們開的賬、拿來算一算 46 你這糊塗東西怎這麼混賬、像你這麼沒有腦子又懶又笨、中甚麼用啊、不配在正經人家做事、你快給我滾出去罷 47 你這是往那裏去。我上花園子去看看園子裏種的子粒出來了沒有、現在那個管園子的人不大妥當我不知道他種的對不對、向來他是給我當苦力、本來不是花兒匠、這幾個月常跟花兒匠在一塊兒現在就懂得一點、因為那花兒匠告了兩個月的假、他就給他當替工 48 這兩條路都是往北京去的、西邊的雖然近一點、可不好走走了不遠、就是石頭道、那石頭道好幾殼了、我打算到那裏拿銀單取錢可有一層、這銀單是在這銀行開的、應當在本處取錢、我不知道在分行扣不扣、怕是要扣、那有限、光景是一兩銀子抽一厘罷40聽他的口氣、是不願意辦這個事、他們行裏的規矩、不準他們櫃上人辦外頭的事情、這個章程他不好意思直告訴你、所以他含糊着答應了41你僅自囉唆我幹甚麽、我簡直的告訴你、你那怕怎麽求我決不答應42這個時候去、天氣太冷、等天暖和再說罷43這些孩子們眞淘氣竟貪玩、我若不是耐心煩的人、我簡直的受不得了44那馬尾巴、你爲甚麽給鉸短了、爲的是好看、就是了、你想着好看、可不體諒那馬、你想這麽樣的熱天、蠅蠅鬧的、你那蠅蠅刷老不離開手、馬尾巴也是人的都不好麼、你謙遜一點纔是 36 我明天請了幾位朋友吃飯聽戲、我約了他們在城外頭同和樓飯館子準四點鐘吃飯、我們兩個人不拘泥、所以我沒給您下請帖、我現在就算是口請了遵命遵命您打算上甚麼戲園子去。這個我是要請教您的因為我不常上戲園子去不知道那個班子好 37 我們的街坊下月初五要辦喜事聽說要很熱鬧要辦甚麼喜事呢、是辦生日啊、是娶媳婦呢、是給他們二少爺娶媳婦。您去不去怎麼不去呢多年的交情必得去 38 您來的真巧、我正要打發人請您過來、你明天上南邊去帶的錢彀不彀足彀了、我手裏有一百兩銀子的現錢還有您給我的那五百兩銀子的銀單、這兩筆錢湊在一塊兒一定是着騾子、現在我們太太上北邊避暑去了、得兩個多月纔囘來、這個工夫騾子也舒坦我也放了心了 32 每逢遇見他的時候、他抬着頭過去不愛理我、他從前窮的時候我們兩個人多麼親熱現在做大官了、就戴高帽子了、唉、俗語說的好、一步登高不認得老鄕親了 33 你們兩個人吵嚷甚麼、有話好好的說、爲甚麼要嚷呢。不是我要嚷、不過是他待我太不公道、我們兩個人合着夥做小買賣了、賺了錢各人分一半我的分兒他不給我、你說、這可怎麼好 34 你瞧、這地板有多麼骯髒了、看起來一定是你這幾天沒掃、你快快給我掃乾淨了罷再這麼樣趕到了月底你不用想和我要工錢 35 你這個人竟愛說嘴難道說就是你一個人的好、別回瞧見您納、他不知道是甚麽樣的人、您坐兩三回車、他知道您是老實人、不要催他、他自然就不踢了、不瞞您說、我這個騾子最嫌的是太太們、太太們裏頭頂嫌的是我們太太、一瞧見他來、要上車、他就知道要受罪了、就撩蹶子、怎麽說哪、我們太太不管騾子怎麽樣、竟愛快走、一上去啊、就說趕車的、你快走、他不管道兒好走不好走、天熱不熱、常叫我打騾子、叫他快跑、我若是不勤打他、他說我是和騾子一類的懶畜生、有時候拿傘把騾子擂一下兒、趕回來的時候、那騾子一身汗、甚麽食餧他都不吃、老爺您想、我這個騾子我仗着他過日子、這麽趕着他、若是趕出病來、我怎麽對得起我們老爺、我常和太太說過這個話、他不管、他說我老護不答應我[29]你問他那件事、他怎麽囘答的他說他肯辦、就怕他東家不答應、上囘人家請他幫個忙、他東家不準他去[30]這裏水深了、往上去一點就淺了、這裏有脖子那麽深、那裏不到踝子骨[31]趕車的、你那個騾子倒不錯、是多少錢買的。唉、老爺的眼力好瞧得出好牲口來、這個騾子買的時候我們老爺沒告訴我價錢、在我估摸着得七八十兩銀子哪也値、他不過七歲口沒瘸過吃的很香您看他多麽漂亮、他到了我手裏的時候、瘦的甚麽似的、現在上了膛、都是我心疼他不累他的緣故。唉、我的老爺、車的時候、他撩蹶子來着要踢我現在好了、大概是認生罷、咳、我的老爺、不是那麽着、那騾子雖然是個啞吧畜生、心裏可明白也認得人他頭一鋪、那個錢鋪不錯、您是要票子、是要錢。你給我一個五吊錢的票子、兩個一吊錢的臢下的給錢罷 23 您讓一點地罷、我們好過去。您請罷借光了 24 我今天來給您道謝您若不出來說合那個人一定要在衙門裏告我一下完了雨、我就出去溜搭溜搭、順着大道走、沒有多少泥、一離開大道、 25 打草地過靴子都濕了連襪子也濕了今天早起要穿的時候那靴子硬的板子似的、不能穿怎麽好、怕壞了。壞不了、把油抹上使勁往裏擦、囘來 26 我擱在火旁邊、可別太近了、烤了一烤、一會兒那油化了、靴子就頓了的刮臉刀不快不能刮臉、我得送到鐵匠鋪裏去叫他們磨一磨 27 我叫了你好幾囘、你爲甚麽不荅應 28 是時候了、我該走了、我若是到晚了、他回去不收、那做靴子的沒有法子 20 若雇車、按日子筭得多少錢一天。那都看您要上那裏去、若道兒遠錢就多了、若不出城自然錢少了、我們按里數兒筭行不行。您打筭給多少錢。你先說個價錢、我告訴你合我的意不合我的意。您看一百錢一里怎麼樣、那趕車的飯錢自然在外、另外還有那酒錢。那酒錢得多少。那是隨您的便、愛給多少就給多少、一百錢筭洋錢多少。那看行市、大概說、一塊洋錢可以筭一吊錢。就這麼着罷、這就筭定了。21 我告訴那趕車的快趕、不然我們趕不上你了、那騾子走的那麼慢、趕到了城門的時候、你們已經走了。22 我沒有零錢、這十吊錢的票子你可以給我換罷。您讓我看看、是那個錢鋪的票子。啊、是福順錢叫您惦記着、差不多好了。
們千金定親的事情定了沒
爺的大兒子那一位李大老爺、
老爺不是文官是個武官現
我姓東、東西的東、您高壽
令郎我有兩個兒子一個姑娘、
19 我這雙靴子太緊了買的是現成的
尺寸量好了、不知道他怎麼做小了。
腳疼。你爲甚麼不退囘去、若是我的我

我好像記得我們上囘見面的時候您商量
有、早已定了、如今出門子了給的是李大老
是福州知府麽、不是那李家這一位李大
在閒着不做官了 18 您貴姓賤姓春沒領教。
我小哪繞四十八啊、比我大兩歲您跟前幾位
您跟前幾位。沒有運氣、就有一個妞兒
還是定做的。是定做的那皮匠把
你穿過沒穿過。沒穿過、不能穿、穿了
一定要退囘去、您若是沒給錢、退

的材料不要緊、有用處、擦布不殼作擦布用罷 16 我找個底下人、您知道有好的不知道那底下人是要作甚麼的、我要他當廚子您若不很講究、我知道有一個人、他現在閒着平常的菜做的還罷了人乾淨又老實也肯用功就是有一樣、他耳朶有一點聾偶爾他也愛喝杯酒我可沒瞧見他喝醉了、他要多少工錢。要的是二十五塊錢一個月、您可不用給他那麼些個我想二十塊殼了。您叫他今天晚飯後來見我行不行。我想、您還是叫他來一個月、試一試行不行、勞駕的很、叫您費心過兩天我上您那裏去再給您道謝豈敢豈敢 17 久違久違、您這一程子好了。托福、都好了、您府上都好。承間都好、就是我們內人病了兩個月。如今大好了罷。

若不信我的話、就問我兄弟、他不撒謊、你是知道的 12 你上輪船的時候把你的行李數一數兒、看看對不對、我怕落下了一包毡子若落下了到了上海、你給我發個電報、我就上飯店去打聽打聽他們有沒有、若有了、我就送到你那裏去 13 你昨天打圍、怎麼樣、得了甚麼沒有。到了山那邊、那樹林子裏沒走了幾步、就瞧見了個野雞舉起鎗來要打那鎗是空的、忘了裝咯、走了不遠、樹根子絆了脚咯、把我跌躺下了、我的鎗也折了 14 把燈點上、擱在那小桌子上、把桌子挪開一點、別挨着帳子放、怕帳子要著了 15 那布、你在那裏買的。在洋貨鋪裏買的。買那個做甚麼。我打筭做汗衫用。那樣的布做汗衫不行、太粗了、做汗衫、得細一點他賠個不是 5 論理這不是我該辦的事、因爲他今天病了、不能上衙門、若不是我去替他辦、您的事就悞了 6 他聽見您同他去拜李大人、他很喜歡、他本來膽子小、頭一次見人、連一句話都說不出來 7 我的眼鏡子找不著、不記得擱在那裏、我各處找了、在棹子底下、椅子底下、連煤匣子裏都找了、那裏都找不著 8 那個箱子的分量太重、一個人扛不動、怕得兩個人抬着。其實是很輕、裝的不過是草帽子 9 他眞沒運氣去年他蓋了個房子、花了多少錢、剛蓋完了、叫火燒壞了、他也沒保險 10 那兩個人昨天在街上打架來着、看街的瞧見了、就把他們拉到官衙門去、那官並不問誰是誰、不是、就叫各人打五十板子 11 這是我各人做的、你

X.

Chinese Text.

1 把那舊布衣裳擱在洗澡盆裏洗一洗、不用使胰子洗、就擱在熱水裏泡一泡、兩點鐘的工夫囘來擰乾了、掛在太陽地裏曬一曬、好了、就擰起來擱在櫃子裏頭 2 我借給你的那個錢、你多喒有現錢我多喒還、目下連一個大錢都沒有 3 他睡醒了的時候、你告訴他我在院子裏等他、他一來了、我們就吃、越早越好 4 你別怪我說你錯了、他有理他好好的坐着並不和誰說話、你無緣無故的過去罵他、他自然是生氣甚麼人、不論是誰、不願意叫人家白罵他、據我瞧你應該給武官來着、因爲眼睛不好了、沒有法子、就不做官、他現在離北京南門不遠的一個村庄裏住 66 皇上明天出皇宮過的那街兩旁邊的舖子、都得關門 67 他不愛花錢、他若是同人家溜搭去、到了給錢的時候、他總要想法子叫那個人給錢 68 我今天後半天坐車拜客去、告訴跟班的他得跟着我去、還得帶名片他是走啊、還是騎馬跟着您去呢、他可以在車旁邊走我去的不遠 69 太陽很熱、別在太陽地裏坐、樹底下有陰凉兒爲甚麼不在那裏坐 70 那一位好像從前見過可不記得是在那裏見過的 71 別動、有一個螞蜂落在你的領子上、等我把他閧開。唉我最怕的是螞蜂螫了、不是玩的狗跑出來了、把我腿咬了一下兒、過了兩天那腿就腫起來了、請了大夫來瞧了一瞧、他說不要緊、叫我把他給我的一點藥抹上、敢情第二天就不疼了、到了第四天就大好了63把那厚衣裳裝在口袋裏頭、帶到裁縫那裏去告訴他那褂子不合式、得改、那砍肩褲子也不對、褲子太長、砍肩太短、兩個都得改64這奇怪了、你昨天好好的、今天怎麼就病了。我不知道怎麼得的怕是昨天晚晌著了涼、後半天很熱出門的時候就穿了薄衣裳了、到了晚晌八點鐘忽然就涼起來了、當時就有一點不舒坦、可不大理會今天早起睡醒了嗓子就疼、滿身發燒、我打算躺一躺、蓋上被窩、半天大概好了罷、若還不好、我吃一劑藥就是了65李老爺從前做

來的時候我乏的利害連飯都不想吃請問我那裏有工夫瞧朋友去
56 唉、這是往那裏擠蹦了我腳指頭了有錯有錯沒留神 57 那孩子真可
憐他父母都死了他在遠親戚家住那親戚不大喜歡他待他也不好他
如今十三歲了也不上學據我瞧這不對因為那孩子不是白住他父親
留下了一點產業利息都是他那親戚拿那利錢比養活他那個錢多一
倍了 58 那火車三點一刻五開行李三點少十分都得預備好了因為馬
車就是在那個時候到門口兒了坐馬車到車站得一刻的工夫 59 你告
訴他那個笑話兒他說甚麼他沒說甚麼他就樂了 60 中國話眞難學西
國話容易多了 61 五個孩子頂難管的就是你 62 我打他門口兒過他的

把大拇指頭刺破了、下囘要用的時候、沒有了、我好像記得、我在剃頭舖裏拿出來削指甲怕落下了、我囘到剃頭舖裏去問他們瞧見了沒有、他們都說沒瞧見、雖然是這麼說、怕是他們夥計偷了去了52、你給我找一塊木頭來、得上下五尺長三寸厚短的不行53、那個人很有一點學問、筆墨上也罷了、就是記性不好、字寫的也不算十分好54、你看的是甚麼書。我看法國書啊、你還懂得法國話麼。不敢說懂得法國話、也就是知道一點。你把幾句念給我聽罷、我要聽聽那聲音怎麼樣55、這好幾個月你沒來瞧我是甚麼緣故、是我得罪了你了麼、別說那個話、你那裏得罪我了、就是因爲我忙的了不得、連我自己家裏的事都沒有空兒辦、打衙門囘

44 借光請問、打這裏到省城有多遠、

45 遠是不很遠、就是大道不好走、若順着這小道兒走、就近多了車也走得了

46 我給你們二位見一見、這是管大人這是樂大老爺。

47 煤若是成車的買就省錢

48 順風順水、一會兒就到了

49 那兩個人是弟兄、哥哥叫大順子兄弟叫小順子、還有一個姐姐、兩個妹妹、中間是他們弟兄兩個

50 那酒杯不乾淨我告訴你多少回、洗完了玻璃杯得拿擦布擦乾了

51 我的刀子剌不了這樣的大繩子、你把你的借給我罷、就是你去年生日我給你的那把刀子。別提可惜了兒的丢了。你怎麼丢的、不知道、怕是禮拜三、上剃頭舖裏去鉸頭髮那一天丢的、我准知道禮拜三上半天有來着、因爲我使了削筆來着、

局去啊、勞您駕就手兒給我買一塊錢的信票 35 您下囘見他的時候、費

您心把我那個事情提一提 36 放心忘不了 37 您這給我費事多謝的

很 38 您天天甚麼時候上衙門去沒有准時候事情多早一點去事情少

晚一點去、沒有人管我、我愛甚麼時候去就甚麼時候去愛甚麼時候走、

就甚麼時候走、都是隨我的便 39 那鋪子裏掌櫃的、從前是洋行裏的買

辦、去年不知甚麼緣故、不要他了、他有點本錢就做起買賣來了 40 高矮

不要緊寬窄可是要緊的太寬了、就擱不進去、太窄了、就鬆了 41 天這麼

冷、你爲甚麼穿這麼薄的衣裳、你不怕著凉麼 42 颳西北風咯、不到黑下、

怕要下雨 43 那也不定、颳西北風這裏不大下雨、帶雨的風是東南風

要甚麼樣的菜 29 叫他煮一兩個小雞子、烤一塊牛肉、做四五瓶湯、我們也要雞子兒、幾樣點心甚麼的、還有茶葉糖鹽這些個都得預備叫他拿紙包上包兒、我們還要一個茶壺開水的開水壺茶碗碟子湯碗盤子刀子叉子匙子還有那牛奶別叫他忘了、我們不要鮮奶、怕到了第二天就壞了、還是買那鐵盒子裏灌的那外國奶好 30 天氣這麼熱、老爺少帶吃的好、一天沒吃完了的第二天就壞了、還是道兒上隨要隨買好 31 我渴了、給我拿氣水來、老爺是單喝還是對酒喝。若是有紅酒我就對一點 32 把我的煙荷包煙袋拿來、也要自來火 33 這茶很淡、茶葉是在那裡買的、茶葉不是買的、是時老爺送您的、讓您試一試看看好不好 34 您若是上郵政好了、我打算坐上半天的火車上北京去、在那裏過禮拜、禮拜一下半天回來 21 在北京甚麼地方住、我那裏有親戚我昨天給他寫了一封信問他有閒屋子沒有、他若有地方、我就在他房子住、他若沒有地方、只好在客店裏住罷 22 今天早起的新聞紙有新聞沒有。沒有甚麼新聞 23 今天銀子甚麼行市。我還沒聽見說後半天我打銀行過、我就進去打聽打聽 24 您若是上銀行去、勞您的駕、把這銀票給我換錢 25 您要甚麼樣的錢、是要銀子、是要洋錢 26 在這裏使甚麼樣的錢方便、自然是洋錢方便、27 在舖子裏買零碎東西、人家都是用洋錢、銀子大半是做大買賣用的 28 我們後天上鄉下去逛兩三天要帶些個吃的、叫廚子預備幾樣菜。您瓶子、有毛病。像那個樣的毛病不要緊、你瞧、那花兒畫的多麼好看、顏色也好像那樣的瓶子、雖然有毛病、也比他要的那個價錢值多了 17 我們兩個人有多年的交情、他在京城住的時候、我們是常見面的、前年他上鄉下去住、離這裏有五十多里、現在我們不大常會、我明年春天打算去見他、要把他帶回來、到了秋天、他若不在我這裏過冬、我就同他一塊兒囘去、我再不離開他 18 你若和那個人有甚麼事、我勸你留一點心、外面很和氣、心裏可利害、我碰過他的釘子、所以我知道他的脾氣 19 那個馬老實不老實、你若常騎他、少餧他糧食甚麼人都可以騎、你若多餧他糧食、或兩三天擱在馬號裏不騎他、就要鬧脾氣 20 下禮拜六天氣若我薦給他、我就告訴你、你可別告訴別人 7 他父親在的時候、他常給我做活他父親死了、他就開了個小買賣、現在不當木匠了 8 現在幾點鐘。按着那個鐘是三點半鐘那個鐘可慢了、等我上我臥房裏去把我的表拿來我知道那個準了、因為我今天早起和禮拜堂的鐘對了一對 9 這個沒有那個大。兩個差不多 10 天黑的連道兒都瞧不見了、差一點沒掉在河裏 11 這麼大的棹子、那麼小的屋子擱不下 12 既是那麼着你愛怎麼辦就怎麼辦、不用和你的朋友商量 13 我四點鐘三刻準來、萬一有甚麼事把我躭悞了、我就打發一個人給你送個信 14 我指頭疼的利害、昨天晚晌我碰了一下兒疼的我一夜睡不著覺 15 你指甚麼 16 別買那個

IX.

CHINESE TEXT.

1 有一件小事、要請您相幫、您是個很忙的人、我是知道的、本來不要勞動您納、我可實在沒有法子、因為除了您納沒有人能給我辦 2 那沒甚麽、我雖然忙、總要勻一點空兒給您幫個忙、我們是老朋友、您幫了我多少回、我樂得的、給您出一點力 3 您剛纔跟誰說話。那是個做官的、就是去年上英國去的那個人、您不記得麽、在我家裏見過的 4 不錯、您一提我就想起來了、我一見他、我好像見過、一時可忘了、在那裏見過了 5 你給他辦那件事他給你多少錢來着 6 若是別人問我、我一定不告訴你、旣把

58 可不是請了麼
59 把東西擱下、擱得下、擱不下
60 擱得下
61 擱得下
62 擱下了
63 你想一想他怎麼能把這麼些個東西都帶回來、你叫他拿一半就是了
64 你父親為甚麼打他
65 你為甚麼不信
66 因為你老不說實話
67 他父親說、下回他一定要打他
68 因為他老不在家上回他父親叫他的時候他不在家他父親說、
69 花老爺做甚麼官
70 現在他不做官了
71 你去打聽他起來了沒有他若是起來了、你就請他過來
72 他昨天告訴我他姓甚麼、
73 啊、我想起來了、他說他姓長
74 那東西你做起來了沒有
75 還沒做、你甚麼時候要
76 我現在要
77 明天行不行
78 你吃了飯就做好
79 我吃了飯就來做、好不好
80 好

他借幾個錢 38 這是你該做的事 39 他病了不能來 40 他有甚麼病 41 我不知道我就知道我昨天早起去見他的時候他還沒起來、他家裏的人說他病了 42 他姓甚麼 43 他是做官的 44 做甚麼官 45 他管官馬 46 我給他做那個事、你想他給我多少錢來着 47 我知道那個人、他不愛花錢、他給的不多罷 48 我若是知道他是那樣的人我就不給他做 49 他早晚一定要來 50 他老沒有主意 51 你給我出個主意 52 快一點走罷、你這麼慢走、怕今天晚晌到不了家 53 他寫這封信我知道他的意思 54 你要得問他、我不能作主 55 你不用問他那字有甚麼意思連字還不認得他怎麼能告訴你字的意思 56 你是一個人去還是同他們去 57 也請了他們了了 17 你甚麼時候去 18 你愛甚麼時候去、就甚麼時候去 19 那兩個東西的大小不同 20 怎麼不同、都是一個樣 21 你就去告訴他我現在有事他在那裏住、我若是明天沒有事我就去見他 22 他在那裏住。他現在在那裏住 23 我明天要早起來、你天天是起來的早、請你把我叫起來 24 你不要給我罷 25 來罷我有話和你說 26 你要說甚麼、那你不用管、你來就是了 28 他昨天晚晌來了、我還沒見他 29 去年他不在這裏、今年他也不來他明年不來、怕他後年要來 30 今天怕要下雨 31 那一個太長、把短的拿來 32 這幾年他長大了 33 那板子的長短你知道不知道 34 他短不了錢 35 我短幾個錢、你借給我罷 36 他該你多少錢 37 我去跟

VIII.

CHINESE TEXT.

1 你昨天叫我上他家裏去打聽那事、我忘了沒去 2 我也知道他不行 3 你還在這裏麼你爲甚麼沒去 4 因爲他不叫我去、他聽見說我還沒吃飯他說我得先吃飯我就去 5 你打那裏來 6 我打鄉下來 7 打這裏到那裏有多少路 8 不遠不過一天的道 9 你上那裏去麼我也去、你同我去行不行 10 怎麼不行、你是甚麼時候去 11 我要一點紙擱在這上頭、你去給我找一找 12 這個行不行 13 怕不行太小了 14 這個行了罷 15 您做完了告訴我我就請他給您的兒子寫一封信叫他明天來拿 16 我來晚說他要了、後來他沒要 69 我說的是實話、你怎麼不信 70 我實在不能給你那個 71 那是我的事你不用管 72 那做不得 73 那個你都知道不用我告訴你 74 那就是了、你若記得是甚麼人給你的、你就去問他是甚麼時候買的 75 天氣這麼熱你穿這麼些個衣裳做甚麼 76 你說熱麼我看冷 77 飯好了麼 78 快好了 79 他姓甚麼 80 把椅子擱在這裏 81 你是走了來的、是坐車來的 82 他不聽話做甚麼。我等他們開門 45 你說錯了 46 我怎麼說錯了 47 你告訴我他買東西去了、他沒買東西去 48 我沒說那個話、我說他出去了、這有甚麼錯 49 你說了那個話麼 50 不錯、是我說的 51 那個你做錯了 52 錯不錯、我不管 53 那是我的錯兒 54 你告訴他、他不聽我的話 55 我上他家裏去了、問他那個事、他出門去了 56 他家裏的人說、他們不知道他甚麼時候回來、我就沒等他了 57 你做得了沒有 58 明天就得 59 那個做不了 60 你不去、我得去 61 他得說他要那個、他不說我怎麼能知道給他那個 62 你聽聽、外頭有甚麼人說話 63 千萬不要說是我說的 64 那個太貴、我不買 65 這個賤多了 66 那個是前那個是後 67 我在前頭走、你在後頭走 68 前幾天他做的不好。

22. 他一囬來你就告訴他、買的那些東西我要看。
23. 你甚麼時候去、我就去。
24. 這個行不行、是行就是行、不行就是不行。
25. 那是甚麼人做的、他說是他做的。
26. 我可不能給你他的東西。
27. 他說甚麼我都不信。
28. 你要我的東西我就給你、你要多少就拿多少。
29. 把那個東西拿來給我看。
30. 那個東西沒有把兒、我怎麼拿。
31. 你是怎麼來的、我是走了來的。
32. 你明天上我這裏來吃飯行不行。
33. 我明天有事、不能來。
34. 他若是請我、我不能去。
35. 這怎麼好、我不能告訴他。
36. 你告訴他、我有事就是了。
37. 我若是告訴他、那個話、他不信。
38. 他信不信、我不管。
39. 把門關上。
40. 門關了。
41. 門沒關上。
42. 開門。
43. 把門開開。
44. 你坐在那裏。

VII.

CHINESE TEXT.

1 你給了他多少錢 2 我不記得 3 你看見了多少人 4 我看見了十幾個人 5 這些東西都是你的 6 我數了數兒 7 我給他說明白了 8 他不懂得我的話 9 他白日不在家 10 這些字都是你寫的麼 11 有不是我寫的 12 他是甚麼時候回來的 13 他說他明天要回來的 14 他回來的時候你告訴他我要見他 15 我聽見說你寫字寫的很好 16 這是甚麼話我不會寫字 17 他給我寫了一封信說他明天不能來 18 我給他寫了回信、請他後天來 19 他來了五回、我都沒在家 20 你能做就做、我不會 21 我能做、就是

VI.

Chinese Text.

1 八十六 2 四百七十九 3 六百零五 4 一千五百二十八 5 三千零一 6 一萬五千 7 一百一十六 8 二十七萬四千六百十九 9 他是頭一個我是第二 10 他是頭裏來的我沒來過 11 你有零錢沒有 12 他有五個兒子兩個在這裏、那三個我不知道在那裏 13 五五二十五 14 第十五 15 第十五個 16 五兩二錢。五兩二

你問他[118]請問、這是上那裏的道兒[119]那看東西的大小[120]外頭有一個賣東西的、你要看他的東西不要

93 他是過來人
94 他過來了沒有
95 我不知道他的買賣好不好
96 他要不了那麼些個東西
97 那裏頭有甚麼
98 請他上來我有話說
99 你看這個好不好、是好、沒有那個好
100 好、是好、沒有那個好
101 這是你的、不是
102 這是你的、不是你的、
103 不是你的、
104 拿這裏來給我看一看
105 你過來、
106 我給你說一說
107 你要說甚麼、等我說了你知道
108 他說甚麼了、你知道
109 我不知道、我來問你
110 不要問我、問他
111 等不等在你
112 那個不是我的、我給了他了
113 你要知道那東西好不好、你問他、他沒有甚麼不知道的
114 拿來給我看
115 這個道、那東西好不好、你問他、他沒有甚麼不知道的
116 是道兒、你知道不知道
117 我不知道、我沒有走過這個道兒
那裏有人來、

62 了那個東西沒有了 63 那是他頭裏說的話 64 我不要問他那個 65 我不好問他那個 66 你不來他要說 67 那沒甚麼 68 他來了我要見他 69 他見我不見我 70 他說他甚麼人不見 71 我看見了你了、你沒看見了 72 你要這個我給你、那個我不給你 73 那個東西的大小你知道不知道 74 不知道 75 我有你那麼些個錢我不賣那個東西 76 你是那麼說等 77 你有錢看 78 你是他的兒子麼 79 上來 80 你過這裏來、我要問你話 81 他來過沒有 82 他沒來過、 83 他說過這個話沒有 84 不是沒有、 85 他不給我 86 他要了錢沒要 87 我要走了 88 請你 89 你問他 90 他要不要、他不要、我給你 91 這個你看見過沒有 92 我沒看見過請麼 31 我不知道他賣甚麼 32 他說你的東西是在他那裏買的 33 他說了那個了麼 34 這些人是那裏來的 35 我沒有那麼大的東西 36 他做甚麼買賣 37 他不是買賣人 38 我沒有錢買那個 39 我有錢我來買 40 你不要說他、 41 他問你甚麼 42 你要甚麼東西 43 我不要甚麼 44 你給我那個不給 45 我不給你、 46 我的兒子你看見了沒有 47 他說甚麼話 48 不要說話 49 我問他要不要、他說不要 50 我不知道兒 51 你請他等我 52 他說他不等 53 你請他坐下等我、他說甚麼 54 他說要買東西、不等你來 55 你沒來了他走了 56 那裏頭有甚麼 57 你問我做甚麼 58 你看這個好不好 59 在我說不是很好的 60 那個我做不了 61 那裏我坐不

V.

Chinese Text

1 這個是你的
2 這個是你的麼
3 我們不要那個
4 你要甚麼
5 他們在那裏
6 那個是甚麼
7 他在那裏
8 他在那裏做甚麼
9 那個是甚麼東西
10 你做甚麼
11 我不做甚麼
12 你要不要
13 他來了沒有
14 他的兒子來了
15 錢拿來
16 你有錢沒有
17 他在裏頭
18 那是我做的
19 你看見了沒有
20 我沒看見了
21 那個人要甚麼
22 我不知道
23 他要甚麼
24 我等你的兒子
25 你在這裏做甚麼
26 我的錢他沒給了我了
27 坐一坐等他來
28 他的買賣大不大
29 他的買賣沒有我的大
30 他賣甚

XII.

The student having now mastered a thousand characters and having been introduced to a few of the many combinations which they can be made to form, the important point is to retain them in the memory. The system of writing each character on a separate slip and recognising these when selected at random answers well enough to begin with, but more than this is wanted, as they must be recognised in all their combinations, and the different meanings or shades of meaning they assume in these varied combinations must also be gradually appreciated. By constantly reading through the list at the end of this volume he will be able to refresh his memory, but it is obviously by constant reading and speaking that progress in the language will best be made, for the words and phrases in common use will go on repeating themselves, both in reading and in speaking, and will thus impress themselves on the memory. Such a system of study presupposes in due course the services of a native instructor, for no one who has not the opportunity of studying with an instructor by his side can ever hope to speak accurately or to pronounce his words well. It will not be so difficult to acquire a paper knowledge of the spoken language, but the assistance of an expert is indispensable for obtaining a correct pronunciation and the rhythmic swing and intonation which are so essential to elegant speaking. A point should be made daily of reading, sentence by sentence, after the "teacher," and endeavouring to mimic his intonation and his style as closely as possible. Mimicry is the great element of success, and no one will ever speak Chinese well who adheres to his ordinary accent and emphasis. A good teacher will correct errors of tone and pronunciation again and again until they have been overcome, and if at the commencement the student finds that he is not constantly brought to a pause and told to pronounce a word or a sentence over again, he may be sure that his instructor is either careless or incompetent.

There is always a temptation, when examinations are looming in the distance, to limit the attention to allotted text books and to learn these by heart, but it is not the best way to learn Chinese, and as soon as the student feels himself fairly firm on his feet he should endeavour to cover as much ground as he can, making a note, as he goes along, of new characters and combinations. He should get away from foreign text books as soon as he can read them with comparative ease, and should turn his attention to colloquial novels in which he will find a vast store of phrases, and will at the same time be introduced by degrees to a useful form of the written language with which all novels are interlarded. He will find poetry there too, but that he would do well to leave alone for some time. Newspapers in the vernacular are now published in Peking, and doubtless in other parts of China, which will be found very useful reading. Efforts should be made at the very outset to get away from disconnected sentences, for one of the initial difficulties is the stringing of sentences together. This, it will have been noticed by a study of the examples previously given, is done by means of a few words or particles judiciously used. It will be found very good practice to write down a short connected story made up of words which have already been learnt or are to be found in one or other of the many vocabularies now procurable, and to submit it to some authority for correction. The study of the corrections by a competent hand of a composition of one's own is a more valuable lesson than pages of ready-made sentences.

One of the most useful books with which the student can provide himself, when he has made a certain amount of progress, is a *Dictionary of Chinese*, by MacGillivray, formerly known as *Stent's Vocabulary*. In this book he will find a translation of every word and combination of words he is likely to come across for many years.

Mention has frequently been made of the "Radicals." These have to be mastered sooner or later if a dictionary is ever to be used, and some authorities call upon the learner to start with them. They are so dry and so uninteresting that many people who only think they would like to learn Chinese give up the task in despair after labouring at them for a few days. The preferable way seems to be to take them by degrees. A fair number consists of words in colloquial use, some of which will already have been met with in the preceding exercises. When the new colloquial words have been added to the stock the balance that remains will not be a formidable one, and it will be sufficient for practical purposes if these are recognised as radicals and their place in the series is more or less established in the mind. A list of radicals in the order of their strokes is appended, and colloquial words are indicated by an asterisk. Of the rest, some are used in writing only, others are never used at all except as radicals.

THE RADICALS.

Colloquial Radicals are indicated by *. Modifications are indicated by †, and placed at the foot of the page.

1 Stroke.

1	i¹	*	一	one.
2	kun³		丨	perpendicular, to pass through.
3	chu³		丶	a point, dot.
4	p'ieh³		丿	a stroke to the left.
5	i⁴		乙	curved.
6	chüeh²		亅	a barb, hooked end.

2 Strokes.

7	êrh⁴	*	二	two.
8	t'ou²		亠	above.
9	jên²	† *	人	a man.
10	jên²		儿	a man.
11	ju⁴	*	入	to enter.
12	pa¹	*	八	eight.
13	chiung³		冂	border waste land.
14	mi⁴		冖	to cover.

† 9 亻

222 THE CHINESE LANGUAGE

15	ping¹			冫	an icicle.
16	chi¹			几	a stool, bench.
17	k'an³			凵	a receptacle, unfilled vessel.
18	tao¹	†	*	刀	a knife, sword.
19	li⁴		*	力	strength.
20	pao¹			勹	to wrap.
21	pi³			匕	a ladle.
22	fang¹			匚	a basket.
23	hsi³			匸	a coffer.
24	shih²		*	十	ten.
25	pu³			卜	to divine.
26	chieh²	†		卩	a stamp.
27	han⁴			厂	a projecting cliff.
28	ssŭ¹			厶	private, selfish.
29	yu⁴		*	又	again, also.

3 Strokes.

30	k'ou³			口	a mouth.
31	wei²			囗	an enclosure.
32	t'u³	†	*	土	earth.

† 18 刂   26 㔾   32 士

33	shih⁴	*	士	a scholar.
34	chih⁴		夂	to follow.
35	ts'ui¹		夊	to walk slowly.
36	hsi⁴		夕	evening.
37	ta⁴	*	大	great.
38	nü³	*	女	a female, woman, girl.
39	tzŭ³	*	子	a son.
40	mien²		宀	a roof, shelter.
41	ts'un⁴	*	寸	an inch.
42	hsiao³	*	小	little, small.
43	wang¹	†	尢	bent, as an ailing leg.
44	shih¹	*	尸	a corpse.
45	ch'ê⁴		屮	sprouting, a sprout.
46	shan¹	*	山	a hill.
47	ch'uan¹	†	巛	streams.
48	kung¹	*	工	labour, work, leisure.
49	chi³	*	己	self.
50	chin¹	*	巾	a napkin, towel, cap.
51	kan¹	*	干	arms, to concern.
52	yao¹		幺	small, immature.
53	yen³		广	a covering, roof.

† 43 兀 兀   47 〈 巜 川

54	yin³		廴	to move on.
55	kung³		廾	hands folded in salutation.
56	i⁴		弋	an arrow, to shoot.
57	kung¹	*	弓	a bow.
58	ch'i⁴	†	彐	head, pointed like one.
59	shan¹		彡	hair, streaky.
60	ch'ih⁴		彳	a step, to step short, or with the left foot.

4 Strokes.

61	hsin¹	† *	心	mind, heart.
62	ko¹		戈	a spear.
63	hu⁴	*	戶	a door.
64	shou³	† *	手	the hand.
65	chih¹	*	支	a stem, prop, to advance money.
66	p'u¹	†	攴	to tap, rap.
67	wên²	*	文	stripes, streaks, literature.
68	tou³	*	斗	a Chinese peck measure, a bushel.
69	chin¹	*	斤	a Chinese pound, a catty.
70	fang¹	*	方	square.
71	wu²	†	无	not, without.

† 58 彑 彐   61 忄 小   64 扌   66 攵   71 无

72	jih⁴	*	日	the sun, day.
73	yüeh¹		曰	to speak.
74	yueh⁴	*	月	the moon, month.
75	mu⁴	*	木	wood, trees.
76	ch'ien⁴	*	欠	to owe, to be wanting in, deficient.
77	chih³	*	止	to stop.
78	tai³	† *	歹	bad.
79	shu¹		殳	a quarter staff.
80	wu²		毋	do not, not.
81	pi³	*	比	to compare.
82	mao²	*	毛	hair, fur, wool.
83	ch'i⁴	*	气	vapour.
84	shih⁴	*	氏	surname, clan name.
85	shui³	† *	水	water.
86	huo³	† *	火	fire.
87	chao³	† *	爪	claws.
88	fu⁴	*	父	father.
89	yao²		爻	blending, crosswise.
90	ch'iang²		爿	Radical 91 reversed.
91	p'ien⁴	*	片	a slab, leaf, strip, slip.
92	ya²	*	牙	the back teeth, a tooth.

† 78 歹　　85 氵水　　86 灬　　87 爫

93	niu² † *	牛	an ox, cattle, oxen.
94	ch'üan³ † *	犬	a dog.

5 Strokes.

95	yüan²		玄	black.
96	yü⁴ † *		玉	jade, a gem.
97	kua¹ *		瓜	a melon, gourd.
98	wa³ *		瓦	earthenware, a tile.
99	kan¹ *		甘	sweet, pleasant.
100	shêng¹ *		生	to produce, to live, alive, to be born, raw.
101	yung⁴ *		用	to use, use.
102	t'ien² *		田	fields, arable land.
103	p'i³ *		疋	a bale, roll.
104	ni⁴		疒	disease.
105	po⁴		癶	back to back.
106	pai² *		白	white.
107	p'i² *		皮	skin, bark, peel, fur.
108	min³		皿	dish, utensil.
109	mu⁴ *		目	the eye.
110	mou²		矛	a lance.

† 93 牛　94 犭　96 王

111	shih³		矢	an arrow.
112	shih²	*	石	a stone.
113	shih⁴	† *	示	to show, revelation.
114	jou²	†	内	a footprint.
115	ho²		禾	grain.
116	hsueh⁴	*	穴	a cave.
117	li⁴	*	立	to set up, stand up, erect.

6 STROKES.

*118	chu²	*	竹	bamboo.
119	mi³	*	米	uncooked rice.
120	ssŭ¹		糸	silk.
121	fou³		缶	earthenware.
122	wang³	† *	网	a net.
123	yang²	*	羊	a sheep.
124	yü³		羽	wings, plumes, feathers.
125	lao³	*	老	old.
126	êrh²	*	而	and, yet, but, still.
127	lei³		耒	a plough.
128	êrh³	*	耳	the ear.
129	yü⁴		聿	a pencil.

† 113 禾　　114 内　　122 ⺲　⺳　冗　冈

130	jou¹ † *	肉	flesh, meat.
131	ch'ên² *	臣	a minister, statesman.
132	tzŭ⁴ *	自	self, from.
133	chih⁴ *	至	to reach, arrive at.
134	chiu⁴	臼	a mortar.
135	shê² *	舌	the tongue.
136	ch'uan³	舛	perverse, erroneous.
137	chou¹	舟	a ship.
138	kên⁴	艮	perverse, limitation.
139	sê⁴ *	色	colour.
140	ts'ao³ †	艸	grass, herbs.
141	hu³	虍	a tiger.
142	ch'ung² *	虫	insects, worms.
143	hsüeh³ } * hsieh³ }	血	blood.
144	hsing² } * hang² }	行	to go, do; hang², a row.
145	i¹ † *	衣	clothes.
146	hsi¹ † *	西	west.

7 STROKES.

147	chien⁴ *	見	to see, perceive.
148	chiao³ } * chüeh² }	角	horns, a corner.

† 130 月　　140 艹　　145 衤　　146 覀

149	yen²	*	言	words.
150	ku³	*	谷	a valley, ravine.
151	tou⁴	*	豆	a bean.
152	shih³		豕	swine.
153	chai⁴		豸	reptiles.
154	pei⁴	*	貝	precious, a cowry.
155	ch'ih⁴	*	赤	flesh colour.
156	tsou³	*	走	to walk.
157	tsu²	† *	足	the foot, enough.
158	shên¹	*	身	the body.
159	ch'ê¹	*	車	a cart, carriage.
160	hsin¹		辛	bitter.
161	ch'ên²	*	辰	time, one of the twelve divisions of the day.
162	ch'o⁴	†	辵	moving and stopping.
163	i⁴	†	邑	a hamlet, a camp.
164	yu³		酉	one of the twelve divisions of the day.
165	pien¹		釆	to discriminate, sort out.
166	li³	*	里	a Chinese mile, a hamlet.

† 157 ⻊   162 辶   163 阝

8 Strokes.

167	chin¹	*	金	gold, metals.
168	chang³ ch'ang²	* †	長	to grow; ch'ang², long.
169	mên²	*	門	a door, gate.
170	fu⁴	†	阜	a mound.
171	tai⁴		隶	to reach to.
172	chui¹		隹	short-tailed birds.
173	yu³	† *	雨	rain.
174	ch'ing¹	*	青	azure.
175	fei¹	*	非	wrong, not.

9 Strokes.

176	mien⁴	*	面	face, surface.
177	ko²		革	to flay, strip, a hide.
178	wei²		韋	dressed leather.
179	chiu³		韭	leeks.
180	yin¹	*	音	sound.
181	yeh⁴	*	頁	the page of a book.
182	fêng¹	*	風	wind.
183	fei¹	*	飛	to fly.

† 168 镸   170 阝   173 ⻗

184	shih²	*	食	to eat, food.
185	shou³	*	首	the head.
186	hsiang¹	*	香	fragrant, fragrance, incense.

10 Strokes.

187	ma³	*	馬	a horse.
188	ku³	*	骨	bones.
189	kao¹	*	高	high.
190	piao¹		髟	bushy hair.
191	tou⁴	*	鬥	to fight, wrangle, tease.
192	ch'ang⁴		鬯	a sacrificial bowl.
193	li⁴		鬲	an incense urn.
194	kuei³	*	鬼	a ghost, spirits of the dead.

11 Strokes.

195	yü²	*	魚	a fish.
196	niao³	*	鳥	a bird.
197	lu³		鹵	coarse, salt.
198	lu⁴	*	鹿	a deer.
199	mai⁴	*	麥	wheat.
200	ma²	*	麻	hemp.

12 Strokes.

201	huang²	*	黃	yellow.
202	shu³	*	黍	panicled millet.
203	hei¹	*	黑	black.
204	chih⁹		黹	embroidery.

13 Strokes.

205	min³		黽	frogs, toads.
206	ting³		鼎	a sacrificial tripod.
207	ku³	*	鼓	a drum.
208	shu³	*	鼠	a rat.

14 Strokes.

209	pi²	*	鼻	the nose.
210	ch'i²	*	齊	even, complete.

15 Strokes.

| 211 | ch'ih³ | | 齒 | the front teeth. |

16 Strokes.

212	lung²	*	龍	a dragon.
213	kuei¹		龜	the tortoise.

17 Strokes.

214	yo⁴	龠	flute, pipe.

XIII.

As has been remarked more than once, the way to fix the characters in the memory is to pass them constantly under review. The characters in the following list have been arranged more or less in the order in which they appear at the foot of each page in Volume I. This list should be referred to frequently as the student progresses. When he passes on to the study of other text books he is strongly advised to enter in a note-book each new character he comes across, arranged in the same manner as those in this list. The addition of a second thousand words to his stock, so arranged as to be handy for reference and verification, will be an immense help. A third thousand will probably be all that he will ever require to learn. The figures to the left of each character indicate the Radical under which it will be found in the Chinese dictionaries.

THE CHINESE LANGUAGE

162	這	1. chê⁴, this
9	個	2. ko⁴, piece
73	是	3. shih⁴, is
9	你	4. ni³, you
106	的	5. ti, 's, -ing, one, -ly
200	麽	6. mo, an interrogative
62	我	7. wo³, I
9	們	8. mên, plural of pronouns
1	不	9. pu⁴, not
146	要	10. yao⁴, want, will
163	那	11. na⁴, that; na³, which?
99	甚	12. shên² (with mo), what?
145	裏	13. li³, in
9	他	14. t'a¹, he
32	在	15. tsai⁴, at
75	東	16. tung¹, east
146	西	17. hsi¹, west
9	做	18. tso⁴, do, make
9	來	19. lai², come
6	了	20. liao³, past tense (-ed)

236 THE CHINESE LANGUAGE

85	沒	21	mei², not	111	知	31 chih¹, know
74	有	22	yu³, have	162	道	32 tao⁴, way
10	兒	23	êrh², son, noun indicator	118	等	33 têng³, wait
39	子	24	tsŭ³, son, noun indicator	120	給	34 kei³, give
167	錢	25	ch'ien², money, "cash"	32	坐	35 tso⁴, sit
64	拿	26	na², hold, take	154	買	36 mai³, buy
181	頭	27	t'ou², top, end, head	154	賣	37 mai⁴, sell
109	看	28	k'an⁴, look, read	37	大	38 ta⁴, great
147	見	29	chien⁴, see	149	說	39 shuo¹, speak
9	人	30	jên², man	7	些	40 hsieh¹, some

30	問	**41** wên⁴, ask	1	一	**51** i¹, one
149	話	**42** hua⁴, talk, language	7	二	**52** êrh⁴, two
149	請	**43** ch'ing³, please, invite, request	1	三	**53** san¹, three
1	下	**44** hsia⁴, down, below	31	四	**54** ssŭ⁴, four
60	很	**45** hên³, very	7	五	**55** wu³, five
42	小	**46** hsiao³, little, small	12	六	**56** liu⁴, six
1	上	**47** shang⁴, above, upon, to	1	七	**57** ch'i¹, seven
162	過	**48** kuo⁴, pass, cross, exceed	12	八	**58** pa¹, eight
156	走	**49** tsou³, walk, go	5	九	**59** chiu³, nine
38	好	**50** hao³, good	24	十	**60** shih², ten

106	百	**61** pai³, hundred	60	得	**71** tê², obtain, succeed; tei³, must
24	千	**62** ch'ien¹, thousand	163	都	**72** tou¹, all
140	萬	**63** wan⁴, myriad	66	數	**73** shu³, count; shu⁴, number
173	零	**64** ling², fraction, zero	72	明	**74** ming², bright
11	兩	**65** liang³, two, ounce	106	白	**75** pai², white
118	第	**66** ti⁴, number, indicator of ordinal numbers	61	懂	**76** tung³, understand
36	多	**67** to¹, many, more	72	日	**77** jih⁴, day, sun
42	少	**68** shao³, few	39	字	**78** tzŭ⁴, character, letter
52	幾	**69** chi³, some, how many	40	寫	**79** hsieh³, write
149	記	**70** chi⁴, remember, record	72	時	**80** shih², time

9	候	81 hou⁴, wait	130	能	91 nêng², can
31	囘	82 hui², return, turn	43	就	92 chiu⁴, then, only, immediately
37	天	83 t'ien¹, day, heaven	144	行	93 hsing², suit, proceed
30	告	84 kao⁴, tell, accuse	37	太	94 t'ai⁴, too
149	訴	85 su⁴, tell	30	可	95 k'o³, but, can
128	聽	86 t'ing¹, listen, hear	64	把	96 pa¹, take hold of; pa⁴, a handle; pa³, handful
73	會	87 hui⁴, able, a society	61	怎	97 tsên³, how?
41	封	88 fêng¹, envelope, classifier of letters	30	吃	98 ch'ih¹, eat
9	信	89 hsin⁴, letter, believe	184	飯	99 fan⁴, cooked food
60	後	90 hou⁴, after, behind	6	事	100 shih⁴, affair

61	情	**101** ch'ing², feelings	36	外	**111** wai⁴, out, outside
140	若	**102** jo⁴, if	154	貴	**112** kuei⁴, expensive, honourable
118	管	**103** kuan³, care, take charge of	9	便	**113** p'ien², cheap; pien⁴, convenient
169	關	**104** kuan¹, shut	40	宜	**114** i², proper
169	門	**105** mên², door	18	前	**115** ch'ien², before, front
169	開	**106** k'ai¹, open	40	實	**116** shih², true
167	錯	**107** ts'o⁴, wrong	101	用	**117** yung⁴, use
28	去	**108** ch'u⁴, go	83	氣	**118** ch'i⁴, vapour; breath, anger
17	出	**109** ch'u¹, out, forth, issue	86	熱	**119** jo⁴, hot
40	家	**110** chia¹, home, family	116	穿	**120** ch'uan¹, wear, to go through

145	衣	**121** i¹, clothes		**131** hsien¹, before, first
145	裳	**122** shang¹, clothes	10 先	**132** shêng¹, beget, born, raw
15	冷	**123** lêng³, cold	100 生	**133** tso², yesterday
61	快	**124** k'uai⁴, fast, quick, sharp	72 昨	**134** chiao⁴, order, call cause
38	姓	**125** hsing⁴, surname	30 叫	**135** ta³, beat, from
75	椅	**126** i³, chair	64 打	**136** wang⁴, forget
64	擱	**127** ko¹, put	61 忘	**137** yeh³, also
159	車	**128** ch'ê¹ cart, carriage	5 也	**138** hai², yet, still; huan², repay
61	您	**129** nin², you sir	162 還	**139** wei⁴, for, because; wei², to do
120	納	**130** na⁴, collect, pay taxes	87 爲	**140** yin¹, cause, reason
			31 因	

163	鄉	**141** hsiang¹, country
18	到	**142** tao⁴, to, arrive at
162	遠	**143** yuan³, far
30	同	**144** t'ung², same, with
203	點	**145** tien³, a little, dot, point
220	紙	**146** chih³, paper
64	找	**147** chao³, search, seek
61	怕	**148** p'a⁴, fear, expect
122	罷	**149** pa⁴, a final particle
40	完	**150** wan², finish
72	晚	**151** wan³, late
61	愛	**152** ai⁴, to like
75	樣	**153** yang¹, fashion, kind, pattern
96	現	**154** hsien⁴, now, ready
9	住	**155** chu⁴, live, tight, fast, stop
72	晌	**156** shang³, noon
72	早	**157** tsao³, early
156	起	**158** ch'i³, rise, get up, commence
173	雨	**159** yü³, rain
51	年	**160** nien², year

9	今	**161** chin¹, now	187	馬	**171** ma³, horse
168	長	**162** ch'ang², long; chang³, grow	61	想	**172** hsiang³, think
111	短	**163** tuan³, short	85	準	**173** chun³, positive, accurate, sanction
75	板	**164** pan³, board	140	花	**174** hua¹, spend, flower
9	借	**165** chieh⁴, borrow	40	定	**175** ting⁴, fix
149	該	**166** kai¹, owe, ought	125	老	**176** lao³, old, ever
157	跟	**167** kên¹, with, from, follow, heel	3	主	**177** chu³, master, ruler
104	病	**168** ping⁴, illness, ill	61	意	**178** i⁴, intention, idea
40	官	**169** kuan¹, official, officer	61	思	**179** ssŭ¹, think, reflect
123	着	**170** cho, verbal particle	61	慢	**180** man⁴, slow

162	181 連	lien², connect, even (adv.), and
149	182 認	jên⁴, recognise, admit
50	183 帶	tai⁴, carry with one, girdle
24	184 半	pan⁴, half
172	185 雖	sui¹, although
86	186 然	jan², but, yet
89	187 父	fu⁴, father
147	188 親	ch'in¹, relative, self
89	189 爺	yeh², sire, grandfather
30	190 啊	ah¹, an exclamation
49	191 已	i³, already, final particle
120	192 經	ching¹, past, a religious, "office," canon, ritual.
149	193 許	hsu³, may, might, promise, possibly
9	194 件	chien⁴, item, a classifier
75	195 相	hsiang¹, mutual
50	196 幫	pang¹, help
61	197 忙	mang², hurry, busy
75	198 本	pên³, root, source
41	199 將	chiang¹, take, on the point of
62	200 或	huo⁴, or, perhaps, if, either

64	挨	**201** ai², suffer; ai¹, close to	20	勻	**211** yün², divide, set apart
145	被	**202** pei⁴, suffer, endure, coverlet	74	朋	**212** p'êng², friend
29	受	**203** shou⁴, receive, suffer, endure	29	友	**213** yu³, friend, friendly
94	狗	**204** kou³, dog	75	樂	**214** lo⁴, pleasure, laugh; yüeh⁴, music
19	勞	**205** lao², trouble, toil	19	力	**215** li⁴, strength, force
19	動	**206** tung⁴, move, touch	18	剛	**216** kang¹, just now, hard
85	法	**207** fa², remedy; fa³, rule	120	纔	**217** ts'ai², then, just now
116	空	**208** k'ung¹, empty	149	誰	**218** shui², who
170	除	**209** ch'u², except	31	國	**219** kuo², country, kingdom
120	總	**210** tsung³, all, generally	140	英	**220** ying¹, English, eminent

64	提	221 t'i², mention; ti¹, lift up	22	匠	231 chiang⁴, mechanic, workman
9	像	222 hsiang⁴, like, likeness, image	167	鐘	232 chung¹, bell, clock
160	辦	223 pan⁴, manage, transact, arrange	64	按	233 an⁴, according to; ên⁴, press down
18	別	224 pieh², another, do not, distinguish	131	卧	234 wo⁴, recline, lie down
71	既	225 chi⁴, since	63	房	235 tang², house, room
140	薦	226 chien⁴, introduce, recommend	145	表	236 piao³, watch
85	活	227 huo², alive, moveable, work	113	禮	237 li³, worship, ceremony, offerings
50	常	228 ch'ang², constantly, often	64	拜	238 pai⁴, salute, pay calls
102	當	229 tang¹, ought, at time of; tang⁴, suitable, pawn	32	堂	239 t'ang², hall, chapel
75	木	230 mu⁴, wood	41	對	240 tui⁴, to compare, correct, opposite, a pair

48	差	**241** ch'a¹, differ; ch'ai⁴, to send, depute	158	訊	**251** tan¹, delay
203	黑	**242** hei¹, black, dark	61	悞	**252** wu⁴, hinder, neglect
109	瞧	**243** ch'iao², look, look at	105	發	**253** fa¹, put forth
64	掉	**244** tiao⁴, fall	162	送	**254** sung⁴, send, present to, escort
85	河	**245** ho², river, canal	64	指	**255** chih³, point; chih², finger
75	棹	**246** cho¹, table	104	疼	**256** t'êng², pain, ache, love dearly
44	屋	**247** wu¹, room	18	利	**257** li⁴, gain, interest
30	商	**248** shang¹, consult, merchant	40	害	**258** hai⁴, injure, injury
166	量	**249** liang², estimate; liang⁴, capacity	112	碰	**259** p'êng⁴, bump, strike against, collide
18	刻	**250** k'o⁴, carve, quarter of an hour	109	睡	**260** shui⁴, sleep

147	覺	261	chiao^{4}, chueh^{2}, perceive, feel
98	瓶	262	p‘ing^{2}, jar, bottle
82	毛	263	mao^{2}, hair, fur
120	緊	264	chin^{3}, tight, pressing
102	畫	265	hua^{4}, draw, picture
181	顏	266	yen^{2}, colour
139	色	267	sê^{4}, colour
81	比	268	pi^{3}, compare, compare with
9	價	269	chia^{4}, price
9	值	270	chih^{2}, price, worth

8	交	271	chiao^{1}, deliver to, friendship
8	京	272	ching^{1}, metropolis
32	城	273	ch‘êng^{2}, walled city, city wall
176	面	274	mien^{4}, surface, face
172	離	275	li^{2}, distant from, separate from, part from
166	里	276	li^{3}, a Chinese mile
72	春	277	ch‘un^{1}, spring
118	算	278	suan^{4}, reckon
35	夏	279	hsia^{4}, summer
115	秋	280	ch‘iu^{1}, autumn

		281			291	
15	冬	tung¹, winter	187	騎	ch'i², ride
13	再	282 tsai⁴, again	184	餧	292 wei⁴, feed (animal or child)
19	勸	283 ch'uan⁴, advise, exhort	119	糧	293 liang², grain
102	留	284 liu², keep, retain, detain	184	食	294 shih², food
61	心	285 hsin¹, heart, mind, centre	141	號	295 hao⁴, mark, label, stable, name
30	和	286 ho², with, harmony, unite	31	圈	296 ch'uan¹, circle, encircle; chuan⁴, coop, pen
167	釘	287 ting⁴, nail, to nail	191	鬧	297 nao⁴, bustle, tumult, break out
63	所	288 so³, place, which, all which	86	火	298 huo³, fire
9	以	289 i³, according to, use	21	北	299 pei³, north
130	脾	290 p'i², temper, disposition	32	地	300 ti⁴, ground, place

70	方	301 fang¹, square, region		銀	311 yin², silver
62	戚	302 ch'i¹, relative	162	進	312 chin⁴, enter, advance
169	閒	303 hsien², disengaged, leisure	187	駕	313 chia⁴, chariot
30	只	304 chih³, only	64	換	314 huan⁴, exchange
40	客	305 k'o⁴, stranger, visitor, guest	113	票	315 p'iao⁴, ticket, banknote
53	店	306 tien⁴, inn, hotel	85	洋	316 yang², ocean, foreign
69	新	307 hsin¹, new, recently	32	塊	317 k'uai⁴, bit, piece
128	聞	308 wên², hear, smell	9	使	318 shih³, employ
144	行	309 hang², business firm, row, order in series	132	自	319 tzǔ⁴, self, from
50	市	310 shih⁴, market	112	碎	320 sui⁴, fragments, broken into bits

THE CHINESE LANGUAGE

162	逛	**321** kuang⁴, ramble, visit	142	蛋	**331** tan⁴, egg
53	廚	**322** ch'u², a cook	85	湯	**332** t'ang¹, soup, gravy
140	菜	**323** ts'ai⁴, vegetables, provisions, food	140	茶	**333** ch'a², tea
181	預	**324** yü⁴, beforehand	140	葉	**334** yeh⁴, leaf
9	備	**325** pei⁴, prepare	119	糖	**335** t'ang², sugar
86	煮	**326** chu³, boil	197	鹽	**336** yen², salt
196	鷄	**327** chi¹, chicken, fowl	20	包	**337** pao¹, wrap up, wrapper, bundle
86	烤	**328** k'ao³, roast	33	壺	**338** hu², kettle, pot
93	牛	**329** niu², ox, cow	112	碗	**339** wan³, bowl
130	肉	**330** jou⁴, flesh, meat	85	水	**340** shui³, water

251

		341				351	
108	盤		p'an², plate	85	灌		kuan⁴, to water, pour into a bottle, &c.
112	碟	342	tieh², saucer, small plate	170	隨	352	sui², follow, comply with
18	刀	343	tao¹, knife, sword	85	渴	353	k'o³, thirsty
29	叉	344	ch'a¹, fork, forked	30	喝	354	ho¹, drink
21	匙	345	ch'ih², spoon	30	單	355	tan¹, single, odd (of numbers)
38	奶	346	nai³, milk	65	收	356	shou¹, collect, receive, put away
195	鮮	347	hsien¹, fresh	120	紅	357	hung², red
32	壞	348	huai⁴, spoiled	164	酒	358	chiu³, wine, spirit
167	鐵	349	t'ieh³, iron	86	煙	359	yen¹, tobacco, smoke
108	盒	350	ho², small box, covered box	140	荷	360	ho², lotus

145	袋	**361** tai⁴, bag, pocket, purse
85	淡	**362** tan⁴, weak, watery
149	試	**363** shih⁴, try, test, experiment
149	讓	**364** jang⁴, permit, yield, waive
44	局	**365** chu², depot, store
163	郵	**366** yu², government postal house
66	政	**367** chêng⁴, rule, government
64	手	**368** shou³, hand
154	費	**369** fei⁴, expend, waste
66	放	**370** fang⁴, to place, let go
144	衙	**371** ya², government office, tribunal
149	謝	**372** hsieh⁴, thank
167	鋪	**373** p'u⁴, shop; p'u¹, spread out
64	掌	**374** chang³, control, palm of the hand
75	櫃	**375** kuei⁴, till, counter, cupboard
60	從	**376** ts'ung², from
120	緣	**377** yuan², because, affinity
66	故	**378** ku⁴, cause
189	高	**379** kao¹, high, tall, eminent
111	矮	**380** ai³, short, low

	381
40	k'uan¹, broad, indulgent
	382
116	chai³, narrow
	383
190	sung¹, loose, slack, loosen
	384
140	pao², thin
	385
30	lo¹, final particle
	386
85	liang², cool
	387
140	chao², hit the mark, catch (as a cold)
	388
182	fêng¹, wind
	389
182	kua¹, blow (of wind)
	390
24	nan², south

	391
10	kuang¹, bright, rays, flame, only
	392
109	shêng³, province, economise
	393
181	shun⁴, following, obedient
	394
9	wei⁴, gentleman, seat
	395
162	chin⁴, near
	396
4	chiu³, long since, a long time
	397
9	yang³, look up to, look up
	398
86	mei², coal
	399
62	ch'êng², accomplish, complete, fractional part
	400
57	ti⁴, younger brother

10	兄	**401** hsiung¹, elder brother
30	哥	**402** ko¹, elder brother
38	姐	**403** chieh³, elder sister
38	妹	**404** mei⁴, younger sister
2	中	**405** chung¹, centre; chung⁴, to pass an examination
169	間	**406** chien⁴, space between
75	杯	**407** pei¹, cup, tumbler
5	乾	**408** kan¹, dry, clean
85	淨	**409** ching⁴, pure, clean
85	洗	**410** hsi³, wash
96	玻	**411** po¹, vitreous
96	璃	**412** li², vitreous substance
64	擦	**413** ts'a¹, rub, wipe
50	布	**414** pu⁴, cotton cloth
18	刺	**415** la², to cut with a knife
120	繩	**416** shêng², rope, string
61	惜	**417** hsi¹, pity, regret
1	丟	**418** tiu¹, lose
18	剃	**419** t'i⁴, to shave the head
167	鉸	**420** chiao³, to cut with scissors or shears

190	髮	421 fa³, hair of the head		44	尺	431 ch'ih³, foot measure, a linear foot
18	削	422 hsiao¹, pare		41	寸	432 ts'un⁴, inch
118	筆	423 pi³, pen, pencil		39	學	433 hsueh², learn; hsiao², imitate
64	拇	424 mu³, thumb		32	墨	434 mo⁴, ink
112	破	425 p'o⁴, break		61	性	435 hsing⁴, disposition
102	甲	426 chia³, nails of finger or toe, armour		18	分	436 fên¹, divide, division, distinguish
140	落	427 lao⁴, to alight, fall, drop; la⁴, leave behind		73	書	437 shu¹, book
36	夥	428 huo³, comrade, partner		66	敢	438 kan³, venture, dare
149	計	429 chi⁴, calculate, plan		30	句	439 chü⁴, sentence
9	偷	430 t'ou¹, steal		61	念	440 nien⁴, recite, read aloud, study

128	聲	**441** shêng¹, sound, tone
180	音	**442** yin¹, sound, musical tone
74	月	**443** yueh⁴, month, moon
122	罪	**444** tsui⁴, fault, sin, punishment
49	己	**445** chi³, self
4	乏	**446** fa², tired
30	唉	**447** ai¹, exclamation of regret or annoyance
64	擠	**448** chi³, push, shove
157	跐	**449** ts'ai³, tread on
130	脚	**450** chiao³, the foot

113	神	**451** shên², deity, spirit, attention
39	孩	**452** hai², child
109	眞	**453** chên¹, true
61	憐	**454** lien², pity
80	母	**455** mu³, mother
78	死	**456** ssŭ³, die
30	喜	**457** hsi³, happiness, joy
76	歡	**458** huan¹, rejoice, happy
60	待	**459** tai⁴, treat, behave towards, wait
38	如	**460** ju², if, as, like

77	歲	461 sui⁴, year of age	48	工	471 kung¹, work, leisure, space of time
64	據	462 chu⁴, according to, evidence	37	夫	472 fu¹, man
100	產	463 ch'an³, bear, produce	118	笑	473 hsiao⁴, smile, laugh
75	業	464 yêh⁴, pursuit, property	172	難	474 nan², difficult
61	息	465 hsi², proceeds, breathe	40	容	475 jung², contain, endure
184	養	466 yang³, rear, nourish	72	易	476 i⁴, easy
9	倍	467 pei⁴, times, fold	73	最	477 tsui⁴, very, most
75	李	468 li³, prune, plum	181	頂	478 ting³, superlatively, top, oppose
30	口	469 k'ou³, mouth	157	跑	479 p'ao³, run
117	站	470 chan⁴, stand, stand up	130	腿	480 t'ui³, leg

#	字	Entry
30	咬	481 yao³, bite, bark at
130	腫	482 chung³, to swell
140	藥	483 yao⁴, drugs, medicine
64	抹	484 mo⁴, rub on; mo³, rub out
145	裝	485 chuang¹, pack, pretend
27	厚	486 hou⁴, thick
145	裁	487 ts'ai², cut out
120	縫	488 fêng², sew
145	褂	489 kua⁴, coat, outer jacket
30	合	490 ho², in harmony with, unite, fit
62	式	491 shih⁴, form, pattern
66	改	492 kai³, alter
112	砍	493 k'an³, to cut with a sword or chopper
130	肩	494 chien¹, shoulder
145	褲	495 k'u⁴, trousers
37	奇	496 ch'i², strange, wonderful
61	怪	497 kuai⁴, weird, strange, object to
61	忽	498 hu¹, suddenly
135	舒	499 shu¹, ease, comfort, open out
32	坦	500 t'an³, quiet

96	理	501	li³, heed, arrange, principle	18	劑	511 chi⁴, dose
164	醒	502	hsing³, awake	77	武	512 wu³, military
30	嗓	503	sang³, gullet, larynx	109	眼	513 yen³, eye, opening
85	滿	504	man³, full	109	睛	514 ching¹, iris, eyes
158	身	505	shên¹, body	75	村	515 ts'un¹, village
86	燒	506	shao¹, burn, burning	53	庄	516 chuang¹, village, farm-house
158	躺	507	t'ang³, lie down	106	皇	517 huang², emperor, imperial
140	蓋	508	kai⁴, cover, build	40	宮	518 kung¹, palace
116	窩	509	wo¹, nest, den, nook	144	街	519 chieh¹, street
75	概	510	kai⁴, the whole	70	旁	520 p'ang², side

162	邊	521 pien¹, edge, margin, side	142	螞	531 ma³, wasp
85	溜	522 liu¹, ramble, flow	142	蜂	532 fêng¹, wasp, bee
64	搭	523 ta¹, add	181	領	533 ling³, collar, guide, lead, receive, draw
96	班	524 pan¹, troupe, rank, class	191	鬨	534 hung⁴, frighten off, clamour
30	名	525 ming², personal name, name, reputation	142	螫	535 chê¹, sting (of a wasp, scorpion, &c.)
91	片	526 p'ien⁴, strip, slip	96	玩	536 wan⁴, play
170	陽	527 yang², sun (with t'ai), convex	9	令	537 ling⁴, honourable
75	樹	528 shu⁴, tree	40	寶	538 pao³, precious
53	底	529 ti³, below	109	眷	539 chüan⁴, family
170	陰	530 yin¹, shade, cloudy, concave	9	偏	540 p'ien¹, deflected, partial

		舊	**541** chiu⁴, old			目	**551** mu⁴, eye
134				109			
85		澡	**542** tsao³, bathe	170		院	**552** yuan⁴, courtyard, college, &c.
108		盆	**543** p'ên², basin	64		擺	**553** pai³, spread out, arrange
130		胰	**544** i², soap	156		越	**554** yueh⁴, exceed, the more
85		泡	**545** p'ao⁴, soak, bubble, blister	1		並	**555** ping⁴, all, moreover, together with
64		拧	**546** ning², wring, twist	86		無	**556** wu², not
72		曬	**547** shai⁴, dry in the sun	122		罵	**557** ma⁴, abuse, curse
64		挂	**548** kua⁴, hang up	149		論	**558** lun⁴, discuss, discourse
64		疊	**549** tieh², fold up	181		願	**559** yüan⁴, wish, desire, a vow
30		喒	**550** tsan², we two (with *to*, when)	61		應	**560** ying¹, ought; ying⁴, answer

154	賠	561	p'ei², forfeit, make good		抬	571 t'ai², carry between two, lift up

154	賠	**561** p'ei², forfeit, make good		64	抬	**571** t'ai², carry between two, lift up
73	替	**562** t'i⁴, substitute, in place of		12	其	**572** ch'i², the, he, she, it
130	膽	**563** tan³, courage		159	輕	**573** ch'ing¹, light
76	次	**564** tz'ŭ⁴, occasion, order, inferior		50	帽	**574** mao⁴, hat, cap
167	鏡	**565** ching⁴, mirror		162	運	**575** yun⁴, revolve, transport
30	各	**566** ko⁴, each, every; ko², self		9	保	**576** pao³, protect, guarantee
22	匣	**567** hsia², casket, box		170	險	**577** hsien³, danger, dangerous
118	箱	**568** hsiang¹, box, trunk		75	架	**578** chia⁴, frame, stand, staging
166	重	**569** chung⁴, heavy, grave		64	拉	**579** la¹, drag, pull
64	扛	**570** k'ang², carry on the shoulders		64	撒	**580** sa¹, let go, let loose

149	謊	581 huang³, lie, falsehood		野	591 yeh³, wild, rude, desert
137	船	582 ch'uan², boat, ship	134	擧	592 chu³, raise, introduce
159	輪	583 lun², wheel	167	鎗	593 ch'iang¹, gun, firearm
82	毡	584 chan¹, blanket, felt	75	根	594 kên¹, root
85	海	585 hai³, sea	120	絆	595 pan⁴, trip, lasso
173	電	586 tien⁴, electricity	157	跌	596 tieh¹, tsai¹, tumble, fall
32	報	587 pao⁴, report, requite	75	折	597 shê², snap; chê², decide
31	圍	588 wei², surround, enclose	86	燈	598 têng¹, lamp
75	林	589 lin², wood, forest	64	挪	599 no², remove
77	步	590 pu⁴, pace, step	50	帳	600 chang⁴, curtain, tent

154	貨	601 huo⁴, goods, wares		51	平	611 p'ing², level, even
85	汗	602 han⁴, perspiration		29	又	612 yu⁴, again, moreover
145	衫	603 shan¹, shirt		130	肯	613 k'ên³, willing
119	粗	604 ts'u¹, coarse		19	功	614 kung¹, meritorious, service, labour
120	細	605 hsi⁴, fine, delicate		128	耳	615 êrh³, ear
141	處	606 ch'u⁴, place; chu³, punish		75	朶	616 to³, bud, lobe
75	材	607 ts'ai², material		128	聾	617 lung², deaf
68	料	608 liao⁴, material, estimate		9	偶	618 ou³, accidental; with the following, occasionally
149	講	609 chiang³, explain, expound, argue		89	爾	619 êrh³, with above, occasionally; you (classical)
116	究	610 chiu¹, investigate		164	醉	620 tsui⁴, intoxicated

57	殼	621 kou⁴, enough	167	金	631 chin¹, gold
151	豈	622 ch'i³, how?	47	州	632 chou¹, departmental district
162	違	623 wei², oppose, disregard	67	文	633 wên², civil, literary
115	程	624 ch'êng², stage in a journey	154	賤	634 chien⁴, common, vulgar, cheap
64	托	625 t'o¹, rely on, carry on the palm	66	教	635 chiao⁴, teach, creed
113	福	626 fu², felicity, prosperity	33	壽	636 shou⁴, longevity
53	府	627 fu³, your house, palace, prefecture	30	哪	637 na¹, final particle
64	承	628 ch'êng², receive, be recipient of	163	郎	638 lang², son, youth
11	內	629 nei⁴, within, interior	38	姑	639 ku¹, girl
61	惦	630 tien⁴, anxious, think of	38	娘	640 niang², mother, woman

38	妞	641 niu¹, lass	154	賸	651 shêng⁴, overplus, balance
172	雙	642 shuang¹, double, pair.	85	泥	652 ni², mud
177	靴	643 hsüeh¹, boots	140	草	653 ts'ao³, grass
162	退	644 t'ui⁴, reject, retreat	85	濕	654 shih¹, wet, moist, damp
107	皮	645 p'i², skin, fur, leather	145	襪	655 wa⁴, stockings
172	雇	646 ku⁴, hire	112	硬	656 ying⁴, hard, obstinate
30	另	647 ling⁴, separate, in addition	9	似	657 shih⁴, ssŭ⁴, like, similar
30	吊	648 tiao⁴, a thousand cash	85	油	658 yu², oil, grease, paint
156	趕	649 kan³, drive, by the time that, pursue	19	勁	659 chin⁴, muscle
187	騾	650 lo², mule	21	化	660 hua⁴, melt, transform

159	輭	**661** juan³, soft	9	倒	**671** tao³, pour, reverse, on the contrary
18	刮	**662** kua¹, scrape	93	牲	**672** shêng¹, animals
130	臉	**663** lien³, face, reputation	9	估	**673** ku¹, estimate, guess
112	磨	**664** mo², grind, rub	64	摸	**674** mo¹, feel for, grope for; ma¹, stroke
118	答	**665** ta¹, consent, reply	104	瘸	**675** ch'üeh², lame
85	深	**666** shên¹, deep	186	香	**676** hsiang¹, fragrant, incense
85	淺	**667** ch'ien³, shallow	85	漂	**677** p'iao¹, drift; with the following, sleek
130	脖	**668** po², neck	8	亮	**678** liang⁴, bright
157	踝	**669** huai², ankle-bone	104	瘦	**679** shou⁴, emaciated
188	骨	**670** ku³, bone; ku² t'ou, a bone	130	臕	**680** piao¹, corpulent (of animals)

120	累	681 lei⁴, weary, to weary		嫌	691 hsien², dislike, aversion
64	撩	682 liao¹, lift up	117	竟	692 ching⁴, only
157	蹶	683 chueh², heels (of a horse)	19	勤	693 ch'in², diligent
157	踢	684 t'i¹, to kick	154	類	694 lei⁴, class, category
30	啞	685 ya³, dumb	61	懶	695 lan³, idle
30	吧	686 pa¹, dumb, stammer	9	傘	696 san³, umbrella
102	畜	687 ch'u⁴, cattle	64	擉	697 ch'o¹, poke, prod
109	瞅	688 ch'ou³, gaze at, look at	9	仗	698 chang⁴, rely on, battle
9	催	689 ts'ui¹, urge, hasten	149	護	699 hu⁴, screen, protect
109	瞞	690 man², deceive, hoodwink	162	避	700 pi⁴, avoid

72	暑	701 shu³, summer heat		30	嚷	711 jang³, bawl, shout
80	每	702 mei³, each, every		12	公	712 kung¹, public, just
162	逢	703 fêng², meet with, encounter		154	賺	713 chuan⁴, make money, sell at a profit
162	遇	704 yu⁴, meet, happen		188	骯	714 ang¹, filthy
116	窮	705 ch'iung², poor		188	髒	715 tsang¹, dirty
62	戴	706 tai⁴, to wear on the head		64	掃	716 sao³, sweep
9	俗	707 su², common, vulgar		30	嘴	717 tsui³, muzzle, mouth
149	語	708 yu³, language		149	謙	718 ch'ien¹, modest, humble
105	登	709 têng¹, ascend, mount		162	遜	719 hsun⁴, humble, modest
30	吵	710 ch'ao¹,³, brawl, clamour		62	戲	720 hsi⁴, theatre, theatricals

120	約	**721** yo⁴, yüeh⁴, treaty, covenant with	38 媳	**731** hsi², wife
75	樓	**722** lou², an upper storey, two storied house	38 婦	**732** fu⁴, woman, wife
184	館	**723** kuan³, inn, eating shop	61 必	**733** pi⁴, must, certainly
64	拘	**724** chu¹, grasp, restrain	48 巧	**734** ch'iao³, lucky, opportune, skilful, artful
162	遵	**725** tsun¹, conform to, obey, honour	77 正	**735** chêng⁴, straight, orthodox
30	命	**726** ming⁴, command, fate	157 足	**736** tsu², enough, foot
31	園	**727** yuan², garden	85 湊	**737** ts'ou⁴, collect, assemble
32	坊	**728** fang¹, manufactory, ward	29 取	**738** ch'u³, to draw as money, fetch
18	初	**729** ch'u¹, commencement, at first	44 層	**739** ts'êng², a layer, a point
38	娶	**730** ch'u³, marry a wife	64 扣	**740** k'ou⁴, deduct, knock, button, discount

170	限	**741** hsien⁴, limit
72	景	**742** ching³, appearance
64	抽	**743** ch'ou¹, draw out, levy, shrink
166	厘	**744** li², thousandth of a tael
147	規	**745** kuei¹, rule, compasses, usage
111	矩	**746** chu³, rule, pattern
117	章	**747** chang¹, regulation
109	直	**748** chih², straight, straight on
30	含	**749** han², restrain;(with the following), reticent, vague
119	糊	**750** hu², to paste, foolish
9	僅	**751** chin³, barely, scarcely
30	囉	**752** lo², annoying
30	唆	**753** so¹, incite, stir up
51	幹	**754** kan⁴, do, attend to
118	簡	**755** chien³, concise, abridge
85	求	**756** ch'iu², solicit
15	決	**757** chueh², positively, decidedly
72	暖	**758** nuan³, warm
85	淘	**759** t'ao², wash out
154	貪	**760** t'an¹, covet

THE CHINESE LANGUAGE 273

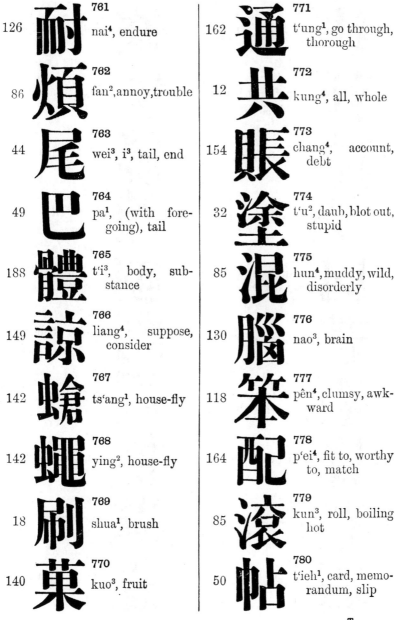

126	**761** 耐 nai⁴, endure
86	**762** 煩 fan², annoy, trouble
44	**763** 尾 wei³, i³, tail, end
49	**764** 巴 pa¹, (with foregoing), tail
188	**765** 體 t'i³, body, substance
149	**766** 諒 liang⁴, suppose, consider
142	**767** 蜦 ts'ang¹, house-fly
142	**768** 蠅 ying², house-fly
18	**769** 刷 shua¹, brush
140	**770** 菓 kuo³, fruit

162	**771** 通 t'ung¹, go through, thorough
12	**772** 共 kung⁴, all, whole
154	**773** 賬 chang⁴, account, debt
32	**774** 塗 t'u², daub, blot out, stupid
85	**775** 混 hun⁴, muddy, wild, disorderly
130	**776** 腦 nao³, brain
118	**777** 笨 pên⁴, clumsy, awkward
164	**778** 配 p'ei⁴, fit to, worthy to, match
85	**779** 滾 kun³, roll, boiling hot
50	**780** 帖 t'ieh¹, card, memorandum, slip

T

		往	781 wang³, towards, go
60			
115		種	782 chung⁴, plant; chung³, seed
119		粒	783 li⁴, grain, seed
38		妥	784 t'o³, satisfactory
30		向	785 hsiang⁴, towards, hitherto
140		苦	786 k'u³, bitter
9		假	787 chia³, false; chia⁴, leave of absence
75		條	788 t'iao², strip, clause
157		路	789 lu⁴, road
112		石	790 shih², stone

		修	791 hsiu¹, repair
9			
32		坑	792 kêng¹, pit, hole
120		繞	793 jao⁴, to wind
145		補	794 pu³, patch
18		刨	795 p'ao², dig
141		虧	796 k'uei¹, deficiency, loss
63		扇	797 shan⁴, fan
64		挑	798 t'iao¹, choose, carry on a pole
76		歇	799 hsieh¹, rest
61		急	800 chi², urgent, impatient

61	悶	801	mên⁴, melancholy, dull	64	撕	811 ssŭ¹, tear
61	慌	802	huang¹, agitated	167	針	812 chên¹, needle
46	山	803	shan¹, hill, mountain	120	線	813 hsien⁴, thread
53	廟	804	miao⁴, temple	177	靪	814 ting,⁴ a patch
9	伴	805	pan⁴, comrade, companion	120	結	815 chieh¹, tie, form; chieh², finish
72	暫	806	chan⁴, temporary, temporarily	181	顯	816 hsien³, apparent, conspicuous
1	且	807	ch'ieh³, moreover	86	照	817 chao⁴, to reflect, according to
130	脫	808	t'o¹, put off, avoid	32	執	818 chih², lay hold on
75	極	809	chi², utmost, extreme	85	添	819 t'ien¹, to add
74	望	810	wang⁴, to hope, towards, look towards	26	印	820 yin⁴, a seal, to print

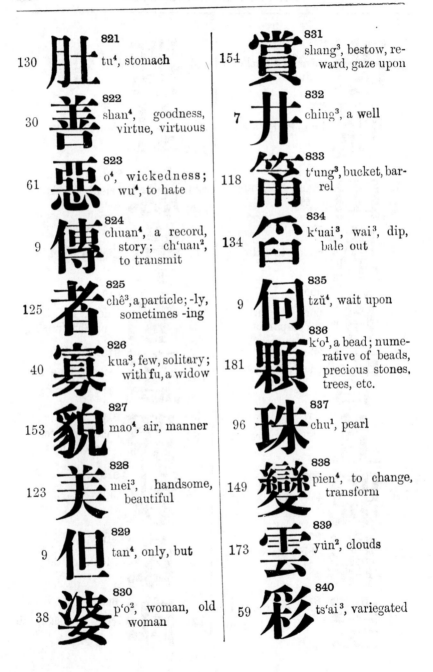

		肚	821 tu⁴, stomach
130			
30	善		822 shan⁴, goodness, virtue, virtuous
61	惡		823 o⁴, wickedness; wu⁴, to hate
9	傳		824 chuan⁴, a record, story; ch'uan², to transmit
125	者		825 chê³, a particle; -ly, sometimes -ing
40	寡		826 kua³, few, solitary; with fu, a widow
153	貌		827 mao⁴, air, manner
123	美		828 mei³, handsome, beautiful
9	但		829 tan⁴, only, but
38	婆		830 p'o², woman, old woman
154	賞		831 shang³, bestow, reward, gaze upon
7	井		832 ching³, a well
118	筩		833 t'ung³, bucket, barrel
134	舀		834 k'uai³, wai³, dip, bale out
9	伺		835 tzŭ⁴, wait upon
181	顆		836 k'o¹, a bead; numerative of beads, precious stones, trees, etc.
96	珠		837 chu¹, pearl
149	變		838 pien⁴, to change, transform
173	雲		839 yün², clouds
59	彩		840 ts'ai³, variegated

182	飄	841 p'iao¹, whirled by the wind, floating in the air	10	免	851 mien³, avoid, dispense with
149	詫	842 ch'a⁴, to brag (classical), surprised	30	吐	852 t'u³,⁴, spit out, vomit
102	異	843 i⁴, strange	9	仙	853 hsien¹, a fairy, genii
2	丫	844 ya¹, forked	93	物	854 wu⁴, things, articles
85	浪	845 lang⁴, waves, dissipated, profligate	75	權	855 ch'uan², power, authority
61	恟	846 mien³, shy, bashful	133	至	856 chih⁴, reach, arrive at. Rad. 133
61	恦	847 t'ien³, shy, bashful	102	由	857 yu², by, through, by means of
164	醜	848 ch'ou³, ugly, offensive	162	遞	858 ti⁴, hand to
157	跳	849 t'iao⁴, jump	27	原	859 yuan², origin
64	撿	850 chien³, pick up, pick out	38	委	860 wei³, depute

64	搖	861 yao², shake	181	頓	871 tun⁴, time, turn, to bow, numerative of meals, beatings, etc.
75	柳	862 liu³, willow	38	媽	872 ma¹, nurse, mother
121	罐	863 kuan⁴, jar, mug, canister	59	影	873 ying³, shadow, vestige
30	噘	864 chueh¹, pout out the lips	142	蝦	874 ha², frog
64	抱	865 pao⁴, embrace, hold in the arms, cherish	142	蟆	875 ma¹, frog
61	怨	866 yuan⁴, resentment, ill-will	30	嗳	876 ai¹, exclamation of pain, pleasure or surprise
130	胡	867 hu², blindly, recklessly	75	棍	877 kun⁴, a stick
55	弄	868 nung⁴, make, prepare, bring about	170	隔	878 ko², separated, a partition
9	傢	869 chia¹, household furniture, effects	90	牆	879 ch'iang², wall
9	伙	870 huo³, household furniture	140	藏	880 ts'ang, hide, conceal

40	密	**881** mi⁴, close together, thick, secret		162	迷	**891** mi², puzzled, bewildered
184	餓	**882** o⁴, hungry		44	屈	**892** ch'ü¹, bent, injustice
30	哭	**883** k'u¹, to cry		30	呢	**893** ni¹, interrogative particle, final particle
167	鑽	**884** tsuan¹, to bore, pierce, a gimlet		66	救	**894** chiu⁴, to rescue
94	猜	**885** ts'ai¹, to guess		115	秀	**895** hsiu⁴, elegant, accomplished
96	王	**886** wang², prince		9	佳	**896** chia¹, good, excellent, fine
61	恰	**887** ch'ia¹, timely		127	耦	**897** ou³, match, pair
61	慈	**888** tz'ŭ², kind, kindness, mercy		64	扶	**898** fu², assist, hold up
61	悲	**889** pei¹, pity, sympathy, sad		64	撫	**899** fu³, pacify
61	忍	**890** jên³, endure		126	而	**900** êrh², and, yet

102	畝	901 mu³, Chinese acre	9	傻	911 sha³, foolish, simple
151	豆	902 tou⁴, bean	134	興	912 hsing⁴, spirits, feelings
102	男	903 nan², male, man	64	扔	913 jêng¹, throw, throw away
44	屠	904 t'u², to butcher	116	窗	914 ch'uang¹, window
63	戶	905 hu⁴, door, family	87	爬	915 p'a², climb, crawl
31	圓	906 yuan², round	148	解	916 chieh³, explain, undo, get rid of
140	藍	907 lan², blue	167	鈴	917 ling², small bell
120	綠	908 lu⁴, green	167	鐺	918 tang¹, pedlar's gong
50	希	909 hsi¹, rare, seldom	180	響	919 hsiang³, to sound, sound
122	罕	910 han³, rare, seldom	30	呀	920 ya¹, exclamation, final sound

64	摔	921	shuai¹, tumble, fall from	159	輩	931 pei⁴, a generation
10	兇	922	hsiung¹, malevolent, cruel	31	困	932 k'un⁴, sleepy
86	爐	923	lu², stove, fireplace, grate	109	盹	933 tun³, nod with sleep
36	夢	924	mêng⁴, a dream, to dream	86	熟	934 shu², ripe, mature, well acquainted with
30	哼	925	hêng¹, to grunt, groan; an exclamation	64	抓	935 chua¹, grab, clutch
66	整	926	chêng³, complete, whole, entire	30	喊	936 han³, cry aloud
94	猪	927	chu¹, pig	30	嘎	937 ka¹, cackle
32	罎	928	t'an², earthenware jar	187	驚	938 ching¹, alarm, terror
85	消	929	hsiao¹, melt, dissolve	64	挾	939 chia¹, carry under the arm
64	推	930	t'ui¹, push	162	追	940 chui¹, pursue

30	哎	941 ai¹, an ejaculation	61	恩	951 en¹, grace, favour, kindness
30	哟	942 yueh¹, an ejaculation	85	江	952 chiang¹, river
130	胖	943 p'ang⁴, fat, corpulent	85	湖	953 hu², lake
30	喘	944 ch'uan³, to gasp for breath	120	縣	954 hsien⁴, department, district
69	斧	945 fu³, axe	118	籍	955 chi², register of population, place of domicile
75	榦	946 kan⁴, stem, trunk	172	雙	956 chih¹, numerative of ships, birds, etc.
154	財	947 ts'ai², property, wealth	85	沿	957 yen², bank, edge
32	埋	948 mai², bury	120	綁	958 pang³, bind, tie up
18	剝	949 pao¹, flay	40	宰	959 tsai³, slaughter animals
39	存	950 ts'un², retain, preserve	61	慘	960 ts'an³, pitiable, pitiful, cruel

46	岸	**961** an⁴, shore, bank
154	贖	**962** shu², ransom, redeem
154	賊	**963** tsei², thief, robber
32	均	**964** chun¹, equal, uniform
64	撐	**965** ch'êng¹, to punt, pole, push off
9	僻	**966** pi⁴, quiet, secluded
174	靜	**967** ching⁴, quiet, still
88	殺	**968** sha¹, kill
12	全	**969** ch'üan², all, complete
60	彼	**970** pi³, that
77	此	**971** tz'ŭ³, this
64	捆	**972** k'un³, bind
30	唧	**973** hsien², hold in the mouth
85	浮	**974** fou², fu², float, swim
156	趨	**975** t'ang¹, wade
30	啃	**976** k'ên³, gnaw
131	臨	**977** lin², to approach, neighbouring
30	嚎	**978** hao², howl, wail
61	愚	**979** yü², simple, foolish
84	民	**980** min², people, subjects

138	良	981 liang², good	75	榜	991 pang³, list of names; with yang, example
170	附	982 fu⁴, near	85	永	992 yung³, everlasting
167	鎮	983 chên⁴, market-town	149	許	993 hsu³, to permit, perhaps, might
64	攏	984 lung³, drag, lie alongside	149	言	994 yen², words
64	搜	985 sou¹, search	196	鳥	995 niao³, bird
137	艙	986 ts'ang¹, hold of a ship	195	魚	996 yu², a fish
154	臟	987 tsang¹, booty	92	牙	997 ya², teeth
1	世	988 shih⁴, the world, a generation	119	米	998 mi³, uncooked rice
154	負	989 fu⁴, ungrateful for	69	斤	999 chin¹, catty, Chinese pound
123	義	990 i⁴, kindness, public, public spirit, loyalty, high-mindedness	209	鼻	1000 pi², nose

INDEX OF CHARACTERS

Arranged under their Radicals.

1. 一 51	7. 二 52	作 same as 18
七 57	井 832	伺 835
三 53	五 55	使 318
上 47	些 40	來 19
下 44		便 113
不 9		俗 707
且 807	8. 亠	保 576
丟 418	交 271	像 869
並 555	京 272	信 89
世 988	亮 678	修 791
		倍 467
2. 丨		備 325
中 405	9. 人 30	個 2
丫 844	今 161	們 8
	他 14	倒 671
3. 丶	仗 698	候 81
主 177	仙 853	借 165
	令 537	傳 824
4. 丿	伙 870	值 270
久 396	以 289	假 787
乏 446	仰 397	做 18
	件 194	偶 618
5. 乙	估 673	偏 540
九 59	你 4	偷 430
也 137	伴 805	傘 696
乾 408	似 657	催 689
	但 829	僅 751
6. 亅	佳 896	像 222
了 20	位 394	價 269
事 100	住 155	儳 911
		僻 966

10. 儿
兄 401
先 131
兕 922
光 391
兒 23
兔 851

11. 入
內 629
兩 65
全 969

12. 八 58
公 712
六 56
共 772
其 572

13. 冂
再 282

14. 冖

15. 冫
冬 281
冷 123
決 757

16. 几

17. 凵
出 109

18. 刀 343
分 436
初 729

別 224
刨 795
利 257
刮 662
到 142
刷 769
刺 415
刻 250
剃 419
削 422
前 115
剛 216
剝 949
劑 511

19. 力 215
功 614
勁 659
動 206
勞 205
勤 693
勸 283

20. 勹
勻 211
包 337

21. 匕
化 660
北 299
匙 345

22. 匚
匠 231
匣 567

23. 匸

24. 十 60
千 62
半 184
南 390

25. 卜

26. 卩
印 820

27. 厂
厚 486
原 859

28. 厶
去 108

29. 又 612
叉 344
友 213
受 203
取 738

30. 口 469
句 439
另 647
只 304
吊 648
叫 134
可 95
吃 98
各 566
合 490
同 144
吐 852
呢 893

哎 941	嚥 864	**33.** 士
名 525	嘎 937	壺 338
向 785	囉 752	壽 636
吧 686	噯 876	
呀 920		**34.** 夂
吵 710		
告 84	**31.** 囗	**35.** 夊
含 749	四 54	夏 279
命 726	因 140	
咬 481	回 82	**36.** 夕
咯 385	圈 296	外 111
和 286	國 219	多 67
哪 637	圍 588	够 same as 621
哥 402	困 932	夥 428
唆 753	圓 906	夢 924
哼 925	園 727	
唉 447		**37.** 大 **38**
喘 944		天 83
啊 190	**32.** 土	太 94
喲 942	在 15	夫 472
問 41	地 300	奇 496
哭 883	坊 728	
商 248	坐 35	**38.** 女
喏 976	均 964	如 460
啞 685	坑 792	奶 346
善 822	坭 same as 652	好 50
喂 same as 292	坦 500	妞 641
嗜 550	城 273	妥 784
喊 936	堂 239	委 860
喜 457	埋 948	妹 404
喝 354	執 818	姐 403
嘲 973	報 587	姑 639
喫 same as 98	塊 317	姓 125
單 355	塗 774	娘 640
嗓 503	墰 same as 928	婆 830
嘴 717	墨 434	
嚷 711	壞 348	
嚎 978		

娶 730,
婦 732
媳 731
嫌 691
媽 872

39. 子 24
字 78
存 950
孩 452
學 433

40. 宀
完 150
官 169
定 175
宜 114
客 305
宮 518
害 258
家 110
容 475
密 881
宰 959
寶 116
寫 79
寬 381
寶 538
寡 826

41. 寸 432
封 88
對 240
將 199

42. 小 46
少 68

43. 尢
就 92

44. 尸
尺 431
尾 763
局 365
屈 892
屋 247
屠 904
層 739

45. 屮

46. 山 803
岸 961

47. 川
州 632

48. 工 471
巧 734
差 241

49. 己 445
巳 191
巴 764

50. 巾
市 310
布 414
希 909
帖 780
帳 600
滯 183

常 228
帽 574
封帛 196

51. 干
平 611
年 160
幹 754

52. 幺
幾 69

53. 广
庄 516
底 529
店 306
府 627
廚 322
廟 804

54. 廴

55. 廾
弄 868

56. 弋

57. 弓
弟 400
彀 621

58. 彐

59. 彡
彩 840
影 873

THE CHINESE LANGUAGE

60. 彳	慈 888	找 147
往 781	憫 847	扶 898
待 459	恤 846	承 628
彼 970	想 172	把 96
很 45	意 178	折 597
後 90	慌 802	抓 935
得 71	惡 823	抬 571
從 376	愛 152	抽 743
	慘 960	抱 865
	憐 454	拉 579
61. 心 285	懂 76	拇 424
必 733	應 560	拏 }26
忙 197	懶 695	拿 }
忍 890		抹 484
忘 136		拘 724
快 124	62. 戈	挪 599
忽 498	成 399	拜 238
念 440	式 491	指 255
怠 97	我 7	按 233
怕 148	或 300	挑 798
思 179	戚 302	挾 939
急 800	戲 720	挨 201
性 435	戴 706	捆 972
怪 497		掉 244
慢 180		搜 985
恰 887	63. 戶 905	推 930
您 129	房 235	掃 716
息 465	所 288	掌 374
怨 866	扇 797	掛 }548
愜 252		挂 }
恩 951		搖 861
愚 979	64. 手, 扌 368	搭 523
悶 801	打 135	提 221
情 201	扔 913	換 314
悲 889	托 625	摸 674
慌 630	扣 740	擺 127
惜 417	扛 570	撒 580
		摔 921

U

290 THE CHINESE LANGUAGE

撫 899
撕 811
撩 682
撐 965
擅 549
擱 697
據 462
擠 448
揑 }
擰 } 546
撿 850
擺 553
擦 413
攏 984

65. 支
救 894

66. 攴
收 356
改 492
政 367
放 370
故 378
敎 635
敢 438
數 73
整 926

67. 文 633

68. 斗
料 608

69. 斤 999
斧 945
新 307

70. 方 301
旁 520

71. 旡, 无
旣 225

72. 日 77
早 157
明 74
易 476
春 277
昨 133
是 3
時 80
晌 156
晒 }
曬 } 547
晚 151
景 742
暖 758
暑 701
暫 806

73. 曰
書 437
替 562
最 477
會 87

74. 月 443
有 22
朋 212
望 810

75. 木 230
本 198
朶 616
李 468
材 607
村 515
東 16
汉 164
杯 407
林 589
相 195
架 578
柳 862
桌 }
椁 } 246
根 594
條 788
椅 126
桶 same as 833
棍 877
業 464
極 809
榜 991
幹 946
概 510
樂 214
樓 722
樣 153
樹 528
櫃 375
權 855

76. 欠
次 564
歇 799
歡 458

77. 止	沒 21	86. 火 298
正 735	河 245	烤 328
此 971	油 658	無 556
步 590	法 207	然 186
武 512	泡 545	煮 326
歲 461	沿 957	煙 359
	泥 652	煤 398
78. 歹	洋 316	照 817
死 456	洗 410	煩 762
	流 p. 141, no. 143	熟 934
79. 殳	活 227	熱 119
殺 968	浮 974	燈 598
殼 621	海 585	燒 506
	淘 759	爐 923
80. 毋	涼 386	
母 455	浪 845	87. 爪
每 702	淡 362	為 139
	淨 409	爬 915
81. 比 268	湖 953	
	深 666	88. 父 187
82. 毛 263	混 775	爺 189
毡 584	淺 667	
	添 819	89. 爻
83. 气	渴 353	爾 619
氣 118	湯 332	
	湊 737	90. 爿
84. 氏	準淮 }173	牆 879
民 980	溜 522	
	滾 779	91. 片 526
85. 水 340	漂 677	
永 992	滿 504	92. 牙 997
求 756	濕 654	
江 952	澡 542	93. 牛 329
汗 602	消 929	牲 672
	灌 351	物 854

94. 犬
狗 204
猪 927
猜 885

95. 玄

96. 玉
王 886
玩 536
玻 411
班 524
珠 837
現 154
理 501
璃 412

97. 瓜

98. 瓦
瓶 262

99. 甘
甚 12

100. 生 132
產 463

101. 用 117

102. 田
由 857
男 903
甲 426
畝 901
留 284
異 843

畜 687
當 229
畵 265

103. 疋

104. 疒
疼 256
病 168
瘦 679
癩 675

105. 癶
登 709
發 253

106. 白 75
百 61
的 5
皇 517

107. 皮 645

108. 皿
盆 543
盒 350
盤 341

109. 目 551
肫 933
直
直 } 748
省 392
看 28
眞 453
睿 539
眼 513

睛 514
睡 260
瞞 690
瞧 243
聰 688

110. 矛

111. 矢
知 31
矩 746
短 163
矮 380

112. 石 790
砍 493
破 425
硬 656
碗 339
碎 320
碟 342
碰 259
磨 664

113. 示
神 451
票 315
福 626
禮 237

114. 禸

115. 禾
秀 895
秋 280
程 624
種 782

116. 穴	**120.** 糸	**124.** 羽
究 610	約 721	
空 208	紅 357	**125.** 老 176
穿 120	納 130	者 825
窄 382	紙 146	
窗 914	累 681	**126.** 而 900
窩 509	細 605	耐 761
窮 705	絆 595	
	結 815	**127.** 耒
117. 立	給 34	耦 897
站 470	經 192	
竟 692	綠 908	**128.** 耳 615
章 747	線 813	聞 308
	緊 264	聲 441
	綁 958	聽 86
118. 竹	緣 377	聾 617
笑 473	縫 488	
第 66	縣 954	**129.** 聿
笨 777	總 210	
筆 423	繞 793	**130.** 肉, 月 330
答 665	繩 416	肚 821
等 33	纜 217	肩 494
筩, 筒 833		肯 613
算 278	**121.** 缶	胡 867
管 103	罐 863	胰 544
箱 568		能 91
簡 755	**122.** 网 罒	胖 943
籍 955	罕 910	腦 776
	罪 444	脚 450
119. 米 998	罵 557	脖 668
粒 783	罷 149	脫 808
粗 604		脾 290
糧 ⎫	**123.** 羊	腫 482
粮 ⎬ 293	着 170	腿 480
糖 335	美 828	膽 563
糊 750	義 990	臉 663
		臕 680 u 2

131. 臣
臨 977
臥 234

132. 自 319

133. 至 856

134. 臼
舀 834
舉 592
舊 541
興 912

135. 舌
舒 499

136. 舛

137. 舟
船 582
艙 986

138. 艮
良 981

139. 色 267

140. 艸
花 174
若 102
苦 786
英 220
茶 333
荷 360
草 653
菓 770
榮 323

萬 63
落 427
葉 334
著 387
蓋 508
薄 384
薦 226
藍 907
藥 483
藏 880

141. 虍
處 606
號 295
虧 796

142. 虫
蛋 331
螞 531
蜂 532
蝦 874
蟾 767
螯 535
蟆 875
蠅 768

143. 血

144. 行 93
行 309
街 519
衙 371

145. 衣 121
表 236
衫 603
袋 361

被 202
裁 487
裝 485
裡 ⎫
裏 ⎭ 13
補 794
裳 122
袖 489
褲 495
襪 655

146. 西 17
要 10

147. 見 29
規 745
親 188
覺 261

148. 角
解 916

149. 言 994
計 429
記 70
許 193 and 993
訴 85
試 363
詫 842
話 42
該 166
認 182
語 708
說 39
誰 218
諒 766
論 558

請 43
謝 372
謊 581
講 609
謙 718
變 838
護 699
讓 364

150. 谷

151. 豆 902
豈 622

152. 豕
豫 324

153. 豸
貌 827

154. 貝
負 989
貨 601
財 947
貪 760
貳 p. 45
賊 963
貴 112
費 369
買 36
賒 p. 146, no. 6
賬 773
賠 561
賤 634
賞 831
賣 37

賺 713
賸 651
贖 962
贅 p. 139, no. 53
藏 987

155. 赤

156. 走 49
起 158
越 554
趕 649
趣 975

157. 足 736
跌 596
趾 449
跳 849
跑 479
跟 167
路 789
踝 669
踢 684
蹶 683

158. 身 505
躭 251
躺 507

159. 車 128
輩 931
輕 573
輪 583
輙 661

160. 辛
辦 223

161. 辰

162. 辵, 辶
近 395
退 644
迷 891
送 254
逛 321
通 771
追 940
逢 703
這 1
連 181
進 312
遇 704
運 575
過 48
遠 143
遜 719
道 32
遞 858
違 623
邊 725
避 700
還 138
邊 521

163. 邑, 阝
那 11
郎 638
郵 366
都 72
鄉 141

164. 酉
配 778
酒 358

醉 620
醜 848
醒 502

165. 釆

166. 里 276
重 569
野 591
量 249
釐·厘 } 744

167. 金 631
針 812
釘 287
鉸 420
鈴 917
銀 311
鋪 373
錢 25
錯 107
鎗 593
鐺 918
鐘 232
鎮 983
鐵 349
鑽 884
鏡 565

168. 長 162

169. 門 105
開 106
閉 303
間 406
關 104

170. 阜
阿 same as 190
附 982
限 741
院 552
除 209
陰 530
陽 527
隔 878
隨 352
險 577

171. 隶

172. 隹
隻 p. 151, 10
雇 646
雖 185
雙 642
雞 same as 327
離 275
難 474

173. 雨 159
零 64
雲 839
電 586

174. 青
靜 967

175. 非

176. 面 274

177. 革
靪 814
靴 643

178. 韋

179. 韭

180. 音 442
響 919

181. 頁
頂 478
順 393
預 324
頓 871
領 533
頭 27
顆 836
顏 266
願 559
類 694
顯 816

182. 風 388
颺 389
飄 841

183. 飛

184. 食 294
飯 99
養 466
餓 882
館 723
餒 292

185. 首

186. 香 676

187. 馬 171	193. 鬲	203. 黑 242
駕 313		點 145
騎 291	194. 鬼	
騾 650		204. 黹
驚 938	195. 魚 996	
	鮮 347	205. 黽
188. 骨 670		206. 鼎
骯 714	196. 鳥 995	
髒 715	雞 327	207. 鼓
體 765		208. 鼠
	197. 鹵	
189. 高 379	鹽 336	209. 鼻 1000
	198. 鹿	210. 齊
190. 髟		
髮 421	199. 麥	211. 齒
鬆 383		
	200. 麻	212. 龍
191. 鬥	麼 6	
鬧 297		213. 龜
鬨 534	201. 黃	
		214. 龠
192. 鬯	202. 黍	

"早期北京话珍本典籍校释与研究"丛书总目录

早期北京话珍稀文献集成

（一）日本北京话教科书汇编

《燕京妇语》等八种　　　　　　四声联珠
华语跬步　　　　　　　　　　　官话指南·改订官话指南
亚细亚言语集　　　　　　　　　京华事略·北京纪闻
北京风土编·北京事情·北京风俗问答
伊苏普喻言·今古奇观·搜奇新编

（二）朝鲜日据时期汉语会话书汇编

改正增补汉语独学　　　　　　　修正独习汉语指南
高等官话华语精选　　　　　　　官话华语教范
速修汉语自通　　　　　　　　　无先生速修中国语自通
速修汉语大成　　　　　　　　　官话标准：短期速修中国语自通
中语大全　　　　　　　　　　　"内鲜满"最速成中国语自通

（三）西人北京话教科书汇编

寻津录　　　　　　　　　　　　北京话语音读本
语言自迩集　　　　　　　　　　语言自迩集（第二版）
官话类编　　　　　　　　　　　言语声片
华语入门　　　　　　　　　　　华英文义津逮
汉英北京官话词汇　　　　　　　北京官话初阶
汉语口语初级读本·北京儿歌

（四）清代满汉合璧文献萃编

清文启蒙	清话问答四十条
一百条·清语易言	清文指要
续编兼汉清文指要	庸言知旨
满汉成语对待	清文接字·字法举一歌
重刻清文虚字指南编	

（五）清代官话正音文献

正音撮要	正音咀华

（六）十全福

（七）清末民初京味儿小说书系

新鲜滋味	过新年
小额	北京
春阿氏	花鞋成老
评讲聊斋	讲演聊斋

（八）清末民初京味儿时评书系

益世余谭——民国初年北京生活百态
益世余墨——民国初年北京生活百态

早期北京话研究书系

早期北京话语法演变专题研究
早期北京话语气词研究
晚清民国时期南北官话语法差异研究
基于清后期至民国初期北京话文献语料的个案研究
高本汉《北京话语音读本》整理与研究
北京话语音演变研究
文化语言学视域下的北京地名研究
语言自迩集——19世纪中期的北京话（第二版）
清末民初北京话语词汇释